Through the Waters

Through the Waters

A Biblical Theology of the Book of Genesis

CALEB S. LEWIS

RESOURCE *Publications* · Eugene, Oregon

Resource Publications
An Imprint of Wipf and Stock Publishers
199 W. 8th Ave., Suite 3
Eugene, OR 97401

www.wipfandstock.com

PAPERBACK ISBN: 979-8-3852-0860-9
HARDCOVER ISBN: 979-8-3852-0861-6
EBOOK ISBN: 979-8-3852-0862-3

04/25/24

Contents

List of Tables and Figures

Acknowledgments

Throughout the writing of this book and the study which led to its conception, my wife Sara and Pastor Nathan Young have contributed much insight and reflection through hours of conversation. I would like to thank them for these helpful conversations. I would also like to thank them for reading earlier versions of this book and offering comments which have greatly benefited its contents. I would also like to thank Wipf and Stock for agreeing to publish this book and Matt Wimer for his assistance in that process.

Abbreviations

ANE	Ancient Near East
AT	Author's Translation
BA	The Biblical Archeologist
BT	The Bible Translator
CBQ	Catholic Biblical Quarterly
DBI	Dictionary of Biblical Imagery
ESV	English Standard Version
HALOT	The Hebrew and Aramaic Lexicon of the Old Testament
HBT	Horizons in Biblical Theology
JBL	Journal of Biblical Literature
JETS	Journal of the Evangelical Theological Society
JSS	Journal of Semitic Studies
LXX	Septuagint
NET	New English Translation
NT	Novum Testamentum
SBJT	The Southern Baptist Journal of Theology
TJT	Toronto Journal of Theology
VT	Vetus Testamentum

Introduction

THE BOOK OF GENESIS, rather than being a dry history, consisting of disconnected stories with isolated significance, is a work of literary art. It is a continuous narrative, building upon itself with each new section and linked together by intricate literary structures. Upon this crafted narrative, the book of Genesis builds its teaching and theology for the edification of God's people. Therefore, in order to fully understand what the book of Genesis intends to communicate, the reader would do well to have a working knowledge of the literary techniques that are used. The goal of the present work is to explore the presence and significance of two motifs that are integrated into the literary organization of the book of Genesis. As these motifs are traced throughout the book, attention will be given to the development of the narrative, especially in light of these motifs. These two motifs are the Exodus motif and what I will call the Two-Goats motif.

There has recently been an increase in interest in the use of the Exodus motif throughout the Biblical canon[1]. However, insufficient attention has been given to its presence in the book of Genesis. Some have noted the presence of the Exodus motif in, for instance, the creation account and Abraham's journey to Egypt[2] as isolated incidents but the Exodus motif can be seen throughout Genesis as a core element of the narrative. Likewise, the Two-Goats motif has received discussion (though not under this designation) but, within modern scholarship, it has not received attention as a unifying element of the book of Genesis. The book of Genesis will utilize, intertwine, and expand these motifs such that they become a key component in understanding the message of the book and in shaping the hope of the reader.

---

1. See for example: Estelle, *Echoes of Exodus*; Fox, *Reverberations*, Morales, *Exodus*

2. See for example: Wenham, *Genesis 1–15*, Comment on 12:1, Explanation of 13:1–18; Hamilton, *Genesis Chapters 1–17*, comment on 12:20; Morales, *Exodus*, 21–33; Estelle, *Echoes of Exodus*, 61–91; Postell, *Adam as Israel*, 95–98

METHOD

In setting forth a method for a proper reading of the book of Genesis and the above-mentioned motifs within, the unity of the book needs to be mentioned. If the book were a patchwork of myths and folktales that had little to no unifying editorial work done to it, there would be little sense in searching for literary motifs that span the length of the book. However, if the text as we have it is the editorial or authorial work of a single mind, or unified group of minds, whether written in a single sitting or composed from, and influenced by, preexisting material, the presence of unifying literary structures and themes becomes plausible.

Others have shown that the Torah, as well as the Tanakh, has been crafted as a unified work, tethered by substantial textual connections[3], literary structures[4], and headings[5]. Therefore, space will not be taken here to argue the unity of the book of Genesis nor any other section of the Tanakh. Rather, the present work will operate under the assumption that, regardless of the compositional process, the book of Genesis is to be read as a unified part of the Biblical canon as we have it.

If the Hebrew Bible is indeed the product of a single person or group who played the role(s) of author or editor, then the reader ought to be in search of the intention of those who put the text in its final form. Throughout this work, for simplicity's sake, those who wrote or compiled the text into its final form will be referred to as "the author." Though arguments can be made that to refer to a single "author" is imprecise in both role and number, this will be a helpful and concise label for whoever put the Tanakh in its final form as we search for the authorial intent of any given passage or the book of Genesis as a whole.

In establishing the presence of motifs and themes within the text of Genesis, guidelines must be set forth for substantiating links between any given narrative sections. Shared language is the most important factor

---

3. Postell, *Adam as Israel*, 27–42; Sailhamer, *Pentateuch as Narrative*, 23–27, 33–59

4. See Waltke for proposed literary structures within Genesis (Waltke and Fredricks, *Genesis*, 19–21) and Dorsey for proposed literary structures within Genesis and throughout the Torah (Dorsey, *Literary Structures*, 47–102). Morales discusses other proposals for chiastic structures within the Torah and their differences (Morales, *Who Shall Ascend*, 23–34). Despite differences, there is agreement that there are chiastic structures built into the micro- and macro-structure of the Torah.

5. The book of Genesis is both segmented and unified by the heading "these are the generations (תּוֹלְדוֹת, twldwt) of . . ." Collins, *Reading Genesis Well*, §5.A.2; Waltke and Fredricks, *Genesis*, 17–19

in establishing connections between texts. The greater the concentration and rarity of the words that are shared, the more likely the textual link becomes. If entire phrases are shared, then the likelihood of a connection increases. Likewise, if the shared language is surrounded by similar contexts then, again, the likelihood of a connection increases[6]. This technique of using shared language and contexts to connect passages does not have to be used to connect only verse to verse or paragraph to paragraph, but may be used across the span of "larger narrative units, to sustain a thematic development and to establish instructive connections between seemingly disparate narratives."[7] However similar or unrelated two narrative units may seem, the presence of shared language, in significant concentrations or contexts, are clues to the reader that the author intends to associate these narratives in some way. The author wants ideas shared between the narratives that have been connected, sometimes from the earlier to the latter, sometimes from the latter to the earlier.

Similar to the use of shared and repeated language, the author may also utilize the repetition of concepts[8]. For instance, take the following two sentences:

> A man was exiled to the wilderness and became a nomad for the remainder of his days.

> He was cast out to a wasteland to be a wanderer for the rest of his life.

These two sentences communicate two very conceptually similar events, despite the fact that they share no significant wording. There are six shared concepts within these sentences: (1) a man/He is (2) exiled/cast out (3) into the wilderness/wasteland to (4) become a nomad/wanderer (5) for the remainder/rest (6) of his days/life. If only one or two of these elements were shared, there would be little reason to suspect an intended connection between the two. But given that there is a concentration of similar concepts/elements in sequential order, there is reason to investigate further to confirm a connection between the two sentences.

---

6. Leonard, "Identifying Inner-Biblical Allusions," 246; see also Schnittjer, *Old Testament*, xxiv–xxviii

7. Alter, *Narrative*, 118

8. Meir Sternberg points out that repetition is a technique and art found on all levels of the text: linguistics, plot, themes, and generic (literary structure) (Sternberg, *Poetics*, 365–366).

If an investigation into the context of the two illustrative sentences above, or similar Biblical passages, yielded no further linguistic repetitions, it may be that no connection is intended and the conceptual similarities are coincidental. Or perhaps even the author may have realized the similarities in the two scenes and varied his language in order to intentionally dissociate them. However, if shared language is found in the context of the conceptual similarities, then the shared language and concepts should be read as elements working together to link the narratives.

The fact that repetition and shared language and concepts are used to connect narratives does not mean, however, that the author must repeat the exact same words, phrases, and concepts each time they wish to make a connection to a given text or motif. The author may use different sets of words and concepts to link to the given text or motif in different places. The author may use these varied connection points to connect one narrative to multiple narratives or to string together a series of narratives as they construct a theme or motif.

Throughout the book of Genesis, the narratives in which the Exodus motif is seen do not all display connections to the Exodus of Israel in the same way. Some instances of the Exodus motif will share language with the Exodus of Israel that is shared by other instances of the motif, while others will utilize an entirely new set of words and phrases found in the Exodus of Israel. So the Exodus motif ought not to be expected to manifest itself in the exact same way each time that it is present. The same is true of the Two-Goats motif. Perhaps this is due to the artistry of the author and their wishing to not tell the exact same story multiple times, becoming predictable and uninteresting. Perhaps this is due to the author wishing to show the motif in a wider variety of contexts to more fully teach about and display Yahweh. It is also possible that the author does not wish for the reader to see all the connections until they reach the Exodus of Israel to increase the tension and resolution of that narrative section. In any case, the author has placed these motifs throughout the book of Genesis in order to connect the narrative sections of Genesis to one another and to the narrative of the Exodus of Israel.

Some may disagree with specific connections proposed in this book. Ultimately, identifying these connections is more of an art form than a science, as is their creation. However, the study of literary connections within the Bible has yielded helpful guidelines to prevent the reader from seeing connections where there are none. With any connection between narratives, guards need to be in place to protect from false positives. One of the main goals of this work is to reasonably present the mentioned motifs as part of the authorial intention. The principles outlined above will serve as guards to the means by which this goal is achieved such that the Exodus and Two-Goats motifs can be displayed as clearly within the text.

When this work was begun, there was no intention of it being a Biblical theology of the book of Genesis; rather only to display the mentioned literary motifs. However, as will be seen, they are found pervasively throughout the text of Genesis. In my opinion, the Exodus and Two-Goats motifs are so pervasive that they are a fundamental component of the Genesis narrative. The author of Genesis utilizes these motifs in an effort to shape the reader's expectations about the promised seed of the woman and build toward the climax of Israel's exodus out of Egypt, which climaxes in the Day of Atonement[9]. Therefore, throughout this book, comment is given, not only to the literary structures which are a part of the immediate scope, but to the development of the narrative as well. Not every stone will be overturned, but features will be highlighted and explained that assist the reader in feeling the narrative tension that the author has attempted to create and to see the resolutions, twists, disappointments, or escalations that follow. If the book of Genesis is an inspired story, intended for the teaching and edification of God's people, then it will not be enough to know of the literary features found within, but the reader must also be able to understand and live within the world of that story. By living within the world of Genesis, we will be able to understand the ideas that the author intends to place extra stress on, and better interpret the text. More importantly, as we allow our minds to wrap around the story and world of Genesis we will be better able to be shaped by the inspired text and think with the wisdom of God's inspired author.

STRUCTURE OF THE MOTIFS

Understanding the structure of any writing is a key component to grasping its intended meaning(s). The book of Genesis as a whole is primarily structured by ten occurrences of the phrase "these are the generations of

---

9. The Day of Atonement is both the chiastic center of the Torah as well as the institution of the ritual which enabled Yahweh to dwell among the people he had just brought out of Egypt, bringing a resolution, though temporary, to the story. Morales, *Who Shall Ascend*, 23–34

(אֵלֶּה תוֹלְדֹת, 'lh twldwt) . . .," separating the book into eleven sections[10]. The book is further structured by the use of various parallel and chiastic narrative patterns[11]. Additionally, changes in genre (from narrative to, for example, poetry or genealogy) are used to structure, segment, or accentuate the text throughout. While understanding these structuring techniques is important for a comprehensive reading of the book of Genesis, they fall outside the immediate scope of this work. The primary focus, as mentioned, will be on the presence, structure, and contribution of the Exodus and Two-Goats motifs. As we make our way through the book, we will see that the motifs are so prevalent that they themselves become a common structuring technique used by the author. It has been discussed that these motifs are presented in different ways throughout the book, but it will be beneficial to here lay out the basic pattern found within these motifs. In its most basic form the Exodus motif within Genesis contains the following elements:

1. The elect one is in a place of violence/oppressors, often in exile

2. Yahweh sees, hears, or knows of the situation

3. The enemies are defeated/struck

4. The elect come out, often as a mixed multitude with increased possessions

5. There is an act of new creation

6. The elect are put in Yahweh's dwelling/temple

7. The elect is commissioned/blessed, sometimes to serve within the dwelling/temple

8. There is an act of disloyalty that results in exile

The Two-Goats motif is patterned on the following elements:

A. A younger brother is elected as firstborn/bearer of the "seed of the woman" promise

B. The older brother acts with jealousy against the elect

C. The older brother is given protection

D. The older brother is exiled into the wilderness

10. "These are the generations of . . ." occurs at the following locations as narrative headings: Gen 2:4; 5:1; 6:9; 10:1; 11:10; 11:27; 25:12; 36:1; 37:2.

11. Waltke and Fredricks, *Genesis*, 17–21; Dorsey, *Literary Structure*, 47–102

E. The older brother is multiplied into a nation

F. The nation becomes hostile to God's people

G. The elect brother is brought to Yahweh's dwelling/exalted

H. The elect brother is sometimes associated with an offering

Others may wish to refine or modify these elements, however, they will be beneficial as a basic framework for the purposes of this work. As discussed, these patterns will show up with variation. There may be missing or additional elements depending on the needs of a particular narrative. Regardless, these patterns are found throughout the book of Genesis such that they begin to create expectations within the reader, which the author can then meet, challenge, or exceed according to the ideas desired to be communicated through the story. These patterns cause the reader to recognize the standard tensions of the narrative, and reflect correctly on the ways in which those tensions are handled by the author. The reuse of these structures also contributes to the cohesion of the narrative, as even seemingly disparate narratives are naturally seen as connected and building on similar concepts due to their structural similarity. As the elements of these motifs are explored, the basic elements will be labeled with the above numbering/lettering for clarity.

One final note ought to be made about the continued reference to the *narrative* of Genesis. To refer to the book as only a narrative would be an oversimplification as multiple literary genres are found within. However, the book is an account of connected events, intending to use its multiple literary types to develop a single story. For this reason, as well as for simplicity, the book of Genesis will be referred to as a narrative. Also, the continued use of the phrase *narrative sections* is not intended to demarcate precise sections separated by literary features. Rather, this phrase is used simply to refer to the current general section of the Genesis story which is under discussion. These imprecisions must be forgiven as I do not wish to impede the discussion with the exploration of precise literary breaks throughout the entire book of Genesis, as this exercise lies outside of the scope of this present work.

As we progress through Genesis, the above structures will be highlighted, as well as any additional elements that connect a given narrative to the Exodus of Israel or Day of Atonement. Note will be given to the development of the immediate narrative; to the tensions being created or resolved; to the ways in which the presence of the motif causes a passage

to be read in light of others; and to the inferences that the author is leading the reader to make. It is beneficial to see the presence of the motifs
that will be explored within this book, but it ought to be kept in mind that
the author of the book of Genesis did not create these motifs in a vacuum.
They are an integral part of the narrative that the author has crafted and
of their communicative strategy. Therefore, the narrative surrounding
the motifs will be given attention. After walking through the Genesis narrative, reflections and interpretive implications of the examined motifs
will be briefly discussed.

HOW TO USE THIS BOOK

This book has been written alongside a careful study of the book of
Genesis and will examine sections of text in the order presented by the
narrative. This book will also expand its arguments according to the development of the Genesis narrative. Therefore, I believe this book will be
used best when read alongside the book of Genesis. It may be useful to
read this work by itself to quickly and concisely understand the points
and evidence presented, but it has been designed in tandem with the
book of Genesis. Because of this, this work will make brief references
to narrative elements, assuming the reader's familiarity with the book of
Genesis. This work is also designed such that it may be quickly referenced
for points concerning a specific narrative. The chapters are arranged such
that they follow the narrative order of Genesis and that the main points
about a given narrative section can be found within the corresponding
chapter of this book.

Following each section containing an exploration of the Exodus
motif is a table that concisely presents the links between the examined
narrative, the Exodus of Israel, and other narratives in Genesis. The sections of Genesis compared in these tables will vary based on the exodus
elements that the author has chosen to utilize in the particular section,
but all exodus cycles will be compared to the exodus of Israel within
these tables. These tables have been constructed in order that they may
be quickly referenced by the reader for reminders of the narrative links.
However, it should be noted that, while looking up the verses in the tables
may at times present clear connections, some noted connections within
the tables ought to be accompanied by the explanation found in the previous section. There may be linguistic, conceptual, or contextual data that

needs to be considered in order to make the referenced verses present substantial connections. The verses in the tables are reminders, not the arguments themselves. Whether read on its own or as a companion to the biblical text, I hope that this work illuminates and deepens the text of Genesis for the reader and that it shapes the expectations of the biblical reader such that later biblical texts may be read with greater academic and devotional clarity.

Creation

THE FIRST THING THAT comes to mind when reading the creation narrative may not be the Exodus. However, the creation narrative has the Exodus motif woven through it and it intends to be read as the first in a series of exoduses in Genesis. Because of the uniqueness of the creation narrative within the Bible, and because it is heavily laden with ANE cultural imagery, it can be difficult to see the Exodus motif within. In order to see this motif, we will begin by looking at parallels between the creation of the first humans and the exodus of Israel. Once we have seen that the author of the Torah has crafted these narratives to parallel one another, we will be able to explore the ways in which the parallels and imagery direct us to read the creation as a type of exodus.

The creation narrative begins with darkness and the Spirit (רוּחַ, *rwḥ*) of God over the waters (Gen 1:2). (It should be noted that רוּחַ (*rwḥ*) can be translated as spirit, breath, or wind[1]. The word will be translated in different ways in the texts examined). The waters are then separated (Gen 1:7) and dry land is then caused to appear (Gen 1:9). All of this is to make way for Yahweh's creation of humanity on the sixth day. At the exodus of Israel out of Egypt, Yahweh again creates a new people to be his own, beginning with similar steps. As the people of Israel stand at the edge of the Sea of Reeds waiting for deliverance, with the Angel of God standing between them and the Egyptian army, Ex 14:21 reads:

> Then Moses stretched out his hand over the sea, and the LORD drove the sea back by a strong east wind (רוּחַ, *rwḥ*) all night and made the sea dry land, and the waters were divided.

Just as in the first chapter of Genesis, the event contains water in the darkness/night which is separated, involving wind/spirit (רוּחַ, *rwḥ*). The wind/spirit brings forth dry land, leading to the creation of a new

---

1. Köhler et al., *HALOT*, see entry 8704 רוּחַ

humanity. These beginning similarities are clear enough but now we need to take a look at some of the imagery found in these passages before we can fully see their interconnectedness and richness.

DARKNESS OVER THE FACE OF THE WATERS

Darkness and Light

In the Biblical worldview, the darkness and waters present in Genesis 1:2 have significance beyond their physical properties. Throughout the Bible, darkness is used as a rich and foreboding image. It is found as representing:

- death or Sheol (Job 10:21–22; Ps 88:12)
- a place for the wicked (Prov 2:13)
- wicked deeds (Isa 50:10; 59:9)
- the domain of satanic powers (Eph 6:12; 1 Cor 6:14–15)
- a means of judgment (Jer 4:28, 23:12; Joel 2:10, 31; Isa 10:13)

This is a very short sampling of the usage of "darkness" in the Bible, and there are other ways in which "darkness" is used, but for our purposes this short list serves to show that "darkness is principally associated with evil, opposed to God's purposes of order and goodness" in creation[2].

The use of darkness in this manner can be seen in both the creation narrative and that of Israel's exodus. In the creation narrative darkness is something that Yahweh must restrain with his light (Gen 1:4, cf. Jn 1:4–5). In the exodus narrative, the Egyptians are struck with darkness as one of the plagues (Ex 10:21–28) which are acts of decreation on Egypt[3]. The Israelites also pass through the waters at night (in darkness) and their salvation is complete when the waters sweep over their enemies as the morning appears (Ex 14:26–27). Perhaps from this scene, Mal 4:2 pictures the salvation of the Day of Yahweh as the rising of the "Sun of Righteousness . . . with healing in his wings."

In the Bible, light becomes associated with Yahweh himself. This can be seen explicitly in places such as Ex 34:29, Ps 18:28, and Isa 60:20. 2 Sam 23:4 illustrates the point well:

2. Wilhoit et al., *DBI*, 191–192
3. Imes, "The Lost World" 130–132; see also Currid, *Ancient Egypt*, 115

> [Yahweh] dawns on them like the morning light,
>> like the sun shining forth on a cloudless morning,
>> like rain that makes grass to sprout from the earth.

In this verse, Yahweh is seen to be a light that brings the blessings of fruitfulness to the land and security to the Davidic kingdom. Throughout the Bible, light is also associated with goodness, blessing, righteousness, truthfulness, and other qualities which find their source in Yahweh (e.g. Num 6:25; Job 30:26; Ps 37:6; Ps 43:3; Isa 2:5). Light becomes a positive image of Yahweh and the goodness which emanates from him. For our purposes, it is helpful to see that when light is used in the context of an exodus narrative, light is "the great antithesis and conqueror of darkness"[4]. At times, light or morning will appear in the exodus narratives as the elect are brought out of darkness and the forces of darkness are defeated. In those scenes, light serves as an image of Yahweh's salvation and restraint of the darkness; of his act of new creation and his act of defeating those who dwell in darkness.

Within the creation and exodus narratives, which will be the subject of our study, darkness seems to take on its typical foreboding connotations, as discussed above. Both creation and the exodus begin in a darkness that is contrary to Yahweh's work of order and salvation. It may even be found to oppose Yahweh. Likewise, we have seen, by way of contrast, the opposite symbolism of light and morning, which comes from Yahweh and is used to restrain darkness. Light has become a rich symbol of deliverance, and continues as such throughout the Bible.

Waters

Water can be an image of both life and death in the Bible. Water is essential for life and ritual cleansing (e.g. Lev 16:24). Often Yahweh provides water for his people, both literally (Gen 21:19, Ex 17; Num 20:13) and symbolically (John 4:14). But in other contexts, water can be deadly and a means of judgment (Gen 7; cf. Isa 24:18). Before the connotations of water are discussed further, it would be helpful to first discuss a few details of the shape of the biblical world, or of biblical cosmology.

---

4. Wilhoit et al., *DBI*, 509

ANCIENT ISRAELITE COSMOLOGY

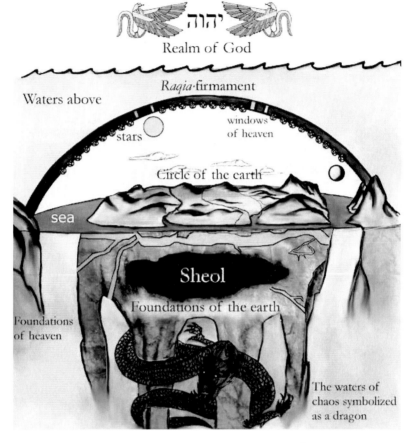

Figure 1. Depiction of Biblical Cosmology[5].

The Biblical authors, as well as most of the ancient world, saw the pre-creation state as endless waters. In Genesis 1:2, these waters are called "the deep (תְּהוֹם, *thwm*)." Yahweh then separated the waters, essentially making a large bubble in which he could make the dry land reside. The deep is then given limits at the shores and is then called seas (cf. Prov 8:29). In this worldview, there are waters above and below the land and sky. Yahweh's throne sits over the waters above (cf. Ps 29:10[6]) and below

---

5. Taken with permission from Stanhope, *(Mis)interpreting Genesis*, 88

6. מַבּוּל (*mbwl*) is another descriptor for the cosmic waters when they are a flood, cf. Gen 7:6, 7, 10, 17

the land are supporting pillars (1 Sam 2:8) and Sheol, the place of the dead (see Fig. 1). In Jonah's prayer, for instance, this worldview is seen at work:

> 2 "I called out to the LORD, out of my distress,
>   and he answered me;
> out of the belly of Sheol I cried,
>   and you heard my voice.
> ³ For you cast me into the deep,
>   into the heart of the seas,
>   and the flood surrounded me;
> all your waves and your billows
>   passed over me.
> ⁴ Then I said, 'I am driven away
>   from your sight;
> yet I shall again look
>   upon your holy temple.'
> ⁵ The waters closed in over me to take my life;
>   the deep surrounded me;
> weeds were wrapped about my head
> ⁶ at the roots of the mountains.
> I went down to the land
>   whose bars closed upon me forever;
> yet you brought up my life from the pit,
>   O LORD my God.

In Jonah 2:2–6, we see Jonah use much of this imagery as he describes his descent into Sheol via the large fish that swallowed him. The great fish takes Jonah on a journey into the deep, bringing him ever closer to death. During this journey, he travels under the land and sees the "roots of the mountains" and the "bars" or pillars of the land. The cosmic waters through which Jonah traveled are not only the way to the land of the dead, but they also threaten to collapse in on creation, sending it back into a pre-creation state of ruin, as exemplified in Genesis 7. It is easy to see why the waters can possess a very ominous overtone.

There is another character, or category of creature, from Genesis 1 that needs to be explored in our brief discussion of the waters: "the great sea creatures." The Hebrew word which is translated as "great sea creatures" (ESV) is תַּנִּינִם (tnynym), תַּנִּין (tnyn) in the singular. Though here in Gen 1:21, it is translated as "great sea creatures" by most major translations, elsewhere תַּנִּין (tnyn) is commonly translated as "snake," "serpent," "dragon," or "sea monster"[7]. Isa 27:1 even equates this creature with Leviathan:

> "In that day the LORD with his hard and great and strong sword will punish Leviathan the fleeing serpent, Leviathan the twisting serpent, and he will slay the dragon (תַּנִּין, *tnyn*) that is in the sea."

Likewise, Ps 74:13–15 makes the same equation:

> [13] You divided the sea by your might;
>   you broke the heads of the sea monsters (תַּנִּינִים, *tnynym*) on the waters.
> [14] You crushed the heads of Leviathan;
>   you gave him as food for the creatures of the wilderness.
> [15] You split open springs and brooks;
>   you dried up ever-flowing streams.

While the "great sea creatures" are docile in Gen 1, the same creature will later become the typical image for ruin and hostility to Yahweh and his people in the Hebrew Bible[8]. Notice also that the sea (יָם, *ym*) is divided just as the sea monster and Leviathan are broken. The two are often equated in the minds of the biblical authors and this equation would have already been in the minds of the Ancient Israelites as well[9]. Israel's neighbors had myths in which a serpent deity, which was the personification of the sea, opposed the creator. We find clear examples of this in Mesopotamia and Ugarit. In the Ugaritic Baal Cycle[10], Baal faces a serpent deity named Yam and Nahar, meaning sea and river, respectively. Yam is not only named after the seas and rivers, but he is the power behind them. Before Baal can establish his rule over the cosmos, he must defeat Yam. When Baal battles Yam, he achieves victory when he "[strikes] the skull of Prince Yam" with his mace[11]. Once the serpent's head is crushed, Baal is able to build his house and establish his rule.

Similarly, in the Mesopotamian creation myth, Enuma Elish, Marduk must defeat the sea deity, Tiamat, mother of serpents[12], before He can establish his rule. Marduk makes a deal with the gods of the pantheon;

---

7. See, for example: Ex 7:9–12; Job 7:12; Isa 51:9; Jer 51:34; Ezek 32:2

8. See verses referenced in n7

9. Heiser, *The Unseen Realm*, 153

10. A Canaanite mythology discovered in Ugarit which tells a story of Baal, the Canaanite deity often found in being worshiped by the unfaithful Israelites throughout the Hebrew Bible.

11. Wyatt, *Religious Texts from Ugarit*, 67

12. Foster, *Before the Muses*, 446

if he can defeat Tiamat, he will be their king. Once the gods agree to this proposal, Marduk goes off to battle Tiamat and her armies. Marduk, like Baal, achieves victory when he crushes Tiamat's head and splits her body in half. He then proceeds to make half of her body into the dome that holds up the waters above, and the other half he forms into the land[13]. Marduk is then made to be king of the gods and cosmos.

These narratives and concepts were in the cultural air of the ANE and would have been brought to mind for both the writers and readers of passages such as Isa 27 and Ps 74. The rebellious serpent and the waters themselves are often used together or interchangeably to represent enemies or forces of ruin in the Hebrew Bible. Similar language can be found throughout the Bible, often comparing the same serpent imagery to nations that are hostile to Yahweh's people. We see this in Num 24:17:

> I see him, but not now;
> I behold him, but not near:
> a star shall come out of Jacob,
> and a scepter shall rise out of Israel;
> it shall crush the forehead of Moab
> and break down all the sons of Sheth.

Notice that just as the serpent's head is to be struck and enmity is to be put between the serpent's offspring and the woman's offspring in Gen 3:15, so Moab's *forehead* is to be crushed and the *sons* of Sheth will be destroyed. This passage applies synonymous language to that of Gen 3:15 to Israel's enemies, continuing the convention of referring to Yahweh's and Israel's enemies with language and concepts reminiscent of the serpent. This convention is seen more concretely in Jer 51:34,

> "Nebuchadnezzar the king of Babylon has devoured me;
> he has crushed me;
> he has made me an empty vessel;
> he has swallowed me like a monster (תַּנִּין, *tnyn*);
> he has filled his stomach with my delicacies;
> he has rinsed me out."

And Ezek 29:3,

> speak, and say, Thus says the LORD GOD:
> "Behold, I am against you,

---

13. Foster, *Before the Muses*, 461–462

Pharaoh king of Egypt,
the great dragon (תַּנִּין, *tnyn*) that lies
  in the midst of his streams,
that says, 'My Nile is my own;
  I made it for myself.'

In both of these passages, the kings of the enemies of Yahweh are called תַּנִּין (*tnyn*). Utilizing this same convention, the psalmist refers to his enemies as serpents (Ps 140:3) and the author of the books of Samuel uses various literary strategies to associate Goliath and Nahash with serpents[14]. Throughout the Hebrew Bible, the enemies of Yahweh's people are found likened to serpents and sea monsters.

As can be seen in the passages above, the sea monster is a mythological creature and the cosmic enemy of Yahweh. It opposes Yahweh's creation of a people for himself and acts to destroy them. Often this sea monster works through enemy nations and, therefore, is often seen as present in entities such as Egypt, Moab, or Babylon, that seek to destroy the people Yahweh has created. This is why Ps 74:12–17[15], reflecting on the Exodus, speaks of Yahweh's victory over his enemies as the crushing of the sea monster, to whom Pharaoh was compared in Ezek 29. Interestingly, this psalm blurs the line between sea and sea monster by setting the two in parallel. It would seem that the conquering of the waters and of Leviathan were one unified action, according to the psalmist. As he defeats both sea and sea monster, Yahweh restrains the forces of ruin that threaten the destruction of his people.

It is not surprising, with their common association with hostility and ruin, that this sea monster is treated as the personification of the sea, the deep, and even death. This is why in many passages, waters are crushed alongside the sea monster, and the distinctions between the two seem to dissolve. On many occasions, the sea monster is not crushed or even mentioned as an enemy but, rather, only the sea[16]. This is why Jonah's prayer that speaks of his descent into the waters is so linked with death[17]; he is carried into the deep by a large fish. He sees himself as being

---

14. Verrett, *Serpent in Samuel*, 46–93

15. cf. Ex 15:4–10

16. Job 9:8; Ps 43:2–3; 69:14–15; 77:16–20; Jer 47:2

17. Jonah's speaking of death could be explained by the fact that he is at great physical risk during his prayer, but both the genre and use of other cosmological features would lend to a cosmological interpretation of the connected uses of death and waters.

carried to the realm of the dead. This is why Isaiah can refer to the king of Assyria as a flood (Isa 8:7–8). This is why David says in Ps 18:16–17:

> [16] He sent from on high, he took me;
>   he drew me out of many waters.
> [17] He rescued me from my strong enemy
>   and from those who hated me,
>   for they were too mighty for me.

David, in a place of danger and death, is figuratively in the sea. In this particular Psalm, he is being rescued from his enemies and he describes the enemies of Yahweh's chosen king as "waters." Since the sea is the home of death and the sea monster, this passage can speak of death and enemies through only the image of the sea. This passage, among others, exemplifies the close association of the ideas of death, sea, and sea monster. The lines are blurred between the three to the point that each word can be used to convey the same meaning. This interconnectedness helps us draw connections between the creation and exodus narratives and it will also help illuminate later narrative sections in Genesis as variations of this imagery will be used.

Now that we have been introduced to the sea monster and the sea, it is time to return to creation. In Job 26 and Ps 74:12–17 the authors are meditating on past acts of salvation with the vocabulary of creation. The references to creation are seen in their mentions of the inscription of boundaries, seasons, and light and dark. They describe this act of creation-deliverance as a crushing of the sea monster, yet in Gen 1:21 we see that Yahweh created sea monsters rather than crushing them. Why this difference? Why would these authors link the presence of a rebellious sea monster to creation when Genesis makes clear the sea monster is not rebellious at creation? In Genesis, it would seem the author wishes to display Yahweh's absolute, unopposed control over the elements of ruin in creation. He has no sea monster to defeat before he can create and establish his rule, only to form the dark, but passive, waters and land. Yahweh commands the order of all things by only his word. The passages in Job and the Psalms are meditating on past acts of salvation, the Exodus in particular in Psalm 74, and they see creation as an act of power over both the sea and the sea monster. Because the imagery of the sea and sea monster are so closely linked, other biblical authors can use variations of the imagery without necessarily contradicting the nuances of Yahweh's control presented in the first chapters of Genesis. So neither presentation is wrong or contradicting if it is kept in mind that neither is simply an account of historical events. Rather, using similar imagery, Genesis wishes to portray Yahweh's unopposed sovereignty over the sea, while the authors of Job and the Psalm wish to portray Yahweh's victorious control of the sea and, by extension, the sea monster. The Psalm and Job call upon Yahweh's work of salvation from the sea monsters that attack them; enemies and the accuser, respectively. Since both creation and exodus display Yahweh's conquering of the sea, the images of both can be utilized in their pleas for help. This overlap will lend to our reading of the creation as a type of exodus. What is most significant from this discussion is that the biblical authors did not see the creation and the exodus as categorically different events.

Some have supposed that since the sea monsters are created by Yahweh in Genesis, and not a preexisting adversary to the act of creation, the meaning of the waters has been completely neutralized. It is supposed that since the sea monster is made simply a created being, the darkness and waters are also just aspects of nature or "functionless ambiguities" in Genesis 1[18]. However, throughout the Bible, as has been seen and will be further explored, the creation story carries connotations of salvation and exodus. I have proposed an explanation of why the authors chose to change the role of the sea monster which does not require the neutralization of the waters. We ought to be selective and careful in which connotations we remove from a narrative when imagery is changed. The differences in the texts are used to *consistently* display Yahweh's control over creation and the sea monster, but not to ambiguate the meaning of the darkness, waters, and unformed earth.

Before we narrow our meaning of the darkness and waters in Genesis 1, we need to discuss the unformed land in Gen 1:2. The land is described as "formless and void" in the ESV, however, this is not the best translation of the Hebrew phrase תֹהוּ וָבֹהוּ (*thw wbhw*). The first term, תהו (*thw*), is glossed as "wilderness, wasteland, emptiness" in HALOT[19]. John Walton, in a more precise study on the biblical usage of the word, proposes that תהו (*thw*) refers "to any portion of the cosmos that is nonfunctional"[20]. The second term, בהו (*bhw*), is more difficult to define on its own because it appears only in Gen 1:2, Isa 34:11, and Jer 4:23. However, the word

18. Hyers, *Meaning of Creation*, 63, 67, with whom Walton agrees (Walton, *Genesis 1*, 145). cf. Chambers, "Genesis 1," 220–221

19. Köhler et al., *HALOT*, see entry 10056 תֹהוּ

20. Walton, *Genesis 1*, 144

always appears with the word תהו (*thw*). In both Isa 34:11 and Jer 4:23, the words are being used to describe Israel's destruction, and Jerimiah is more explicitly using terms that also refer to a pre-creation (or de-created) state. Given that בהו (*bhw*) is never present without תהו (*thw*), we ought to be able to venture a meaning of the word pair based on their usage. In all three contexts, the word pair can be glossed as "ruin." John Golingay also takes this approach and concludes that the term "chaos" appropriately gives the meaning of תהו וָבֹהוּ (*thw wbhw*)[21]. In an attempt to preserve the alliteration of the Hebrew and maintain the connotations shared by "chaos" and "ruin," Robert Alter aptly translates תהו וָבֹהוּ (*thw wbhw*) as "welter and waste"[22].

Both of the terms "ruin" or "chaos" are accurate, if by them we mean "someplace or someone in a state of disorder that is threatening to Yahweh's imagers." In Genesis 1, Yahweh is in the process of turning the תהו וָבֹהוּ (*thw wbhw*) land into a place for his imagers to dwell, in order that they may serve and guard his garden-temple. In Isaiah and Jeremiah, because of the disobedience of his people, Yahweh is making the land תהו וָבֹהוּ (*thw wbhw*) such that it will be a desolate ruin unfit for human life.

Although this exploration of the pre-creation state has been brief, we have seen that in Genesis 1:2 the pre-creation state has been de-personified by the author, removing any enemies to Yahweh's creative/salvific act. We have also seen that we cannot then say that the pre-creation state was neutral or "ambiguous." Rather we have seen that the land was deadly and unfit for humans. In their most docile form, the darkness and waters are a natural home for death, enemies of Yahweh, and "evokes everything that is anti-God"[23]. All of these elements need to be ordered, restrained, and given exodus from. This work began in Genesis and will be ultimately completed in the final exodus[24] when the beast from the sea is destroyed (Rev 19:20), darkness is no more (Rev 22:5) and the sea is gone (Rev 21:1).

Pertinent to the Exodus motif in creation, the above discussion enables the reader to see that (1) the darkness and waters are the hostile and ruinous environment out of which the elect must be given exodus. These pre-creation elements, despite the fact that the first human is not

21. Goldingay, *Genesis*, 20

22. Alter, *The Hebrew Bible*, 11

23. Wenham, *Genesis 1–15*, 16

24. Estelle, *Echoes of Exodus*, see "Chapter 11: The Exodus motif in Revelation: Redemption, Judgement, and Inheritance"

yet alive, are similar to the violent nations, such as Egypt, out of which future elect ones will be brought and made into a new creation. As in the other exoduses, Yahweh begins his work of making a new humanity with an environment of disarray and destruction. As Yahweh continues and (3) restrains the darkness and waters, he is subduing the ruinous precreation elements, as he will later subdue the enemies of his people, and (4) brings out a couple (5) as a new humanity.

FUNCTIONAL ONTOLOGY AND TEMPLE

Before finishing our preparation for the discussion of the Exodus motif present in the creation story, there are two more facets of the creation that must be explored. The first is the concept of "functional ontology." In *Genesis 1 as Ancient Cosmology*, John Walton has interacted with many ANE texts and ANE scholars and shown that ANE peoples thought primarily in terms of functional ontology as opposed to material ontology. Put another way, when a person in the ANE thought of what it means to be created, or exist, they thought about the function, or purpose, of an object rather than its material composition. If something has purpose and function within creation, it is considered to be something, to have been created. In a material ontology, however, something is considered to exist when it is materially brought into being. As modern Westerners, we would look at a desert and see it as having been created. We would say that if something can be discerned by the senses, if it is materially present in the world, then it has been created, it exists and is something. A person from the ANE would look at the same desert and say that it has not been created. While they would recognize that there are rocks and sand present, they would see this land as the pre-creation dry land that is not yet created, or better "formed," into a place for Yahweh's imagers. It is pre-creation chaos and ruin with no purpose in creation, and is, therefore, nothing. It has not yet been formed or ordered into anything. It is raw material from which nothing has yet been made.

As the ANE had a primarily functional ontology and thought less often of material ontology, we as moderns have a primarily material ontology and have a less prominent, but still present, concept of functional ontology. Highlighting an example of functional ontology in our own context may help us. When a brick house is made, for instance, it is created at the point in time when the clay is dried into bricks and the bricks are stacked together. Before that point, the clay existed, but the house did not. The house is simply reformed clay. No new material came into being, yet we still may say that a house did not exist until the clay was formed into one. If one goes to look for the house and sees only a pile of clay, one may very well say, "there is nothing here." All that was found was the pre-creation material, which for all intents and purposes, is nothing.

In the ANE, darkness, waters, and ruined land were the pre-creation materials. They were nothing. They had not yet been formed by Yahweh and given a purpose within his world. Walton has pointed out that in ANE texts, creation takes place by a separation of part of the pre-creation material from the rest then naming or giving function to the separated material. This pattern is activated by various language used to denote the separation and naming/assigning of functions. This pattern will be seen in the creation narrative and throughout our discussion of the Exodus motifs in Genesis.

In Genesis 1, light is seen separated from darkness, then both are named. Next the waters are separated and the created expanse is named "sky" or "heaven." Waters were then gathered (made distinct from the rest of the waters) and named "seas." Likewise, Yahweh caused the land to appear out of the waters and named it. In the next three days of creation, Yahweh fills the spaces he has created with lights, plants, animals, and humans, giving them each functions within the world (i.e. ruling, producing seed/offspring, to be food). We also learn in chapter 2 that the plants, animals, and humans came from the ground (i.e. separation, vs. 7, 9, 19). Everything in the account has been created from the pre-existing material and given a function. There is much more to say on the topic, as Walton's book is almost entirely devoted to this topic, but for our purposes of exploring the Exodus motifs within Genesis, this will suffice.

We see this principle of functional ontology reappear at the Exodus of Israel as the Breath (רוּחַ, *rwḥ*) of God divides the dark waters and causes dry land to appear. Israel is brought through this new act of creation after being separated from the nations (Deut 32:8–9) and given a new function as a nation of priests (Ex 19:5–6)[25]. This idea appears again in the New Testament as Paul sees the Church as a new creation or new humanity (e.g. 2 Cor 5:17, Eph 2:15, 4:24). This is more than a clever metaphor. Paul

---

25. Carmen Imes also argues that Israel's exodus is to be read as an act of functional creation given that Israel's exodus, as well as the creation narrative, fit the ANE creation pattern of naming, separating, and temple building. Imes, "The Lost World," 126–141

sees that Jesus has undergone and led a new exodus[26] through the waters of death by the power of the Breath of God and called a new people to the priestly calling of Ex 19:5–6 (see 1 Pet 2:9). Having been separated from the nations, undergone exodus in Jesus, and given a new purpose, the assembly of Christ is not just *like* a new creation but *is*, ontologically, a new creation. As we continue, we see this concept reappear in Genesis as part of the Exodus motif.

We should keep in mind that these acts of new creation are also linked to coming through the waters by the work of the Breath of God. We have already explored the presence of parting waters and breath/wind in the creation narrative and in Israel's exodus. We will also see these elements present as an act of new creation in the flood narrative. The pattern of water and breath continues as Israel renews the covenant and crosses the Jordan in Josh 3 (breath (רוּחַ, *rwḥ*) is not mentioned here but it is portrayed as a reenactment of Israel's exodus) and in Jesus' baptism (Matt 3:16). This motif of re-creation through water and breath is why Jesus tells Nicodemus that he must be born of water and breath/spirit[27] in order to enter the kingdom of Heaven in John 3. Notice that when Jesus tells Nicodemus he must be born of water and breath, he is rephrasing his former statement, that one must be born again (or "from above")[28]. Jesus here equates being born from above, being re-created so to speak, and being born of water and breath. This fact strengthens the argument that when someone is brought through the waters, or through metaphorical waters, we ought to see them undergoing an act of re-creation from Yahweh. They are separated out from the ruin around them and formed into a people for Yahweh's restorative purposes.

Lastly, we need to discuss the intertwined concepts of temple and creation. John Walton has also surveyed ANE creation texts, demonstrating that biblical creation was viewed as a temple[29]. G.K. Beale has conducted a similar study of ANE material while also investigating the Hebrew Bible and early Jewish literature, giving an account of the cosmic

26. For a discussion of Exodus themes in the new testament see Estelle, *Echoes*, Chapters 7–11 and Fox, *Reverberations*, Chapters 6–9

27. The Greek word here, πνεῦμα (*pneuma*), is commonly used in the LXX to translate רוּחַ (*rwḥ*) and can likewise be translated as "spirit, breath, or wind."

28. It is likely that to be born "from above" is the better translation, as the Greek word (ἄνωθεν, *anōthen*) can mean either "again" or "from above."

29. Walton, *Genesis 1*, 100–119

and Edenic symbolism found in the tabernacle/temple and its utensils[30]. These studies have shown that both the Biblical authors and the people of the ANE viewed creation accounts as the creation of temples. Often these temples were intended to consist of the entire cosmos, as in the Bible. These cosmic temples were often identified as fertile gardens, from which life-giving waters flow, and likewise, temples were often decorated with gardens and water features[31]. These first temples are also depicted as mountain tops, as the Garden of Eden is said to be in Ezek 28:13–14, and are the place in which the deity rests when his temple/world-creating work is done. Also significant to our prior discussion of light and sunrise is the fact that ANE temples are often identified as the place from which the sun rises[32].

The original audience of Genesis would have clearly perceived that the creation narrative was also a temple creation narrative. They also would have perceived this particular garden-temple to be a precursor to the Tabernacle and Jerusalem Temple. The Tabernacle/Temple was decorated with garden imagery, and like the Garden of Eden, had Cherubim on the east side, protecting the path to the Most Holy place. These Cherubim were woven into the curtain rather than real, but these images were to symbolize that to enter the Tabernacle/Temple was to reenter the Garden. The Tabernacle/Temple was a "copy and shadow of the heavenly things" but the Garden was the substance, the heavenly temple[33]. Notice also that the Tabernacle/Temple faced East (Ex 26:18–22, cf. Ezek 43:4) just as the Cherubim were put on the East to guard the Eastward entrance into the Garden. This may give us reason to think that the "east wind (רוּחַ, rwḥ)" that parted the waters during Israel's exodus was the Spirit (רוּחַ, rwḥ) of God who had hovered over the waters in the beginning.

It is also significant that, within the Bible, humanity is created to be kings and priests in the garden-temple. In the ANE, a king was the image of a god and, as such, was endowed with the authority to rule on behalf of the deity[34]. Humanity's creation in the Image of God is our creation as kings of creation on behalf of Yahweh. The first human was

---

30. Beale, *Temple*, 29–80

31. Walton, *Ancient Near Eastern Thought*, 83

32. Walton, *Genesis 1*, 104

33. This is why Jesus tells the believing thief that they will be together in paradise (Lk 23:43). The word "paradise" is simply an English transliteration of the Greek word for garden (παράδεισος, *paradeisos*), used in the LXX in reference to the Garden of Eden.

34. Walton, *Genesis 1*, 175–176

also given the kingly command to subdue (כבשׁ, *kbš*) the land[35] (Gen 1:28). Adam is commissioned as a priest when he is told to "work (עבד, *ʿbd*)" and "keep (שׁמר, *šmr*)" the garden-temple (Gen 2:15). A similar charge is given to the Levites as they "work (עבד, *ʿbd*)" and "attend to (שׁמר, *šmr*)" the tabernacle and temple (Num 3:7–8, 8:25–26, 18:5–6; 1 Chr 23:32 ; Ezek 44:14). Also contributing to humanity's priestly status in the garden-temple, Yahweh makes (עשׂה, *ʿsh*) garments (כֻּתֹּנֶת, *ktnt*) and clothes (לבשׁ, *lbš*) the man and woman (Gen 3:21) just as Moses makes (עשׂה, *ʿsh*) priestly garments (כֻּתֹּנֶת, *ktnt*) and clothes (לבשׁ, *lbš*) the priests (Ex 28:39–41; 29:8; 39:27; 40:14; Lev 8:7). The garden-temple structure is complete with a ruling priest within it.

While not exhaustive, the points demonstrate that the creation of the Garden is to be read as the creation of Yahweh's temple in which (6) humanity was created to be placed and (7) take up a kingly/priestly role within. Now that we have taken a detour to explore the pre-creation state, functional ontology, and the Garden's temple status, we are better able to explore the similarities between the exodus of Israel from Egypt and the exodus of creation. We will then be better able to see how these exodus/creation motifs run throughout the rest of Genesis.

THE EXODUS MOTIF: CREATION

We have already briefly discussed a couple of the exodus features at the beginning of the creation narrative. In both the exodus of Israel and creation, dry land is brought out of the dark waters by the Breath of God. As the story continues and a new creation of humanity is brought out of these conditions, we see several more interesting parallels between the creation and the exodus out of Egypt.

In the second creation account of Gen 2, the land is present, but the Garden could not be grown because the land was dry. So, Yahweh caused a life-giving stream to come up and water the ground (Gen 2:6). The first man was then created out of the, now wet, ground before the creation of the garden-temple. He was created outside of the area where the garden-temple would be. Once Yahweh had made the garden-temple, he put (נוח, *nwḥ*) the man in it. Yahweh then commissioned the man as a priest and gave him a command (צוה, *ṣwh*) to not eat of the Tree of the

---

35. The Hebrew word כבשׁ occurs four other times in the Torah and Joshua (Gen 1:28; Num 32:22, 29; Josh 18:1) and only refers to the subduing of Canaan by Israel in these verses outside of Gen 1:28.

Knowledge of Good and Evil so that he does not die. The man is then given a wife. After this, seeking authority which is not theirs, the first man and woman take from the Tree of the Knowledge of Good and Evil. The man and woman are visited by Yahweh, sentenced with difficulty in their fruitfulness, and exiled east.

In the exodus out of Egypt, once the people have come through the waters as a new creation, and both sea and sea monster have been defeated, we see more similarities emerge. We see the repeated motif of life-giving waters and being put in Yahweh's dwelling. After leaving the Sea of Reeds and wandering for three days, the people become thirsty and find a water source. However, this water source is bitter and undrinkable. Yahweh instructs Moses to throw a tree[36] into the water which makes the water into a source of life for the people. The people then come to the twelve springs and seventy trees of Elim (which means "Oak trees"); to a garden-like oasis fed by water that comes up from the ground. In Ex 17, again the people are thirsty and test Yahweh, but he provides a spring out of a rock to give life to the people before they come to Yahweh's dwelling. Yahweh, just as at creation, turns bad waters into good and provides springs which foster the life of his new creation.

As the people reach Sinai, the hope of Israel found in Ex 15:17 is fulfilled for the first time,

> You will bring them in and plant (נוח, *nwḥ*) them on your own
>   mountain,
>   the place, O Lord, which you have made for your abode,
>   the sanctuary, O Lord, which your hands have established.

After the exodus, (6) Yahweh brings his people to his mountain dwelling on Sinai, just as he brought the man to his mountain abode at the Garden of Eden. He does this with intentions to, next, plant (נוח, *nwḥ*) the people in Canaan, at his mountain dwelling in Jerusalem.

> [9]for you have not as yet come to the rest (נוח, *nwḥ*) and to the inheritance that the Lord your God is giving you. [10]But when you go over the Jordan and live in the land that the Lord your God is giving you to inherit, and when he gives you rest (נוח, *nwḥ*) from all your enemies around, so that you live in safety,

---

36. The word עֵץ (*ʿṣ*) is often translated as "tree" or "wood" but also as other items made of wood, such as "beam" or "shaft." The idea behind this word is of a tree or anything made from a tree. A separate word is not used for what we may consider to be "dead" wood.

[11]then to the place that the LORD your God will choose, to make
his name dwell there. —Deut 12:9–11

We find the expectation of being rested in the land of Israel throughout Deuteronomy and Joshua[37]. This promise is fulfilled in Josh 21:44 as
the people are finally given rest (נוח, *nwḥ*) from their enemies in the land
after they have subdued (כָּבַשׁ, *kbš*) them (cf. Gen 1:28) and set up the
tabernacle in Canaan (Josh 18:1). We should also note here that, in Deut
7:11–16, Israel is given the Edenic blessing of fruitfulness, multiplication,
and subduing and the Abrahamic blessing of the land on the basis of their
obedience to the commandments (צוה, *ṣwh*). On this same basis, Israel
is again promised the ability to subdue their enemies in Canaan in Deut
11:8–12. Interestingly, in this passage, the land of Canaan is described
as a garden which is tended by Yahweh himself. In these passages we see
Israel given rest in the land after subduing their enemies and setting up
in Yahweh's garden-like dwelling, just as the first man was given rest in
the Garden and commissioned to subdue the land. The people then must
continue in obedience to the commandments to remain in the garden-
land with the blessings of Eden and Abraham, just as was true for Adam.

In the first 9 verses of Ex 19, the people reach Sinai and are (7) given
a priestly commission and covenant, to which they agree. They are now
set aside from the nations, with a new purpose: to be Yahweh's priests
who will bless the nations and make Yahweh known. This role is based on
the covenant between Yahweh and Israel, which consists, in part, of the
commandments found throughout the Torah. In Deut 30:15, once Moses
has finished expositing the covenant and commandments, he says, "See, I
have set before you today life and good, death and evil." It has been noted
that just as Yahweh gave Adam and Eve the command to not eat from
the Tree of the Knowledge of Good and Evil lest they die, so Moses sets
before Israel a command that he refers to as "good and evil"[38] to follow,
lest they "perish" (Deut 30:18). Moses goes on in this passage to briefly
recount the blessings Israel will have if the commands are kept, and the
curses that will be on them if not. Deut 28 more fully describes the blessings of loyalty to the covenant, as well as the consequences of disloyalty.
When speaking of the curses, Moses speaks in terms of unfruitfulness
and the Babylonian exile. Just as Israel, Adam was given a command concerning good and evil with the consequences of disloyalty being death.

---

37. See also Deut 3:20; 25:19; Josh 1:13–15; 22:4; 23:1

38. Sailhamer, *Pentateuch as Narrative*, 474

When Adam broke the commandment, rather than immediate death, the ground was made unfruitful and he was exiled East[39] with only the hope of a seed that would be his redemption.

Another parallel between the Exodus and Creation may be found in Gen 3:8. Jeffrey Niehaus has reexamined the verse[40]:

> And they heard the sound (קוֹל, *kwl*) of the LORD God walking (מִתְהַלֵּךְ, *mthlk*) in the garden in the cool (רוּחַ, *rwḥ*) of the day (יוֹם, *ywm*).

To be brief, the word קוֹל (*kwl*) can be translated as "sound" or "voice" (e.g. Gen 27:22; Ex 19:19) but is also used to denote "thunder" (Ex 20:18). The root of the term מִתְהַלֵּךְ (*mthlk*), הלך (*hlk*), is often translated "to walk" but can also simply mean "to go." The current verb form (hithpael) denotes a "walking throughout" or "going to and fro," as is more clearly seen in places such as Gen 13:17 and Deut 23:14. We have already looked at the word (רוּחַ, *rwḥ*), and seen that it means "breath," "wind," or "spirit." The word "cool" may come from an assumption that the "*wind* of the day" must denote a cool breeze (cf. NET). Lastly, the term יוֹם (*ywm*) is the word for "day," but also is a homonym with a less-used word meaning "storm." Taking these facts into consideration, Gen 3:8 may be better translated as:

> And they heard the thunder of Yahweh God going throughout the garden with the wind of the storm (AT)

Here we see a parallel with Sinai in that Israel met with Yahweh in a fiery storm on his mountain dwelling, and here Yahweh meets with Adam and Eve in a storm on his mountain dwelling. Though יוֹם (*ywm*) is rarely used for "storm," seeing Yahweh as coming in a storm is conceptually aligned with the image of Yahweh as coming in a storm seen in the Torah and throughout the Psalms, Prophets, and Job. Therefore, the proposed translation may reveal the intended meaning of the author and reveal conceptual connections within the text.

39. Throughout the biblical story, East is the direction of exile away from Yahweh's presence. This is seen, for example, with Cain (Gen 4:16), humanities movement to Shinar (Gen 11:2), and Israel and Judah's exiles to the eastern nations of Babylon and Assyria.

40. Niehaus, "In the Wind"

Marriage and Covenant

A brief word needs to be said about Adam's marriage and its relation to the Sinai Covenant. Adam's statement in Gen 2:23, "This at last is bone of my bones, and flesh of my flesh," is familial language[41]. In this statement, Adam is making a marriage covenant and recognizing the woman as family. In Eph 5:31–32, Paul sees this marriage ceremony as programmatic for the marriage between Christ and the church. G.K. Beale and Benjamin Gladd have shown that when Paul speaks of Gen 2:24 being a "mystery" that refers to Christ and the Church, he is not simply using an Old Testament metaphor or fabricating an enigmatic interpretation, but he is using *mystery* in a technical sense[42].

Paul's use of *mystery* refers to something that was only partially revealed but now is fully revealed. That is to say, Paul believes the author of Genesis meant for the reader to apply Gen 2:24 to the relationship of God and his people, though Genesis is not overtly clear on that interpretation. Paul gets this understanding of Gen 2:23–24 because of the rest of the Hebrew Bible's understanding that the Sinai covenant was a marriage covenant between Yahweh and Israel (e.g. Jer 31:32; Ezek 16:1–14[43]). The import into our discussion is that Adam receives his bride and Israel is received as a bride as part of their exodus events. Adam and Israel are both brought through the parted waters and made into a new creation. Each is then presented with a marriage. To say that these marriages have a one-to-one correspondence would go too far, but they are linked by interbiblical interpretation as well as by their climactic placements within exodus cycles. This pattern of exoduses climaxing in the reception of a bride will show up again later in Genesis. While the brides of the Genesis narratives are not clearly symbolic of Israel, it is beneficial to see that the author has set up, within the Exodus motif, a theme of delivered and received brides, beginning with the first man and woman and climaxing with Yahweh's reception of his bride at Sinai.

However, the first man and woman, after their own receiving of a commandment, commissioning as priests, and marriage, quickly (8)

---

41. cf. Gen 29:14; Judg 9:2; 2 Sam 5:1; 19:12–13

42. Gladd and Beale, *Hidden,* for use of *mystery* in Ephesians 5, see section "Marital Mystery in Ephesians 5."

43. Ezek 16 speaks in a marriage metaphor but is a description of Yahweh bringing the people out of Egypt, covenanting with them, and adorning them with the law (compare v14 to Deut 4:5–6).

rebel and choose their own wisdom over Yahweh's. This brings about a frustration of their fruitfulness and exile east. Likewise, Israel rebels until their divided kingdoms face the curses for disobedience (Lev 26; Deut 28) and are exiled east. Even within the immediate context of Israel's exodus, Israel rebels and makes an image to worship. Because of this, Moses is then chosen to survive as all Israel perishes for their sin (Ex 32:10, cf. Gen 6:12–14). Moses is able to intercede for the people but it is clear that Yahweh cannot dwell continually with Israel. Purification is required. This is not a new problem in the biblical story, but rather it is a problem that has been in the biblical narrative since Gen 3: Yahweh and humanity cannot dwell together.

This rebellion narrative in Exodus is building to the heart of the entire Torah. L. Michael Morales has shown that, because of this problem, and because Yahweh desires to bring humanity back into his presence, the Day of Atonement[44] in Lev 16 is the literary and narrative center of the Torah[45]. This is a climax within Israel's exodus story since it accomplishes the goal of purifying the people so that Yahweh can dwell with them after he has performed the exodus. This element of purification after exodus will appear in Genesis. In the creation narrative, this element does not appear as humanity is still clean and without sin until Gen 3. The garden-temple is created and it has no need of further purification. Yahweh has taken the unclean dark waters and cleansed them. But for every future exodus, sinful humans are the subject of the exodus, so every temple or new creation will need purification. Although no purification or Day of Atonement is needed at creation, it is worth noting that both Israel's exodus narrative and the creation narrative *do* climax with a functioning temple system, serving as the dwelling of both humans and Yahweh together.

Through our exploration of the world-creation narrative and the Israel-creation narrative, we have seen that the author has intentionally and sequentially modeled these events off one another. The author demonstrates that in these two events, he sees Yahweh completing very similar acts, and for the same purpose. Yahweh seeks to create a bride which he

---

44. Better translated "the Day of Purgation" as Israel and the tabernacle are purged of impurity (Milgrom, *Leviticus 1–16*, 1079–1084). For simplicity sake I will continue to refer to the events of Lev 16 as the Day of Atonement.

45. Morales, *Who Shall Ascend*, see pages 23–38 for a discussion of Leviticus 16 within the structure and narrative of the Torah.

loves and intends to commission to expand the goodness of the Garden[46]; to be a light to the nations (Ezek 16:14; Deut 4:5–6). In both narratives we see the Breath of Yahweh interacting with (1) the dark, foreboding waters, and the ruined land. (3) These elements are subdued and dry land is caused to appear, which becomes the means of the creation of (5) a new humanity[47]. This new humanity is then (6) brought to the Garden/mountain temple of Yahweh, (7) commissioned as priest-kings, given a commandment, married, and made pure. Our stories ought to end here, with humanity and Yahweh enjoying one another's presence as humanity works to expand Yahweh's goodness and as they represent him to creation. However, the parallels between Adam and Israel continue as both (8) disobey, causing exile from Yahweh's abode and a rift in the human family. So, the author leaves the reader awaiting a new and permanent exodus. While this permanent exodus is not found in Genesis, there is a prevalent presence of intrahuman and intrafamilial strife and disloyalty to Yahweh, which he overcomes using chosen individuals, or by bringing individuals through their own exodus events to rectify these problems introduced into creation.

---

46. Beale, *Temple*, 81–121
47. cf. Isa 43:1

Table 1

Correspondences to the exodus of Creation

	Creation	Exodus
(1)(3) Dark waters separated involving the Breath of God	Gen 1:2, 6	Ex 14:21
(1)(3) Sea/sea monster/enemies defeated/restrained	Gen 1:4, 6	Ex 14:21, 26–28; 15:1–12; Ps 74:12–17
Dry land appears	Gen 1:9	Ex 14:21
Salvation at morning	Gen 1:4	Ex 14:24, 27
(5) New humanity	Gen 1:26; 2:7	Ex 19:4–5; Isa 43:1
Creation of temple	Gen 2:8	Ex 15:17; 35–40
Spring/well	Gen 2:6	Ex 15:25–27; 17:6
(6) Rested at Yahweh's garden/dwelling	Gen 2:15	Ex 15:17; Lev 26:11–12, Deut 11:8–12; Josh 21:44
(7) Blessing: fruitful, multiply	Gen 1:28	Lev 26:3–10; Deut 11:7–16
(7) Commissioned to subdue	Gen 1:26, 28	Lev 26:6–8; Deut 7:16; Josh 18:1
(7) Act as Priests	Gen 2:15	Ex 19:5–6
Given command (regarding Good and Evil) on pain of death	Gen 2:16–17	Deut 30:15
Results of failure to keep the commands	Gen 2:17	Deut 30:17–18
Marriage	Gen 2:22–25	Ex 19:5–8; Jer 31:32; Ezek 16:8
(8) Rebellion	Gen 3:6	Ex 32:1–8; 2 Kings 17:6–18; Micah 1
(8) Fruitfulness frustrated/ Exile East	Gen 3:16–19, 23–24	Lev 26:14–27; Deut 28:15–68; 2 Kings 17:6–18; Micah 1

Cain and Abel

THE STORY OF CAIN and Abel is one of family strife, to say the least. The introduction of rifts within the human family took place when Adam and Eve ate from the Tree of the Knowledge of Good and Evil. They became ashamed to be in one another's presence and began to blame shift, and were subsequently exiled from the Garden. The story of Gen 3 sets up problems that the biblical narrative must resolve: separation from God and disunity among humans. The book of Genesis does not resolve these problems, nor does the rest of the Hebrew Bible, and even now, we await the final resolution to our story, after having seen the firstfruits of the Bible's resolution in Jesus. As we read through the book of Genesis we need to keep these two central problems from the Garden in mind. All future problems we face in Genesis are rooted in separation from Yahweh and the disunity of the human family. Likewise, all resolutions we see in the biblical narrative are small-scale types of the ultimate resolution to these two problems. These small types of the resolution we are looking for *give us pictures of what the final solution will look like* and show us that Yahweh is consistently pursuing the unification of Yahweh and the human family. This makes sense in light of the hope of the Hebrew Bible: Yahweh's return to enact an exodus, bringing the people, purified, to his holy mountain, and a reunification of the Israelite tribes under the Davidic king. All of these elements will be presented in Genesis as the book shapes the eschatological hope of the reader, with the exception that the book of Genesis looks to a Judahite king and not yet to the more narrow scope of the Davidic king.

The Cain and Abel story clearly presents family strife, which is part of another motif present in this section of Genesis. This motif is the Two-Goats motif mentioned above. The reasoning for the motif being called the "Two-Goats" motif is because the characters that take part in this motif each play a distinct role that climaxes in the roles of the two goats used in the Day of Atonement ritual. In some of these stories, there are words and concepts that link the narrative to the two goats found in the Day of Atonement in Leviticus 16. As is typical of the biblical authors, they will show us this motif a handful of times then will use the, now recognizable, motif in different ways in order to make different points or subtly give the reader additional insight into the narrative. Before we can recognize these motifs in Genesis, we need to acquaint ourselves with the roles that the two goats play in the Day of Atonement.

THE DAY OF ATONEMENT

It has already been mentioned that the Day of Atonement lies at the literary and narrative center of the Torah. The Day of Atonement provides yearly cleansing for the people of Israel so that they may continue to have Yahweh in their presence. On this day, the high priest must bring a bull to be a purification offering for himself, along with the two goats, to the Tabernacle. Lots are then cast over the goats in order to determine which will be for Yahweh (the purification offering) and which will be for Azazel (sent out with the sins of the people). Once the destinies of the goats are determined, he bathes and changes his high-priestly garments for holy linen garments. He then slaughters the bull and brings the blood into the Tabernacle. Before proceeding, he adds burning coals and incense to the incense altar. He proceeds to sprinkle the blood on and next to the lid of the Ark, thereby making purification for himself and his household. The goat for Yahweh is then slaughtered as a purification offering and its blood is sprinkled on and by the lid of the Ark, as was done with the bull's blood, in order to make purification for Israel. The blood of both the bull and the goat is then put on the altar, cleaning it from Israel's impurities. The goat for Azazel is then brought to have the sin of Israel confessed over it by the high priest, then it is sent out into a barren desert, bearing the sins of Israel away. The high priest then bathes and puts on his high-priestly clothes once again, having purged Israel of impurity by the two goats of the Day of Atonement.

The two goats are, significantly, *elected* for their roles. It would be easy to assume that since lots were cast, the decision of the goats' fate was as random as possible. However, lots are used in the Bible as a form of Yahwistic divination; a way of seeking Yahweh's will. Within the priestly system and monarchy of Israel, Yahweh authorized individuals to discern his will through this method. So, rather than being random, the decision that comes from the cast lot is from Yahweh (Prov 16:33). The decision, then, of each goat's fate was not random, but each goat was (A) elected by Yahweh to its role[1]. One goat is then (G) brought closer to Yahweh as it is (H) slaughtered and its blood is brought into the Tabernacle to purify Israel, while (D) the other goat is sent out into the wilderness bearing the sins of Israel. It is important to note that the sending away of the goat for Azazel is not a punishment upon the goat nor a means to afflict it, despite what some later Jewish tradition may suggest[2]. By taking the sins of Israel upon itself, the goat does not become sinful. The role of the goat for Azazel within scripture is not to be punished on behalf of Israel or suffer as an embodiment of sin but, rather, to be the means by which the sins are removed from the community of Israel. This is why the goat is set free (Lev 16:22), presumably in peace, rather than killed. This is significant to note given that most of the brothers that fit within this motif are not removed from the elect community as a punishment and are, rather, blessed through their exile[3].

Throughout Genesis, we will see repeated words and concepts that are meant to draw attentive readers to the Two-Goats motif and the goats' roles within the Day of Atonement. We will highlight these words and concepts as we go and trace their development through Genesis and up to the Day of Atonement in Leviticus. Andrei A. Orlov, drawing from various modern and ancient scholars, has discussed the connections between the two goats from the Day of Atonement and the brothers Cain and Abel, Isaac and Ishmael, Jacob and Esau, and Joseph[4]. Much of the discussion in this work of how these particular characters fit within the Two-Goats motif will be based on his work. He highlights connections within Genesis and Leviticus and demonstrates how these connections were seen by early rabbinical writers as well as other early Jewish writers. However, our discussion will remain germane to the texts of the Torah and explore the meaning that the author of the Torah intended readers to perceive.

1. Milgrom, *Leviticus 1–16*, 1019–1020

2. Moscicke, "Jesus as Scapegoat," 246, 250–254. In the Second Temple period, the scapegoat was severely abused before being killed in the wilderness and banished to the underworld. This practice, however, is a later development and not in view within the Hebrew Bible.

3 See also Douglas, *Jacob's Tears*, 49–52

4. Orlov, *The Atoning Dyad*, 6–42

THE TWO-GOATS MOTIF: CAIN AND ABEL

Gen 4 begins with Cain and Abel being born to Adam and Eve. Cain is the eldest, and in the ANE this would put him in the role of firstborn. Along with the duty of leading the family, this role entitled him to a larger inheritance and preeminence over his brothers. Ideally, this cultural convention enabled the oldest male of the family to care for and lead the next generation of the family. With this role naturally came the largest and best inheritance as well as honor within the family. In the story of Genesis, however, the firstborn right often does not go to the eldest, but rather Yahweh selects a firstborn, disregarding birth order, and gives to them the blessings of the Garden of Eden. The purpose of giving this blessing is that this firstborn, whom Yahweh elects, would be a blessing to all peoples, bringing humanity back to a state of blessedness in Yahweh's presence, as it was in the Garden. We will see this play out as we continue through Genesis.

Although Abel is nowhere given this firstborn blessing, while other elect individuals in Genesis are, it is implied that Abel is given the blessing by a few facets of the narrative. The fact that his offering is looked on with favor, the fact he is the first to fit in the slot of the goat for Yahweh, and the fact that Seth is said to replace Abel (Gen 4:25) all suggest to the reader that Abel was given the firstborn blessing. The fact that Seth is Abel's replacement is significant because Seth is the father of the chosen line of Noah and Abraham. Seth passes the role, promises, and Edenic blessings on to his children, which he received when he replaced Abel as the woman's seed. Notice that Yahweh has not selected only an individual, but the father of a family, and subsequently, that family; from Seth all the way to Israel. That is why the blessing flows through family lines and firstborn rights as opposed to the random selection of unrelated individuals.

The narrative of Gen 4 is intentionally sparse in detail but communicates much in light of the story of the Torah. Just as with Abel's firstborn status, later scripture will cause gaps in the present narrative to be filled. Cain and Abel bring unnamed offerings to Yahweh, Cain from the "fruit of the ground" and Abel from the "firstborn of his flock and of their fat (best) portions" (parentheses mine). Abel's sacrifice is looked on by Yahweh, marking him as the (A) elected firstborn and (G) accepted before Yahweh, while Cain's is not. Because of this, (B) Cain is jealous and enraged that his birthright has been removed from him and given to his younger brother. At this point, we could move beyond the nature of the sacrifice, which we are told so little about, but an exploration of it will help us see the pervasiveness of cultic[5] language in this passage.

We know that, since Abel took his sacrifice from the flock, his sacrifice was a blood sacrifice. We are also told in Gen 9:4 that the life of a creature is in the blood. This same statement is later expounded upon in Lev 17:11 when Yawhweh says,

> For the life of the flesh is in the blood, and I have given it for you
> on the altar to make atonement for your souls, for it is the blood
> that makes atonement by the life.

In the Bible, and in much of the ancient world, blood functioned as a ritual detergent, cleansing those offering sacrifices from impurity[6]. Blood was given by Yahweh so that it could be used by people to cleanse themselves and make themselves fit to be in Yahweh's presence, as is done on the Day of Atonement. Whether Abel's offering was a burnt offering or a purification offering, the blood of his sacrifice cleansed him for entry into holy space or communion with Yahweh.

Cain's vegetables did not have the same effect. A non-animal purification offering is only allowed to the poorest worshipers in Lev 5:11, but even then, this individual is part of the Israelite community which is purified each year by blood on the Day of Atonement. These considerations from elsewhere in the Torah help us to step into the worldview of the biblical author and give us a reasoning for why Abel's sacrifice may have been looked onto by Yahweh while Cain's was not. Once we have this understanding of Gen 4:3–5, we must make some more detailed comments about Gen 4:7 that will lend support to this offering being a purification offering and show how thoroughly the cultic world of the bible is ingrained in this text.

In Gen 4:7 Yahweh is encouraging Cain after he has been rejected as firstborn. The ESV reads,

> If you do well, will you not be accepted? And if you do not do
> well, sin is crouching at the door. Its desire is contrary to you,
> but you must rule over it.

This translation is representative of the major modern translations. However, I contend that there is a better way to translate the verse. There are

---

5. I use the term "cultic" not in the popular sense, referring to unorthodox religions, but rather in the technical sense, referring to the ritual system of a religion.

6. Milgrom, *Leviticus 1–16*, 254

several terms that we need to discuss in detail, so it will be helpful to look at the verse in Hebrew, though I will structure the discussion such that those without knowledge of Hebrew can follow along. I will also provide a transliteration, reading from left to right, for those unfamiliar with the Hebrew script. The Hebrew of Gen 4:7 reads:

הֲלוֹא אִם־תֵּיטִיב שְׂאֵת וְאִם לֹא תֵיטִיב לַפֶּתַח חַטָּאת רֹבֵץ וְאֵלֶיךָ
תְּשׁוּקָתוֹ וְאַתָּה תִּמְשָׁל־בּוֹ ⁷

hlw' 'm tytyb s't w'm l'tytyb lptḥ ḥt't rbṣ w'lyk tšwktw w'th
tmšl bw

Much of the argument regarding this verse comes from an article written by L. Michael Morales[8], but I will be adding to his arguments in some places. To begin, the word חַטָּאת (*ḥt't*), which is translated here as "sin" in most translations, contains the same Hebrew consonants translated as "sin offering" or "purification offering" elsewhere. Often context makes clear whether חטאת (*ḥt't*) is to be translated as "sin" or "purification offering," but the present verse requires greater attention. In the popular translation, *sin* is an animal ready to pounce on Cain and master him, but imagery of the like is not again found in scripture. The Bible is a very self-referential book, reusing the same sets of words and motifs throughout the canon, adding to the Bible's richness and depth of meaning. However, we do not again see a personification of *sin*. To render חטאת (*ḥt't*) as "purification offering" here, as opposed to "sin," may be a better reading of the text[9]. While repetition of cultic imagery, and lack of animalistic imagery, throughout the Torah may not be enough to make a convincing argument for translating חטאת (*ḥt't*) as "purification offering" as opposed to "sin," a further examination will show that this is the more natural understanding.

The word רֹבֵץ (*rbṣ*) is typically rendered "crouching" and has connotations of a violent prowling animal. However, of the 30 uses of this lemma in the Hebrew Bible, its primary, and arguably only, meaning is one of peacefully lying down. In the other uses of רֹבֵץ (*rbṣ*), violence is markedly absent from the context, and peace is the implied connotation[10].

7. From The Lexham Hebrew Bible (Bellingham, WA: Lexham Press, 2012), Gen 4:7.

8. Morales, "Crouching Demon"

9. Morales also notes that the difficulty of having feminine חַטָּאת (*ḥt't*) referred to with masculine words is removed when the חַטָּאת (*ḥt't*) is a purification offering. While חַטָּאת (*ḥt't*) is feminine, it is possible to have it referred to as masculine when the animal of the purification offering is masculine. Morales, "Crouching Demon," 187–188

10. See for example Ex 23:5, Num 22:27, Deut 22:6, Ps 23:2

Rather than a violent animal on the prowl, we now see an animal, which is to be a purification offering, peacefully lying down.

Next, the word פֶּתַח (pth) is accurately translated as "door" (though it more broadly means "entrance"), but we must narrow our understanding of this word in this context. This is not an abstract, symbolic door for the sin-creature to crouch behind, nor the entrance of Cain's dwelling, but instead, we ought to understand this as the entrance of the Tabernacle/Temple. In the previous chapter, we saw that the Garden is to be understood as the first temple. In the Biblical sacrificial system, sacrifices are brought to the entrance (פֶּתַח, pth) of the Tabernacle (eg. Lev 1:3; 3:2; 4:4; 8:3) which was a prototype of the temple. Furthering the correspondence between the Garden and the Tabernacle, the door of the Tabernacle also had Cherubim worked into the curtain (Ex 26:1) which represent the Cherubim stationed at the East edge of the Garden, each guarding the way to the holy place. Right before the beginning of chapter 4, Adam and Eve were exiled out of this holy place, so it is not unnatural to think that Cain and Able would offer their sacrifices at the entrance of Yahweh's dwelling, just as any Israelite would. Both would take their sacrifices along the path to the holy place, Yahweh's dwelling, until they were met by Cherubim, guarding Yahweh's dwelling from impurity. There they would offer their sacrifices to purify themselves, making themselves fit for communion with Yahweh.

The last term we must look at is the term תְּשׁוּקָתוֹ (tšwktw). This term only appears in the Hebrew Bible in Gen 3:16, 4:7, and SoS 7:10. Because of its sparse usage, it has been a difficult word to define, as can be seen in the history of the word's interpretation. The word is typically translated as "desire" but this translation is, in fact, a later development and does not best fit the word's usage. In examining the use of תְּשׁוּקָה (tšwkh) in the Dead Sea Scrolls and Hebrew Bible, alongside its historical translations, Macintosh concludes that the word is appropriately glossed by "concern, preoccupation, (single-minded) devotion, [or] focus"[11]. Perhaps a more

---

11. His argument utilizes the traditional translation of Gen 4:7 and his examination of this verse is the most strained portion of his arguments in my opinion. The translation I am arguing for fits very nicely with the definition of תְּשׁוּקָתוֹ (tšwktw) he has proposed. Macintosh, "The Meaning of Hebrew," 385

appropriate meaning, given the contexts in which the word is found[12], is the idea of giving one's submission or self over to something[13].

Taking the above considerations into the translation of Gen 4:7, the verse reads:

> If you do well, will there not be lifting-up[14]? But if you do not do well, at the entrance [of the garden-temple] lies a purification offering. And to you is his submission, but you must rule him. (AT)

In this translation, rather than having sin as a blood-thirsty animal, Cain is told that a purification offering lies at the door when he does not do well. If he does not do well, and thereby makes himself unclean, Yahweh has provided a way for him to purify himself. This is the purification offering that he should have offered alongside Abel, and even at this moment, there is an animal peacefully waiting for Cain. This animal has given itself over to Cain and waits to be used as purification for him. Since Yahweh informs Cain of this purification offering, it may be the case that Yahweh has provided the animal for this offering, just as he will do for Abraham in Gen 22:13.

We can see from this translation that the cultic motifs and principles of the Bible run throughout this passage. After the previous generation's exile from the garden-temple, Cain and Abel come to offer purifying

12. Macintosh, "The Meaning of Hebrew," 366–379

13. This meaning becomes more likely in light of my proposed translation of Gen 4:7. "Submission" or "the giving over of one's self" makes sense in all contexts, except for Gen 4:7, if it is interpreted as a beast that is on the offense. If I am correct that Gen 4:7 is about a willing sacrificial animal, then its use of תְּשׁוּקָה (tšwkh) agrees more closely with the other examined uses in Macintosh's article. In this context, "submission" fits, but more precisely, the word is a noun referring to one's self being given over. For example, in 1QS 11:22 reads, speaking of man's mortality, man's "תְּשׁוּקָה (tšwkh) is to dust." The verse refers not to man's desire for dust, but his being made from dust and return to it. He is given over to dust; submitted to death.

14. The word שְׂאֵת (s't), outside of this verse has to do with exaltation, sovereignty, or majesty." The "lifting-up" may be of Cain's countenance but also may be a lifting up of his honor and preeminence, i.e. restoration to his state as firstborn. This is uncertain but may be why we have not been told explicitly that Abel, being favored, was chosen as firstborn. If it is proper to understand this passage as Yahweh instructing Cain on how to keep the firstborn blessing, then the more natural understanding of "to you is its devotion, but you must rule it" is "to you is his (Abel's) devotion, but you must rule him." This understanding is possible in the context and though awkward to not have Abel's name mentioned, this would not be out of character for the Biblical text. In this reading, Abel is willing to be ruled by Cain, if Cain proves himself. However, the most natural referent of "him/it" is the purification offering.

sacrifices and come before Yahweh at the entrance of his dwelling. However, Cain offers an improper sacrifice. Yahweh provides him the opportunity to make it right, but consumed by jealousy, he instead murders his
brother. Cain is then met by Yahweh again and confronted. Cain avoids
responsibility for his brother, similar to the way his parents tried to shift
blame during a similar confrontation. Yahweh then says to Cain:

> What have you done? The voice of your brother's blood is cry-
> ing to me from the ground. [11]And now you are cursed from the
> ground, which has opened its mouth to receive your brother's
> blood from your hand. [12]When you work the ground, it shall
> no longer yield to you its strength. You shall be a fugitive and
> a wanderer on the earth." [13]Cain said to the LORD, "My punish-
> ment is greater than I can bear.—Gen 4:10–13

After asking the same question as he asked Adam and Eve after they
ate the fruit ("What have you done?"), Yahweh tells of Abel's blood being spilled on the ground by "[Cain's] hand." While blood on the ground
seems to be a fairly natural way to speak of murder, it is interesting that
in Leviticus, after sprinkling the blood of the purification offering on the
altar, the remaining blood is to be poured on the ground at the base of
the altar (Lev 4:7, 18, 25, 30, 34). The same instructions would presumably apply to the remaining blood of the Day of Atonement purification-
offering goat. Amid the cultic context of the passage it is worth noting
that similar to the blood that purifies being poured out on the ground,
Abel's blood calls to God from the ground after it has been spilled. The
reader expects to see the blood of Cain's purification offering appear in
the narrative, but instead, it is Abel's blood.

Strengthening the link between Abel and the purification offering is
a wordplay on Abel's name in Gen 4:4. Though not true in every instance,
names in the Bible are often not arbitrary but are rather "an integral part
of the literary texture"[15]. The particular literary feature we will see at
work in Gen 4:4 is known as "metathesis." Metathesis is the transposi-
tion of the letters within a word in comparison to another nearby word.
This literary feature is often used in the Bible to "link people's names to
particular characteristics of theirs, things that have happened to them,
or things that they have done."[16] In Gen 4:4 this literary feature is used

---

15. Garsiel, *Biblical Names*, 14

16. Kalimi, *Metathesis*, 50

to link Abel's name to the nearby word meaning "fat portions" or "best parts" of his flock:

> Abel (הֶבֶל, hbl) also brought of the firstborn of his flock and of their fat portions (וּמֵחֶלְבֵהֶן, wmḥlbhn)

The Hebrew word וּמֵחֶלְבֵהֶן (wmḥlbhn) is a compound word built on the root חֵלֶב (hlb), meaning "fat portions." The word חֵלֶב (hlb) contains the same letters as Abel's name, with the second and third letters transposed. Moshe Garsiel, in his work on the use of Biblical names, notes that וּמֵחֶלְבֵהֶן (wmḥlbhn) "seems to be both redundant and grammatically odd" and he therefore concludes that the link between Abel and the "fat portions" is likely deliberate[17]. The author wants his readers to equate, or at least see a similarity between, Abel and the fat portions that are to be sacrificed to make purification. The Biblical author has hinted to the reader that (H) Abel is to be compared to a purification offering. The comparison of Cain to the goat for Azazel will make clear that the particular purification offering that Abel is being compared to is the purification-offering goat of the Day of Atonement.

Cain, after he kills his brother, is "cursed from the ground," which echoes Adam's exile from the Garden. Cain is also cursed to no longer receive the ground's strength, which echoes the pronouncements on Adam and Eve which frustrate their ability to be fruitful and multiply. He is (D) being sent out of the land to a place that is desolate and will not easily produce food. After this sentence of exile has been pronounced, Cain then states that he cannot "bear (נשׂא, nsʾ)" his punishment and that he has been driven away from the land to be a wanderer. Just as the goat for Azazel bears (נשׂא, nsʾ) the sins of Israel and is driven from the land, or camp, of Israel, so Cain bears (נשׂא, nsʾ) his punishment as he is driven from the land. The goat for Azazel is sent to be set free in the wilderness and Cain is sent to be a wanderer in a desolate land. In these parallels, Cain is linked with the goat for Azazel, and Abel is linked with the goat for Yahweh in the Two-Goats motif.

Cain goes on to fear for his life in this new land of wandering. Yahweh (C) gives him protection and he (E) goes on to build a fruitful city in the land of his exile. We will see this protection, exile, city/nation-building, and fruitfulness develop into a pattern continually seen with the goat-for-Azazel character; the non-elect brother. This particular city that Cain builds becomes (F) a city of evil, characterized by Lamech's

---

17. Garsiel, *Biblical Names*, 92

polygamy and proud acts of murder. Likewise, other cities within this pattern will become problems for Israel in the future, but Yahweh shows a love and mercy to their founders similar to the love that he shows to his elect nation. This love is shown to Cain in his mark of protection and his ability to prosper to the point that he builds a city. Though Cain's city ends in the flood, and the other cities of this pattern end in a flood of judgment, Yahweh's wish for these cities is for them to be blessed by his elect one and to be brought to his dwelling through the elect one. Though humans may bring on themselves a different end, Yahweh intends to continue his plan of multiplying humanity, making them fruitful, and bringing them into his dwelling.

Cain's city and the multiplying of humanity lead us to the further fall of humanity in Genesis 6. As the narrative of Cain, Abel, and their parents closes, we are taken through a genealogy of Cain and then through a genealogy of Adam, following the chosen son. This in turn will take us to the story of Noah where the Exodus motif continues.

THE SEED OF THE WOMAN AND THE SEED OF THE SERPENT

Before moving on to the narrative of Noah, a brief word needs to be said about the seed of the woman and the seed of the serpent. In Gen 3:15, as Yahweh is pronouncing a curse on the serpent, we read:

> I will put enmity between you and the woman,
>   and between your offspring and her offspring;
> he shall bruise your head,
>   and you shall bruise his heel.

It has been noted the term "seed" (translated as "offspring") is applied to Seth in Gen 4:25, and therefore "seed" is vicariously applied to Abel as well. This term, however, is not applied to Cain[18]. We will also note from Gen 3:15 that the relationship between the seed of the woman and the seed of the serpent will be characterized by enmity. If Abel, and later Seth, is the seed of the woman through whom the serpent crusher will come, Cain is the seed of the serpent with whom they find enmity. This conclusion is strengthened by the fact that Cain is "cursed from the ground" (Gen 4:11) just as the serpent is "cursed" above all livestock. We

---

18. Verrett, *Serpent in Samuel*, 24–25

have already noted that Cain's curse has similarities with Adam's exile, but it is significant that only the serpent and the ground are cursed in Gen 3. The ground is only cursed because of Adam but the serpent is cursed because of his own deception of Eve. This language of "curse" and the characteristic of hostility toward the seed of the woman links Cain and the serpent[19].

It has been mentioned in a previous section that election and the firstborn blessings travel through family lines. The same is true for the seed of the woman. The ideas of the seed of the woman, Yahweh's elect, and Yahweh's firstborn are intertwined within the Bible. The identity of the seed of the woman, elect, and firstborn will continue through Seth's line to Noah, and on to Abraham. We will see the blessings of the Garden following this elect individual throughout the Genesis narrative. All the while, we are waiting for the Edenic blessings to fall on a seed of the woman who can not only strive against the seed of the serpent but crush the head of the serpent himself.

The seed of the serpent is also seen to follow family lines at times in Genesis (e.g. Cain's line), but the seed of the serpent can come from an unexpected place. This narrative demonstrates that the seed of the serpent is anyone who is at enmity with Yahweh's elect. Cain was part of the family of royal priests and could have maintained this status by submitting to his younger brother. But he becomes the seed of the serpent by his hostilities toward his brother. Members of the elect family can become the seed of the serpent by aligning themselves with the serpent and against Yahweh's elect one.

The idea that the seed of the serpent is any enemy of Yahweh and his elect may feel like familiar territory within this current work. We have already discussed some ways in which serpent imagery is applied to the enemies of Yahweh and his people, and how this imagery relates human enemies to Yahweh's cosmic enemy; the sea monster. This is why we will also see the seed of the serpent restrained or destroyed in many of the narratives ahead as part of the Exodus motif. When we see enemies being destroyed or afflicted we ought to see the restraining or conquering of the waters, the sea monster, and the sea monster's seed. We are seeing Yahweh getting victory in the hostility of the seed of the serpent.

---

19. Verrett, *Serpent in Samuel*, 24–25

Noah

THE STORY OF NOAH is similar to the creation narrative in that it is one of the most well known stories of the Bible. I will attempt to demonstrate that, like the creation narrative, it is also an exodus narrative. Throughout the narrative of Noah, we will see several keywords and concepts that have already been seen in our exploration of the Exodus motif in the creation.

The narrative begins with the further descent of humanity as the Sons of God mix with the daughters of men. There has been much debate over the identity of the Sons of God, but this work will presume their identity as spiritual beings. In short, this conclusion is based on the use of the phrase "sons of God" being used in the Bible to denote spiritual beings elsewhere and due to the ANE backgrounds to this story.[1] In Job 38:7, by way of parallelism, we are told that the Sons of God are also the stars. In the Bible, as well as throughout the ancient world, stars were seen as spiritual beings, placed there by Yahweh on the fourth day of creation to have rule over the marking of various seasons and occasions. We also see the Sons of God as part of Yahweh's council in places such as Ps 82. The Sons of God were given authority and a place in Yahweh's council, and they were to exercise that authority from heaven. However, the Sons of God, just as Eve does with the fruit, "saw" (ראה, r'h) that the daughters of humanity were "attractive" or, literally, "good" (טוב, twb) and "took" (לקח, lkh) of them.

Just as Adam, Eve, and Cain had been before, the Sons of God were dissatisfied with the positions and provisions Yahweh had given them, and they wanted more. So they saw what was good in their own eyes and took it, transgressing the boundaries of their authority. This story

---

1. Mesopotamia likewise had narratives in which gods breed with humans and produce demigods. For example and explanation see Heiser, *The Unseen Realm*, 23–27, 107–109

also serves as an inversion of the narrative of Genesis 3 in that instead of a spiritual being, the serpent, deceiving the woman into "taking" and rebelling, now the spiritual beings are themselves rebelling and "taking" women. Through this "taking," the Nephilim are born, giants who fill the land with violence and become persistent enemies of Yahweh's people[2]. Whether it comes in the form of jealousy and anger, or in the form of "seeing" and "taking" what seems to be good, the desire to transgress the bounds of one's current authority is a repeated motif throughout Genesis. This repetition of this sinful pattern, instigated in Gen 3 by the serpent, displays the rebellion of its subjects. While this pattern does not strictly signify that one is the seed of the serpent (as it was applied to Adam and Eve and will be applied to Abram and Sarai), it does signify one's rebellion, and, in this particular narrative, associate these Sons of God with the seed of the serpent[3].

After this transgression of boundaries takes place, the world and the hearts of humanity are filled with violence to the point of self-destruction. Therefore, Yahweh tells the righteous Noah that "the end of all flesh has come before me" (Gen 6:13) and instructs him to build an ark to withstand the coming flood. In a previous chapter we discussed that, in the Biblical imagination, the world sat inside a bubble in the endless cosmic waters, which were split to begin Yahweh's act of creation. We also discussed the foreboding connotations of the waters and their conceptual links to the sea monster and the enemies of Yahweh and his people. This flood is not just a large amount of water covering the land, but, in order to purify the land from humanity's violence, Yahweh is going to send the dwelling of all things anti-Yahweh to sweep over the land. This flood is an un-splitting of the waters from Gen 1 as the fountains of the deep break forth and the windows of heaven open (Gen 7:11). The world is being de-created on account of its violence, and it will be re-created in a purified state, with the seed of the serpent having been defeated.

Before Yahweh de-creates the world, sending the land back into a watery state of "welter and waste,"[4] he elects one individual, and his family with him, to carry the blessings of the Garden and to make a covenant with. Here, Yahweh's process of election continues in Noah as it did in Abel and Seth. While we do see the appearance of the motif of election with Noah, which is often seen in Genesis as part of the Two-Goats motif,

2. Heiser, *The Unseen Realm*, 183–215

3. Verrett, *Serpent in Samuel*, 25–26

4. Alter, *The Hebrew Bible*, 11

we do not get characters who clearly fit the roles of the two goats. However, the general characteristics of the motif are still present, despite the lack of two specific brothers that fill each role. First, a word must be said about the connotation of the wilderness that the goat for Azazel, and the corresponding brothers, are sent to.

WILDERNESS

In our discussion of the creation account, it was mentioned that the pre-creation state included ruined and chaotic land beneath the waters. After Yahweh had brought the land out of the waters, he continued forming it into something suitable for life and his presence. Greenery and trees are signs of this creative act of life, but wastelands and wildernesses are lands that are still in a pre-creation state. They are unfit for, and hostile to, Yahweh and his imagers.

We also discussed that the cosmos was created in order to be a temple. The Most Holy place, Yahweh's dwelling, *was* the Garden. But as was demonstrated in the creation narrative and by Cain's exile, there are at least three more areas of creation. The second area is the land of Eden, in which the Garden is planted, but is not the Garden itself. The third area, to which Cain goes, is the unfruitful land of wandering outside of Eden. The fourth area is the seas and cosmic waters which surround the land. It has been recognized that these first three areas of the land correspond to the areas of the Tabernacle[5]. The Most Holy place corresponds to the Garden as the dwelling of Yahweh, the Holy place corresponds to the land of Eden, the outer court corresponds to the land of wandering, and outside that is wilderness and uncleanliness corresponding to the seas and cosmic waters (see Fig. 2). This same structure is seen at Sinai. When Yahweh dwells on the mountain, the mountain is separated into three parts. The top is Yahweh's dwelling (Ex 19:20; 24:12, 16–18), The midsection is the Holy Place (Ex 19:24; 24:1–2, 9–15), the base is the outer court (Ex 19:12, 17), and beyond that is wilderness[6].

5. Morales, *Who Shall Ascend*, 64–67
6. Morales, *Who Shall Ascend*, 87

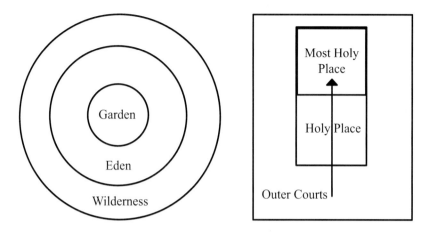

Figure. 2 Representation of the gradations of creation and the Tabernacle

Table 2

Gradations of Holy Space

Garden of Eden	Tabernacle	Sinai
Garden	Most Holy place	Top
Eden	Holy Place	Middle
Land of Wandering	Outer Court	Base
Waters	Wilderness	Wilderness

This list of tiered holy spaces is not exhaustive, but it demonstrates the understanding of the wilderness in the Biblical mind. The wilderness is a place of uncleanness that has not yet been fully formed by Yahweh's creative power into a place fit for Yahweh's dwelling and his imagers. The wilderness is a place of death, where serpents live (Deut 8:15). It is a place of evil spirits (Lev 16:10; Matt 4:1; 12:43), sin (Lev 16:22), and judgment (Josh 5:6; Ezek 20:35). It is also a place to be rescued from and a place that Yahweh will transform into a garden through his creative power (Isa 32:15–16; 43:19; Hos 2:12–15).

There are differences between the waters and wilderness; e.g. the waters are often equated with death itself whereas the wilderness is a deadly place to which people go, often with an expectation of future restoration by Yahweh. However, one can still see that the wilderness is, conceptually, very similar to the waters, and that the wilderness is geographically close to the waters in the temple-shaped world of the Bible. The attributes of the wilderness and those of the waters listed above ought not to be taken as dissociated from one another. Rather, because the waters and wilderness are farthest away from Yahweh's dwelling, it is natural for them to be devoid of plant life, full of unclean spirits and animals, a place of sin and enemies of Yahweh, and a place that is used as a judgment. These attributes also make it all the more astounding when Yahweh sustains a generation of people through the wilderness; when he provides food and water in the wilderness; when he uses it to refine his people; and when he transforms it into a lush garden as he did in Eden. In the prophets, because of these connotations and because of the wilderness wandering after the Exodus of Israel, the wilderness is often depicted as a place to go in order to escape Israel's wickedness and await a new creative act from Yahweh.

Conceptual links, such as those between the waters, the sea monster, Yahweh's enemies, the wilderness, and the area outside the Tabernacle, are often used by the Biblical authors to repeat motifs and meanings while being able to tell different stories with different nuances. It would serve our understanding of scripture to recognize these links so that we can perceive repeated motifs throughout scripture and understand the meaning of a book, or collection of books, as a whole. These conceptual links between the waters and the wilderness will serve us in the flood narrative as we explore Noah's election and the fate of those not elected.

THE EXODUS MOTIF: THE FLOOD

The flood narrative exhibits some characteristics of the Two-Goats motif in Noah's election, but it also exhibits differences from the elements of the motif. Just as is typical of the elected brother, Noah and his family are chosen to carry the Edenic blessing and he is given a covenant with Yahweh for the preservation (blessing) of humanity. He is then, in ef-fect, brought closer to Yahweh as he enters the Ark and ends up in his own Eden-like garden, which we will explore further. However, there is no corresponding non-elect brother who leaves the dwelling of Yahweh, protected by Yahweh, to build his own rebellious city. Rather, those out-side the elect family are all of humanity, and rather than being exiled in the wilderness, they are killed in the waters. The conceptual framework of the Two-Goats motif is still loosely at work: one is elected, blessed, and brought closer, and the rest are enemies of Yahweh that are sent further from his presence. However, in this case, being sent further from Yahweh's presence did not result in a wilderness exile but instead death in the cosmic waters. The people are not protected and given hope of future restoration but are instead cut off from the land of the living and plunged into the deep.

This outline of Noah's generation is more akin to the outline of Yahweh's enemies at the Exodus, who, because they oppressed his people, were faced with acts of decreation and covered by the flood of the Sea of Reeds. Ultimately, the similarities between the Two-Goats motif and Noah's narrative, while perhaps intentionally present, are not woven tight enough to suggest this narrative's inclusion in the motif. While similarities can surely be found, to rely upon the similarities between the waters and wilderness to call this section a part of the Two-Goats motif would be an over-reading of those (only conceptual) similarities. But as was stated, the story of Noah *is* an exodus narrative, so let us turn to examine the presence of that motif in the story.

Just as the Egyptians oppressed the people of Israel, Noah's generation (1) filled the earth with violence (Gen 6:11). Yahweh needed to purify his temple by washing it clean; by decreating and re-creating it. However, he still wished to have his human bride with him in his temple to rule and work as priest-kings. So he elected a righteous man, one who was loyal to Yahweh, to be preserved through the decreation and re-creation by means of an Ark. The Ark itself has tabernacle and garden imagery attached to it as well as narrative similarities. In the creation narrative of Gen 1, the Tabernacle building narrative of Ex 25–39, and the present story in Gen 6, Yahweh speaks, action is commanded, the command is carried out according to his will, and the narrative is concluded with divine blessing (Gen 1:28; 9:1; Ex 39:43)[7].

The Ark is also made of "gopher (גפר, *gpr*)" wood, which is an unknown species of tree, and "covered (כפר, *kpr*)" with "pitch (כֹּפֶר, *kpr*)." It is possible that gopher (גפר, *gpr*) is an Akkadian loan word referring to a reed hut[8], but I find it more likely that gopher wood was chosen in this narrative, and not used again throughout the canon, because it rhymes with the Hebrew words for "cover" and "pitch," both of which are spelled with the same three-letter root: כפר (*kpr*). Noah is to take

7. Sailhamer, *Pentateuch as Narrative*, 125
8. Walton et al., *The Flood*, See "Proposition 8," § Materials.

gopher and *kapharta* (cover) it with *kopher* (pitch)[9]. The Hebrew word
כפר (*kpr*) is actually the word that is most often translated "atonement"
(though better translated "to purge"[10]) in places such as Ex 25:17 to refer
to the *Atonement* cover (lid of the Ark), in Lev 1:4 to refer to the *atonement* made by sacrifices, and throughout Lev 16 to refer to the Day of
Atonement. The author wanted his audience to hear the repetition and
rhyming of כפר (*kpr*) and think of the atonement (purgation of impurity)
made at the Tabernacle. Likewise, though the Tabernacle instructions far
surpass the Ark instructions in length, only the Ark construction narrative and the Tabernacle construction narrative share such meticulous
instructions. The level of detail of the instructions for these two building
projects is not seen elsewhere in the Torah. Having seen some similarities between the Ark and the Tabernacle, let us look at some similarities
between the Ark and the Garden.

Similar to the Garden, Noah is also to fill the ark with every kind
of animal "according to their kinds" (Gen 1:21–25; 6:19–20), male and
female so that they can be fruitful and multiply. He is to fill the ark with
every sort of food, similar to the richness of food found in the Garden
which may be taken from every tree. The Garden and Ark each become
spots in the midst of the waters where animals of every kind are present
with their mates, cared for by the elect human family, and food is abun-
dantly supplied.

On the day when the rains begin to fall, Noah's family and all the
required creatures enter into this floating tabernacle; this miniature and
remnant of the cosmos. When they had all entered into the Ark, Yahweh
was the one who shut them in, protecting the inhabitants of the Ark from
the flood. This is conceptually similar to what happened on the night of
Passover as well. As Yahweh prepares to pass through the land to strike
the firstborn of Egypt, and having given Israel instructions about marking their doors with the blood of a lamb, he tells Israel:

9. Hebrew words originally lacked vowels. After the canon was complete, ancient
scholars known as the Masoretes, came up with a pointing system to denote the vowel
sounds that went with each corresponding consonant. Therefore, when looking at repeated words, a difference in vowels can be superficial.

10. Milgrom, *Leviticus 1–16*, 1079–1084

The blood shall be a sign for you, on the houses where you are.
And when I see the blood, I will *cover-over*[11] you, and no plague
will befall you to destroy you, when I strike the land of Egypt.
—Ex 12:13, ESV with modification in italics

In both the Flood narrative and the Exodus Narrative, Yahweh gives
the elect family instructions for making a place of protection during the
striking of the land of their oppressive enemies. Then, just as Yahweh
protects Israel by covering over their houses, he protects Noah and his
family by shutting them in the Ark. The people of Israel were protected
from the judgment of decreation brought on their violent enemies, and
Noah was protected from (3) the decreation of the world brought on Yahweh's violent enemies.

After the land had been cleansed of violent humanity, (2) Yahweh
"remembered" Noah and the creatures on the Ark (Gen 8:1) as they
floated through the waters, just as he would "remember" his covenant
with Abraham, Isaac, and Jacob as Israel groaned in the "waters" of their
oppressive enemy (Ex 2:23–24; cf. Ps 74:12–17). A wind (רוּחַ, *rwḥ*) once
again blows over the waters and the waters are restrained (Gen 8:1–3),
allowing the dry land to be seen (Gen 8:5). The Ark came to rest (נוּחַ,
nwḥ) on the mountains in the week of the Feast of Booths (Gen 8:4; Lev
23:34), when Israel was to remember Yahweh's provision in the wilderness. Again we are reminded of the Exodus motifs in Yahweh's provision
for Noah through the waters by way of the dates given in Gen 8. Israel
was to remember Yahweh's provision in the wilderness in the same festival season in which Noah was remembered by Yahweh and experienced
his provision through the waters. The waters also finished receding from
the earth on the day that the Tabernacle was erected (Gen 8:13; Ex 40:2,
17–18), signifying that the world was not simply drying, but rather that
the temple-cosmos had been re-created[12].

Being (4) (6) rested (נוּחַ, *nwḥ*) on a mountain in the (5) new
temple-cosmos, Noah builds an altar, discerns and selects the clean animals, and offers a burnt offering to purify the new creation and establish

11. Meredith G. Kline makes the convincing argument that פסח (*psḥ*, typically
translated "passover") ought to be translated as "cover-over," and denotes protection,
based on the word's use within scripture and its correspondence to the Egyptian word
sḥ. Kline, "The Feast of Cover-Over," 497–510

12. LeFebvre, *Liturgy of Creation*, 62–64, 70–71; Michael LeFebvre has demonstrated that dates in the Torah are intentionally structured to compound the significance of
observed festival days, rather than to provide a journalistic Chronology. See LeFebvre,
Liturgy of Creation, Ch. 4–6

communion with God as a priest would naturally do (Gen 8:20). Noah and his family are (7) given the Edenic blessing to "be fruitful and multiply" (Gen 9:1, 7), and in place of a commission to subdue the land, Noah is told that every creature would now be in dread of humans. All animals are given into humanity's hands for food. As Adam subdues the land and the creatures within it to continue Yahweh's order, so here Noah has mastery of the animals, although now the peace between animals and humanity has broken down.

Within the Noah narrative, the phrase "good and evil" is not found, but Noah is given a command that came with the consequence of death just as Adam and Israel were. In Gen 9:4, Noah and his family are given the command to not eat animals with their blood, a command we have already looked at in our exploration of Gen 4. Noah and his family are also commanded not to spill the blood of humans either, since Cain creates the necessity for this instruction. This command comes on pain of death, as those who murder their fellow humans are to be executed.

At this point in the narrative, we may expect a marriage to take place, based on our previous discussion of Adam's marriage to Eve and Israel's marriage to Yahweh at Sinai. We saw that both at creation and at Sinai, the marriage ceremony consisted of covenants or covenantal language. Within the Sinai narrative itself, there is only covenantal language but it was also discussed that later Biblical texts, recognizing that the bond formed between Israel and Yahweh is that of a marriage, inform us that readers ought to view the Sinai covenant as a marriage. After the flood, Noah is given no marriage ceremony but he is given a covenant with Yahweh in Gen 9:8–17 in place of a marriage. Though this is not a covenant of priesthood, such as it was with Israel, Noah has shown his priestly traits in the sorting of animals and burnt offering that he made once exiting the Ark. The covenant itself was one of patient peace toward creation, even if humanity ruins creation again.

In Gen 9:20 Noah plants a garden for himself. At this point in the narrative, again the Breath (רוּחַ, rwḥ) of God has caused the dry land to appear, a new humanity has been (4) brought through the waters from (1) a violent people, (3) the enemies of Yahweh have been crushed, (5) a new temple/creation has been made, the new humanity has been (6) rested (נוח, nwḥ) on/at a mountain, purification has been made, and this new human (7) rules as priest-king in a garden. Again, sadly, our parallels to the creation and exodus continue, complete with (8) a fall narrative, this time also involving fruit and nakedness.

THE FALL OF NOAH'S FAMILY

Much of the Bible is designed to be understood better on a second read-through. We saw in the Cain and Abel narrative that at times we need to know later scripture in order to make more complete sense of our current passage. The same is true of our current narrative. Often Gen 9:20–27 is read in the following way: A father has too much to drink; he disrobes and falls asleep. Ham peeks into his father's tent and sees him sleeping in the buff. He maligns his father to his brothers, making fun of him for what he saw. Upon hearing Ham's ridicule, the noble brothers, Shem and Japheth, determine to cover their father without looking at him. In the morning the father wakes and, knowing that his son has mocked him for his nude slumber, becomes enraged, curses Ham's child, and blesses the other brothers.

On this reading, Ham seems to be simply juvenile and Noah seems to be a man with a very short fuse. However, if we look at a couple of other passages in scripture, we will see that the biblical author has painted Ham as a much more nefarious character, and Noah's family is far more deeply wounded than it seems on the surface. Ham's evil deed consists, it would seem, of seeing his father's nakedness and reporting it to his brothers. Lev 18:7 teaches us something about Ham's actions:

> You shall not uncover the nakedness of your father, which is the nakedness of your mother; she is your mother, you shall not uncover her nakedness.

And Lev 20:11:

> If a man lies with his father's wife, he has uncovered his father's nakedness; both of them shall surely be put to death; their blood is upon them.

In these two verses, we are told that to "uncover the nakedness" of one's father is to have sex with one's father's wife. Immediately the story appears in a more grotesque light. Noah, in becoming drunk, has left his nakedness uncovered. He has left his wife exposed. In Noah's virtual absence Ham takes the opportunity to "see" his father's uncovered nakedness; to lie with his wife. Noah's anger seems justified and is no longer an outburst over a fairly trivial matter. It is also more understandable why Noah curses Ham's son rather than Ham himself. The result of this event is that Noah's wife is carrying Ham's child. This may be alluded to in that Noah curses Canaan to be a servant of his brothers (Gen 9:25) and then curses Canaan to serve Shem and Japheth (Gen 9:26–27). Gen 9:25 may be suggesting that Canaan will be a servant to Ham's other sons but it may also be suggesting that Canaan will be a servant to Shem and Japheth, his half-brothers.

Why would Ham do this and why does the Biblical author include this story? In the Bible, we see quite a few instances where individuals are trying to take more authority than what they have. They become jealous of the status of others and transgress the bounds of their position. We have already seen this in each narrative we have looked at and it will become a pattern found throughout the whole of scripture. Ham is part of this pattern; what he did was attempt to take power through the act of sleeping with the family matriarch. In this cultural setting, to sleep with the matriarch was to seize power within the family. By telling his brothers, Ham is asserting his headship. This same phenomenon is found in 2 Sam 16:21–22. Once Absolom has marched into Jerusalem, seizing the throne from his father David, he sleeps with his father's concubines on the roof of his father's own house. He does this "in the sight of all Israel" so that "the hands of all who are with [him] will be strengthened." Absalom shows that he has taken the place of his father as king and asserted dominance over the Davidic family by taking his father's concubines in his father's own home. He announced this assertion by putting the act on display.

The same cultural assumption is also seen in 1 Kgs 2:22. Adonijah requests that Bathsheba ask Solomon to give him Abishag the Shunammite as his wife. Upon hearing this Solomon replies, "And why do you ask Abishag the Shunammite for Adonijah? Ask for him the kingdom also . . ." In 1 Kgs 1:3, Abishag was given to David in his old age to keep him warm, and though he never slept with her, it was understood that she became part of David's harem. Upon hearing Adonijah's request, Solomon immediately perceived that he wished to have a member of David's harem in order to strengthen his claim to power.

We also see Reuben, the firstborn of Jacob, attempt the same thing. In Gen 35:22 we are told:

> While Israel lived in that land, Reuben went and lay with Bilhah,
> his father's concubine. And Israel Heard of it.

We do not hear of this incident again until Jacob addresses it in his "blessing" to Reuben in Gen 49. In the narratives between Gen 35 and Gen 49, Reuben is continually depicted as one who attempts to lead as firstborn but is motivated by self-interest and is completely ineffective. We will examine his character more in later chapters but knowing of his character now may help us see his motivation for taking Bilhah. As the eldest, he is naturally expected to be the leader but is ineffective and selfish. So, to secure his preeminence, he takes one of his father's concubines on his father's own bed. Therefore Jacob says to him:

> [3] "Reuben, you are my firstborn,
>   my might, and the firstfruits of my strength,
>   preeminent in dignity and preeminent in power.
> [4] Unstable as water, you shall not have preeminence,
>   because you went up to your father's bed;
>   then you defiled it–he went up to my couch!

Reuben is the firstborn and is preeminent over his brothers. But he has shown himself unworthy by taking his father's concubine. His power grab has lost him the blessing of the firstborn. There are others who fit within this pattern without taking their father's wives, such as Nadab and Abihu. In Lev 10:1–3, Nadab and Abihu offer incense that has not been authorized by Yahweh and are consumed by Yahweh's fire because of their actions. In Ex 30:7–9, we are told that it was Aaron, the high priest and father of Nadab and Abihu, who was to offer the incense and we are explicitly told that unauthorized incense is not to be offered. In Lev 10, Nadab and Abihu ignore Yahweh's command and attempt to take the role of their father, thereby taking his high priestly position and authority. There are others within this pattern, but I simply wish to demonstrate its existence and the plausibility of Ham's goal of usurping his father by taking his father's wife.

It is also of interest that Ham is the youngest of the three brothers (Gen 9:24). Ham was naturally not expected to receive the blessing of the firstborn. So, what we have in Ham is another brother, motivated by jealousy and lust for power. He resolves to commit an atrocity to secure a place of preeminence and, just like Cain, it costs him any place in the family.

Shem and Japheth, on the other hand, in the midst of their father's drunken absence, bear the burden[13] of covering[14] the nakedness of their father, i.e. their mother. The narrative keeps with the innuendo of "looking at nakedness" such that a surface reading would suggest that Shem and Japheth cover their naked father. But this action as a whole is strange. There are factors of the situation that may cause the reader to wonder why this action was needed. Their father's nakedness was already concealed in a tent and no longer under threat. The use of this literalistic language may serve more of a narrative function rather than a purely historical one. Within the narrative, Shem and Japheth are playing the covering role that Yahweh played in Gen 3:24. Just as Yahweh covered the shameful nakedness of Adam and Eve to reinstate them as his representatives, Shem and Japheth are now covering the disgraced "nakedness of Noah," which also became vulnerable because of a failure relating to fruit. The author is also careful to continue referring to Noah's nakedness rather than just to Noah. This leaves the possibility open that this is a continued reference to Noah's uncovered wife instead of Noah's naked person. The awkwardness of this part of the narrative and the use of the "seeing nakedness" innuendo are due to the fact that the author is crafting this narrative to bear key markings of the fall in the Garden. The author of this narrative is using his symbols and phrases fluidly and creatively to maintain thematic cohesion throughout the Biblical narrative.

After Shem and Japheth bear the burden required to (symbolically or narratively) cover the shame of what Ham did, the blessing of the first-born is given to Shem. Shem is now to be a source of blessing to Japheth. However, Ham's child, rather than being a source of exaltation as was planned, is to be a slave to Ham's brothers. This curse on Canaan is similar for Ham to the sentences received by Adam and Eve in that the curse frustrates his plans for fruitfulness. Ham sought to make himself ruler of the new humanity but instead, his kingly aspirations were frustrated and turned on their heads. Though the curse differs in that it does not have to do with a curse of exile and unfruitful land in this brief narrative, we do see a resemblance between Ham's curse and Adam's and Eve's curses.

13. The fact that Shem and Japheth laid a garment "on their shoulders" is a somewhat awkward statement and an awkward way to carry a garment. Often when something is laid "on the shoulder" in the Bible, it denotes the taking of a burden. See for instance Gen 21:14; 49:15; Ex 12:34; Num 7:9

14. This is not the word כפר (kpr), which is often translated as to "cover" or "atone," but Shem does act to rectify the failure of his father through the concealment of his nakedness.

This is not to mention the fact that it is indeed a "curse," a type of oration which has thus far only been pronounced in Gen 3 on the snake and land and in Gen 4 on Cain. Ham intended to exceed his station and was instead cursed to be a slave. And just as with Cain, this curse, following Ham's violent actions, literarily aligns him with the seed of the serpent. This curse brings Noah's narrative section to a close as we enter into a genealogy of Noah and his sons.

Though it is very subtle, there is a presence of the Two-Goats motif in this passage. But because of the brevity and subtlety of this narrative, it is best seen on a second reading. In order to see the Two-Goats motif in this passage, we need to first examine the Jacob and Esau narrative. Since the Jacob and Esau narrative will be addressed in this book in detail, with regard to this motif, we will circle back to the presence of the Two-Goats motif in Gen 9 once we have explored that narrative.

Table 3

Correspondences to Noah's exodus through the Flood

	Creation	Flood	Exodus
(1)(3) Dark waters separated involving the Breath of God	Gen 1:2	Gen 7:11–12, 17–24; 8:1–3	Ex 14:21
(1)(3)Sea/sea monster/ seed/enemies defeated/ restrained	Gen 1:4, 6	Gen 7:21–23; 8:2	Ex 14:21, 26–28; 15:1–12; Ps 74:12–17
Covered/protected		Gen 7:16	Ex 12:13
(2) Yahweh remembers		Gen 8:1	Ex 2:24
Dry land appears	Gen 1:9	Gen 8:5, 13	Ex 14:21
(4) Come out as a mixed multitude		Gen 8:15–19	Ex 12:35–36, 38
(5) New humanity	Gen 1:26; 2:7	~Gen 8:15–16	Ex 19:4–5; Isa 43:1
Creation of temple	Gen 2:8	Gen 6:14–21; 8:13, 20	Ex 15:17; 35–40
(6) Rested at Yahweh's garden/dwelling	Gen 2:15	Gen 8:4; 9:20	Ex 15:17; Lev 26:11–12, Deut 11:8–12; Josh 21:44
(7) Act as Priests/ Purification	Gen 2:15	Gen 8:20–21	Ex 19:5–6
(7) Blessing: fruitful, multiply	Gen 1:28	Gen 9:1, 7	Lev 26:3–10; Deut 11:7–16
(7) Commissioned to subdue	Gen 1:26, 28	Gen 9:2–3	Lev 26:6–8; Deut 7:16; Josh 18:1
Given command (Good and Evil) on pain of death	Gen 2:16–17	Gen 9:5–6	Deut 30:15
Results of failure to keep the commands	Gen 2:17	Gen 9:5–6	Deut 30:17–18
Marriage/covenant	Gen 2:22–25	Gen 9:11	Ex 19:5–8; Jer 31:32; Ezek 16:8
(8) Rebellion	Gen 3:6	Gen 9:22	Ex 32:1–8; 2 Kings 17:6–18; Micah 1
(8) Fruitfulness frustrated/Exile East	Gen 3:16–19, 23–24	Gen 9:25	Lev 26:14–27; Deut 28:15–68; 2 Kings 17:6–18; Micah 1

Babel and Abram

AFTER HAM'S FAILED ATTEMPT at seizing control, we enter into a genealogy of Noah's sons in Gen 10. From Ham's line comes many of the future enemies of Israel, e.g. Cush, Egypt, Canaan, Philista; seeds of the serpent. In Gen 10:8 we are told of one of Ham's grandsons: Nimrod. He began to be a mighty man and a mighty hunter. He also was the founder of two more great enemies of Israel: Babylon (Babel[1]) in Shinar and Assyria. The original audience of the Torah, as well as anyone well acquainted with the Hebrew Bible, would read these names and immediately see the darkest of undertones. We have already seen Jeremiah describe Nebuchadnezzar, the king of Babylon in the days of Judah's exile, as a sea monster (Jer 51:34). Before they ever became a threat to Judah, Babylon is described as a violent and devouring nation (Hab 1:6–11). Babylon has consistently remained a place of opposition to Yahweh and a threat to his people from its origin to the time of Daniel.

The narrative resumes in Gen 11 with all people of the land[2] being one and having one language. They journeyed "in the east"[3] until they reached the land of Shinar (or Babylon). This eastward location, similar to the movements of Adam, Eve, and Cain in their exiles, already hints to the reader the treacherous nature of this people. The people wish to unite to build a name for themselves and a tower to bring themselves blessing.

---

1. In Gen 10–11, בָּבֶל (*bbl*) is translated as Babel, elsewhere בָּבֶל (*bbl*) is translated as Babylon based on the common Greek transliteration of the word used in the LXX and New Testament (Βαβυλών, *babylōn*). Since the word "Babylon" is the more common transliteration in English Bibles, "Babylon" will be used to transliterate בָּבֶל (*bbl*) in order to maintain the intended connection between the Tower of "Babel" and Babylon.

2. The Hebrew word often translated "earth" (ארץ, *'rṣ*) simply means "land." This can refer to all lands of the earth or only to a particular land or region.

3. The ESV reads as "from the east" but the usage of מִקֶּדֶם (*mkdm*) would suggest that "in the east" would be a better translation of the word. See for example Gen 3:24; 12:8; 13:11.

In ancient Babylon, towers were built which are often referred to as ziggurats. At the bottom of these ziggurats were often temples and these ziggurats were used to support a staircase that the deity could use to travel from heaven down to the temple. At the temple, the deity could receive worship, bless the people, and make the surrounding city fruitful[4]. The tower of The Tower of Babylon was not an attempt to reach heaven but rather an attempt to bring a deity down to the city to make it fruitful and great. Through this building, the builders' name would be attached to this long-lasting city and remembered throughout the ages; they would maintain their place in this society even in death[5]. These first Babylonians are afraid for their well-being and build this ziggurat for their security. In their pursuit for security, these builders also begin to take on the oppressive characteristics of Israel's later conquerors.

It has been noted that Assyrian inscriptions refer to kings making lands speak "one speech" as a description of their domination or subjugation of a people[6]. If this cultural parallel is in view, that the people of Babylon were of "one speech" may not have been a note about a lack of cultural diversity, but rather a note that associates Babylon with oppression and domination. If the note about "one speech" is to be taken as a parallel to the Assyrian inscriptions, though this is uncertain, it does not seem that it should be taken to mean that there was one dominating people amidst a group of conquered peoples, however. The narrative seems to suggest that this rebellion involved all the peoples of the land and that these peoples are cast out in judgment, rather than liberated from one oppressor when they are scattered. The "one speech" is to denote that the people had not filled the earth as they ought to have and/or that they were a nation with the same domineering intentions as displayed in Egypt, Assyria, and Babylon.

To further add to the negative image of this city, the Tower of Babylon has connections to Cain's violent city and to oppressive Egypt. When looking at the larger motifs of the Torah, one may notice a pattern of mountaintop climaxes and falls throughout the books. This pattern may already be seen in the creation, flood, and exodus narratives that we have already looked at. The beginning of each pattern begins with ruin, which, at times, comes from a previous judgment from Yahweh on a violent people. The pattern then climaxes in a mountaintop sacrifice but ends

4. Walton, *Ancient Near Eastern Thought*, 79–82

5. Mathias, *Paternity, Progeny, and Perpetuation*, 112–123

6. Smith, "What Hope After Babel?"

in the fall of our main characters, necessitating that the story continue until we find the mountaintop purification that changes the hearts of its objects. This pattern begins at creation.

The narrative begins with the deep and then moves to the mountaintop garden, which needs no purification. Humanity falls when they find their wisdom apart from Yahweh and humanity descends into Cain's city of violence. Noah's narrative begins with the violent nations, moves to the waters, and then to Mount Ararat where Noah makes a purifying sacrifice in a new creation. His family then falls through Ham's seizing of power and Noah's failure to guard his "nakedness." Humanity again descends, until it reaches the city of Babylon. Next, we find Abraham, amidst the judgment of the Babylonian dispersion. He travels to Canaan and makes a sacrifice at the Oak of Moreh and in the hill country of Bethel and Ai, then travels to Egypt, which we will speak more about shortly. He is brought, ultimately, to Mount Moriah where he offers Isaac, who is replaced by a ram, as a purification (we will further explore this narrative as well within this study). We next find Israel in the ruin of slavery in Egypt and they are brought out to Sinai where, because of their fall, Moses offers himself on the mountain[7].

I rehearse this pattern in order to show that the city of the Tower of Babylon fits into this thematic pattern within the Torah. The city of Babylon is one of the post-fall rebellious cities, full of the seed of the serpent, as are both Cain's city and Egypt. There is a further link with Egypt in that the root of the term for "bricks" (לְבֵנָה, lbnh) is used three times in Gen 11:3 and is not seen again until it is used once in Ex 1:14 and seven times in Ex 5; in the midst of the description of Egypts oppression toward Israel. The word is only seen again one other time in the Torah in Ex 24:10, used to describe the sapphire brickwork of the pavement under Yahweh's feet. Due to the concentration of the word לְבֵנָה (lbnh) in the Tower of Babylon narrative and in the Egyptian slavery narrative, along with the facts that the bricks are used in both instances to build rebellious cities and play a significant role in the stories, a connection is drawn between Egypt and the city of Babylon. These connections between Babylon, Cain's city, and Egypt are meant to suggest to the reader that the city of the Tower of Babylon was a violent and oppressive city like the others, or at least that it bears the same negative connotations.

7. This pattern is developed throughout *Who Shall Ascend the Mountain of the Lord?* But is summarized here: Morales, *Who Shall Ascend*, 181–183.

The people's lack of trust and reliance on Yahweh, as they build their city and tower, results in their confusion and dispersion. Cain's city of violence ended in the flood, Egypt ended in the flood of the Reed Sea, and this city of Babylon ended in mass exile. The exile of the people of the Tower of Babylon narrative fits within the pattern of judgment found in these other narratives, such that when we come to the end of Gen 11 we are left with a world in a flood of judgment due to their wickedness. This Babylonian exile is thematically similar to the floods that came over Cain's city and the Egyptian soldiers. This is the world into which our next major character, Abram, is born into.

THE EXODUS MOTIF: ABRAM OUT OF BABYLON

When the people of Babylon had built their (1) violent, Egypt-like city, Yahweh (2) came to see the city (Gen 11:5) and determined to (3) disperse its inhabitants. This is the world in which Abram lives; (1) a world exiled far from the Garden and effectively living in a flood of judgment. He has his origins in Ur of the Chaldeans, or in other words, Babylon[8]. Terah, Abram's father, brings his family out of the land of Shinar on a journey to the land of Canaan but stops halfway in Haran (Gen 11:31). In Gen 31:53 we are given a clue that Terah's journey was possibly motivated by Yahweh in the same way that Abram's journey was. In the midst of Jacob and Laban's covenant with one another Laban says:

> "The God of Abraham and the God of Nahor, the God of their
> father, judge between us."—Gen 31:53

Here Laban is saying that Yahweh is the God of Abraham, his brother Nahor, and their father Terah. This reference is rather obscure to be used to fill in a previous narrative, but as we have seen, the authors of the Torah are accustomed to giving little information in one narrative and using later narratives to fill in previous gaps. I would not say this is a hill to die upon, but the authors' intentionality in their writing makes it plausible that we are to read Terah's intended journey to Canaan as a result of Yahweh's commissioning to Terah. Abram's commission to journey into Canaan would then be a continuation of the same commission that Terah previously received yet failed to carry out. Acts 7:2–3 would

---

8. The Chaldeans were a distinct people within Babylon that rose to rule the empire. Therefore, the Bible often will refer to Babylon as Chaldea, despite the fact that this is not technically precise by modern historical standards.

suggest that Abram was called before he journeyed to Haran. This call of Abram could have been part of Terah's call. Alternatively, the passage from Acts may suggest that the original journey was motivated by a call to Abram, not Terah. If the latter is the case, Abram's stop in Haran would have been a failure on his part, and the recorded commission in Gen 12:1–3 would be a recommissioning of Abram rather than a first call. Neither of these readings is necessary for our seeing the Exodus motif in Abram's call narrative, but it is interesting that Abram may have been picking up the dropped torch of the elect lineage or following through on previously ignored commands in his journey to Canaan.

Whether or not Terah was called to Canaan, it is at least clear that Terah did intend to go to Canaan. Upon failing to reach his intended destination, and having been satisfied to dwell in Haran, Abram is called by Yahweh to part with his family and go to Canaan. Abram is elected by Yahweh to "go from [his] country and [his] kindred and [his] father's house to the land which Yahweh will show (ראה, *r'h*) [him]" (Gen 12:1). Despite there being no threat of death, this calling is the command that Yahweh gives to Abram which must be trusted for deliverance to come. Adam must not eat of the tree, Noah must build the Ark, and Abram must travel to the land.

Interestingly the word ראה (*r'h*) is the same lemma used in Gen 1:9 to speak of the dry land "appearing." It is also the same lemma used in Gen 8:5 to tell us that the tops of the mountains "appeared." Keeping in mind the intentional use of words and the use of these exodus-creation patterns throughout Genesis, this is likely an intentional link back to Gen 1. In both stories, land is made to be seen (ראה, *r'h*). This would suggest to the reader that as Yahweh "shows" the land or causes it to "appear," the creation of the temple-land in Genesis 1 is mirrored. No new land is needed to be created in Gen 12, but this land is going to be the temple of Yahweh in the midst of the nations as the garden was in the midst of the waters, once Israel is rested in the land.

There may also be a link in the current context to the division of the waters in Gen 1:6. It is less certain but worthy of note. In Gen 10:25, we are told that in the days of Peleg (פֶּלֶג, *plg*) the earth was "divided (פלג, *plg*)," alluding to the dispersion of the people in the city of Babylon. The Hebrew word used for "divided" in Gen 10 is not found in Gen 1, but conceptually, this may be a link between creation and Babylon. Just as Yahweh divides waters and splits the heads of his enemies and the sea monster, so we may be intended to see him here dividing his enemies.

Interestingly, it has been noted that Ps 55:9 contains an allusion to the Tower of Babylon narrative through the use of "confuse (בלע, *bl'*)" and "divide (פלג, *plg*)" in reference to the Psalmist's enemies[9]. It may be that the Psalmist connects the "division" of Gen 10:25 with Yahweh's thematic judgment of his enemies. I am not convinced enough to call it a certainty, but because of the intentional use of words and patterns in Genesis, it is not outside of the realm of possibility. Additionally, the reuse of the word "divide" in this context of judgment, and that Peleg is in Shem's line, strengthens what was said above that all peoples were involved in this rebellion, rather than some being oppressed by-standers in the rebellion of Nimrod's city, Babylon. Even Shem's family was involved in his city.

Contingent on Abram coming through the flood imposed on the nations, to the land that would be shown to him, he is elected to carry the blessing of Gen 12:2–3:

> [2]And I will make of you a great nation, and I will bless you and make your name great, so that you will be a blessing. [3]I will bless those who bless you, and him who dishonors you I will curse, and in you all the families of the earth shall be blessed.

Abram is given the promise that if he will go to Canaan, (6) a garden-like land (Deut 11:10–12), he will be given (7) the kingship and lasting name that those of the city of Babylon sought. In being separated from the nations and made into the father of a new nation, Abram is also (5) a new creation as Adam and Noah were. This fact is reinforced elsewhere in the Abram narrative and will be addressed, but the current narrative has the marks of a functional-ontological change given the context of the creation pattern of the Bible and ANE. Abram, similar to Israel at Sinai, is separated from the nations and given a new function: to be a new nation which is to be a blessing to the rest of the nations. Yahweh has made something new in Abram, continuing the pattern of "new creation."

Abram is also promised to have all of his enemies defeated by Yahweh. This promise echoes the command to subdue the land given to Adam in Gen 1:26. Though Adam's commission has to do with subduing hostile land and Abram's promise has to do with hostile people, both are subduing that which is not in accordance with Yahweh's act of creation. This promise also echoes the promise that a seed of the woman will crush

---

9. Garsiel, *Biblical Names*, 141. Garsiel notes that בלע, *bl'* is used as a pun upon the name Babylon, though the word does not occur in the Tower of Babylon narrative. See Jer 51:34, 44.

the serpent. We have discussed the connections between the sea monster, the seed of the serpent, the enemies of Yahweh, and the enemies of Yahweh's elect in previous sections. For Yahweh to promise Abram the defeat of enemies, he is also promising the defeat of the seeds of the serpent, all those opposing Yahweh's elect. To have his enemies cursed brings the reader's mind back to the curse on the serpent, as well. Ultimately, to have all of Abram's enemies cursed is to have the serpent crushed, as the serpent is the father of the enemies of Yahweh's elect. The blessing that Abram receives marks him as Yahweh's elect through whom this snake-crushing seed will come. This reality will be manifested throughout Abram's story as Yahweh curses Abram's enemies and subdues them before him.

In this promise to curse those who curse Abram, instead of commissioning Abram to subdue, Yahweh promises that he will be the one to subdue. This new kingdom that Yahweh blesses will not use its power for oppression and self-interest, such as the other kingdoms that have been examined, but from the start, this kingdom is created in dependance on Yahweh. This nation is created in order to bring the blessings of Yahweh, the blessings of the Garden, to the nations. The very nature of Abram becoming a nation means that he must have many children. Therefore we find within this blessing, the blessing to (7) be fruitful and multiply, which has been found to be with Adam and Noah as well.

One will notice that before Abram, Yahweh's blessings were mostly commands. After two repeated patterns of failure, Yahweh has determined to make his plan succeed, despite the inability of his human partner to follow through. Rather than being commanded to be fruitful and subdue the land, Yahweh promises to make Abram a great nation and curse his enemies, if Abram will only go to the land of Canaan. Additionally, while the term "covenant" is not found in the present narrative, by the nature of these promises and Abram's obedience, Abram and Yahweh enter into a covenantal relationship. They each have responsibilities within their new relationship that they must uphold.

So (4) Abram sets out on his journey to Canaan, trusting Yahweh's ability to bless. Lot attaches himself to Abram and "went with him." Lot and his household are here similar to the mixed multitude that came out of Egypt with Israel (Ex 12:38). In places such as Lev 24:10, we see that there were Egyptians, and likely other peoples in the area, that became part of the camp of Israel at the Exodus, constituting this "mixed multitude." They, seeing the great signs and power of Yahweh, trusted in him and chose to abandon their native country and fathers' houses, becoming part of Yahweh's people. This may be the very same motivation behind Lot's going with Abram. Abram, taking his wife and Lot, sets out for Canaan with all of the great possessions they gathered in the place of their exilic dwelling (Gen 12: 5). These possessions are also part of the exodus pattern which we see in Ex 12:35–36, as Israel plunders the Egyptians and leaves the land of their oppression with great possessions.

This short narrative section culminates in Abram coming to the land of Canaan and making sacrifices. Abram, now in fruitful Canaan, first comes to the Oak of Moreh, or Teacher. This oak ought to draw our minds back to the two trees of the Garden. Rather than being at the Tree of the Knowledge of Good and Evil, which gives knowledge, or being at the Tree of Life, which stands in the place of Yahweh, from whom we are to know good and evil, Abram has come to the Tree of the Teacher. The author may be attempting to draw a connection to both trees in order to highlight the fact that Abram is in Yahweh's presence in the land, at the Tree of Life, and that he has chosen to be faithful as Adam and Eve did not do at the Tree of the Knowledge of Good and Evil. Perhaps I have drawn stronger connections than the Biblical author intended, but I believe that the author does intend to use this tree to draw us back to the Garden of Eden. This is also the first mention of a tree since the garden narrative (besides the mention of the gopher wood (עֵץ, ʿṣ) in Gen 6:14) and one that comes with a notable name. We have already established the connections between Canaan and the Garden in a previous chapter, so when we see that our elect person comes immediately to a tree within Canaan, thoughts of the Garden should quickly enter our minds.

At this Oak of Moreh, Abram, as a new creation coming out of the flood of the Babylonian judgment, receives a promise from Yahweh. Having journeyed to the land as Yahweh instructed, Abram is promised that his offspring will receive the land (Gen 12:7). After this promise, Abram builds an altar. Though the narrative does not say so, Abram presumably used this altar by sacrificing to Yahweh, rather than just building it and moving on, as one may do with the memorial pillars that one finds throughout the Biblical narrative. He then moves on to the hill country, between Bethel and Ai, builds another altar, and calls on the Name of Yahweh. The word here translated as "hill country (הר, hr)" is the Hebrew word for mountain, and it is in the singular with the definite article attached. It is often translated as "hill" because the Hebrew word can refer to small mountains, which we may call hills, as הר (hr). The translator selects "hill" or "mountain" based on what they believe best suits the scenario. Literally, Abram moves to "the mountain east of Bethel."

Abram building an altar at a mountain should again, in light of surrounding imagery, make us think of Noah's mountaintop altar, which also had connections to the Garden. The phrase "called upon the Name of Yahweh" is used throughout the Bible to denote simply calling out to or praying to Yahweh, but is also used to denote worship more generally[10]. The phrase, paired with the building of an altar, again suggests that he made an offering, purifying himself and communing with Yahweh as a new creation in the land to which Yahweh has called him. Here, just as with Noah, Abram has been brought out of the flood of judgment on the nations and is in a land that resembles Yahweh's first dwelling. (7) Abram offers sacrifices that mirror Noah's priestly sacrifice within the narrative pattern; sacrifices that purified the new creation and brought about the promise of Yahweh to never flood all the land again. Thus far in the narrative, we see Abram's priesthood in his ability to offer these sacrifices and in his bearing of the blessings first given to Adam, the priest-king. Abram is also to be a mediator of Yahweh's blessing to the world (cf. Num 6:22–27). We will see more of Abram's priestly qualities later in his story[11].

By the time we get to Gen 12:9, we have seen another full exodus cycle with Abram now in the slot of Yahweh's elect. He has been (4) brought out of the flood of (1)(3) judgment that was inflicted on the rebellious people of Babylon and shown a new (6) garden-like land. On Yahweh's instruction, he leaves for this new land with his nephew's household and great possessions. Contingent on this journey, he is also (7) given Edenic blessings, promises of kingship, and a (5) new purpose. He reaches this garden-like land, makes (7) priestly sacrifices, and there sets up his dwelling (Gen 12:8). While Abram is not explicitly "rested" in the land, he does set up his dwelling in the place to which Yahweh has invited him, perhaps mimicking Adam's and Noah's being "rested" in their respective gardens. The narrative section ends with the elect character as a new creation in a figurative Garden of Eden, having set up his dwelling, functioning as a priest, and possessing promises of kingship.

10. Hamilton, *Genesis Chapters 1–17*, see comment on 12:8 and verses cited

11. David Schrock argues for Abraham's priestly nature in these sacrifices and blessings as well. He also sees Abraham's priestly nature in his prayerful and military intercessions for Lot in Gen 14 and 18, his guarding of the covenant ceremony in Gen 15, and in the sacrifice in Gen 22 (Schrock, "Priesthood and Covenant," 71–93). These will be addressed in summary as we continue.

The story continues with a fall that is only mentioned, as it is also the introduction to the next segment of the narrative. In the midst of a famine in Yahweh's promised land, Abram (8) does not trust Yahweh and leaves the land. At this point, we know that the blessings Abram received are tied to the land and it is where he ought to stay. Abram learns this by the end of his story (cf. Gen 24:6), but for now, his self-exile is his fall from the Edenic state of Gen 12:8.

As we discussed in the Noah narrative, there is a general similarity between this exodus and the Two-Goats motif. Yahweh's enemies are dispersed, exiled further from the Garden, while one elect individual and his family are brought closer to Yahweh, to the garden-land where Yahweh will choose to dwell. This similarity will appear throughout exodus narratives because within the nature of a Biblical exodus is the saving of one and the defeat of the other. To have exodus is to be brought out of the rebellious city and into Yahweh's dwelling. By contrast, the rebellious city is either left in exile or cast farther away from Yahweh's presence until they reach Sheol. Going forward I will not address this similarity between the Exodus motif and the Two-Goats motif when present, as it is only a superficial similarity and not an intentional identification of the enemy nations with the goat for Azazel, or the elect people with the goats for Yahweh. I mention these similarities so that we may have a better understanding of the tightly interwoven motifs and patterns that run throughout scripture, particularly those that center around election and being brought to Yahweh's presence.

Table 4
Correspondences to Abraham's exodus out of Babylon

	Flood	Babylon	Exodus
(1) Violent city/people	Gen 4:17, 23–24; 6:2–5	Gen 10:6–16; 11:1–4	Ex 1:8–22
(2) Yahweh remembers/ sees/knows	Gen 8:1	Gen 11:5	Ex 2:24
(1)(3) Dark waters separated involving the Breath of God	Gen 7:11–12, 17–24; 8:1–3	Gen 10:25?	Ex 14:21
(1)(3) Sea/sea monster/ enemies defeated/ restrained	Gen 7:21–23; 8:2	Gen 11:6–9	Ex 14:21, 26–28; 15:1–12; Ps 74:12–17
Dry land appears	Gen 8:5, 13	Gen 12:1	Ex 14:21
(4) Come out with mixed multitude and possessions		Gen 12:5	Ex 12:35–36, 38
(5) New humanity	~Gen 8:15–16	Gen 12:2	Ex 19:4–5; Isa 43:1
Creation of temple	Gen 6:14–21; 8:13, 20	Gen 12:1 (land shown, not created)	Ex 15:17; 35–40
(6) Rested at Yahweh's garden/dwelling	Gen 8:4; 9:20	~Gen 12: 8	Ex 15:17; Lev 26:11–12, Deut 11:8–12; Josh 21:44
(7) Blessing: fruitful, multiply	Gen 9:1, 7	Gen 12:2	Lev 26:3–10; Deut 11:7–16
(7) Commissioned to subdue	Gen 9:2–3	Gen 12:3	Lev 26:6–8; Deut 7:16; Josh 18:1
(7) Act as Priests/ Purification	Gen 8:20–21	Gen 12:7–8	Ex 19:5–6
Given command on pain of death	Gen 9:4	Gen 12:1 (no threat of death)	Deut 30:15
Marriage/covenant	Gen 9:11	Gen 12:1–3	Ex 19:5–8; Jer 31:32; Ezek 16:8
(8) Rebellion	Gen 9:22	Gen 12:10	Ex 32:1–8; 2 Kings 17:6–18, Micah 1
(8) Fruitfulness frustrated/Exile East	Gen 9:25	Gen 12:10, 15	Lev 26:14–27; Deut 28:15–68; 2 Kings 17:6–18; Micah 1

Abram and Sarai in Egypt

THE EXODUS MOTIF: SARAI OUT OF EGYPT

THE NARRATIVE OF ABRAM and Sarai in Egypt is the easiest one in which to see a likeness to Israel's exodus out of Egypt, and it is often recognized by even the casual reader. This narrative, however, utilizes several different narrative features to create points of contact with the Exodus narrative in comparison to those we have examined so far. Up to now, we have begun our exodus cycles with a pre-creation state or with the world in a state of ruin. As we continue through Genesis, these cosmic and creation motifs will be seen less, and new links will be drawn to the exodus. Often the elect will be rescued from a specific enemy instead of cosmic ruin. In order to begin and establish this new set of narrative connections, we are given a narrative that mirrors the Exodus of Israel in such a way that it is almost impossible to miss.

In Gen 12, there is a famine in the land causing Abram to migrate to Egypt. In the last chapter, it was noted that this is Abram's fall from the Edenic climax of the previous narrative. Abram is promised kingship, blessing, priesthood, and a kingdom of descendants, but all this is contingent on his journey to Canaan, and in Gen 12:7 we are told explicitly that Abram's descendants will possess Canaan. This is the land where he ought to stay and trust Yahweh. The understanding of Abram's leaving the land being a fall is strengthened by Abraham's instruction to his servant to never take his son, Isaac, to Mesopotamia in Gen 24:6. Abraham understands that the promises are tied to the land promised to him by Yahweh and, therefore, his son is not to settle outside the land. Another reason that this ought to be understood as a fall is because this journey outside the land will result in the need for a new exodus. Abram could have relied on Yahweh in the land and the narrative would have remained in its Edenic state.

This is not the first time that Egypt has shown up in Genesis. It was seen in Gen 10 that Egypt is from Ham's lineage, alongside the others in his lineage who turn into nations that oppress Israel. When we read the name "Egypt" at this point in the narrative, we are expected to see the nation as being in the lineage of the seed of the serpent; as one who strives for power over and against his brothers (i.e. Cain and Ham). Besides the genealogical connotations, it may very well be expected that the reader's knowledge of the exodus of Israel is to color Egypt as a dark place, knowing the oppression that will soon take place there. Seeing Abram leave Canaan is a disappointment within the narrative, as he too has a form of fall; his entry into Egypt ought to give the reader the feeling that he is walking into (1) the dwelling of an enemy.

This journey to Egypt, due to a famine, closely mirrors the journey of Israel into Egypt. There was a great famine in all the land, which Joseph had predicted. Jacob's sons had already bought grain in Egypt, but upon being reconciled to Joseph the brothers were instructed to bring the family down to Egypt so that they may be cared for throughout the famine (Gen 45:4–13). As Joseph brings his family into Egypt, he devises a plan in order to ensure that his family is able to prosper in their livelihood of shepherding. He instructs his brothers to say that they are "keepers of livestock" when brought before Pharaoh so that they will be able to dwell in a good land away from the general Egyptian populace (Gen 46:31–34). Abram is seen taking similar precautions with Sarai, albeit to the detriment of his family rather than for their well-being. Abram instructs his wife with a prepared speech in order to secure his safety in the land (Gen 12:11–13). Both give instructions to their dependents to tell half-truths to Pharaoh in order to secure well-being.

When Abram and Sarai entered into Egypt, the Egyptians and Pharaoh *saw* Sarai and *took* her into Pharaoh's house. Here, Pharaoh is set in parallel with Eve in Gen 3 and the Sons of God in Gen 6. Just as they "saw" (ראה, r'h) and "took" (לקח, lkḥ) what they saw as good, so Pharaoh's officials "saw" (ראה, r'h) Sarai and he "took" (לקח, lkḥ) her. This suggests to the reader Pharaoh's wickedness and that he has taken what is not rightfully his, despite the fact that he did not know she was another man's wife. Though the events of the story are not fully detailed by the author, the literary patterns communicate to the reader the type of character that Pharaoh is. His oppression of the elect family suggests

that Pharaoh is here the seed of the serpent. While there is no explicit
hostility from Pharaoh, he wrongs Abram and Sarai by taking her as part
of his harem, when she was not his to take. As were the sons of God who
have "seen" and "taken," Pharaoh's actions ultimately make him an adversary to Yahweh and his elect. Pharaoh is the seed of the serpent in this
narrative. Sarai has become possessed and oppressed by Pharaoh similar
to how another Pharaoh possessed and oppressed the Israelites in Ex 1.
Abram's plan, however, seems to have worked fairly well.

Abram has his wife taken from him, but he is able to live in safety.
He is not only living in safety but because of his connection with Sarai,
he is able to acquire great wealth from the Egyptians. In the previous
narrative, we saw that this acquisition of great wealth is also part of the
exodus pattern. This is also seen in Ex 12:35–36 as the Israelites acquire
wealth from the Egyptians. But because Pharaoh has taken Abram's wife,
(3) Yahweh "afflicts" (נגע, *ng ʿ*) Pharaoh and his household with "plagues"
(נגע, *ng ʿ*) (Gen 12:17; cf. Ex 11:1)[1]. Here, there is clear similarity with the
Exodus of Israel. In both cases, Yahweh afflicts Egypt with plagues for
holding his people captive. These plagues also show Yahweh cursing the
enemies of Abram (cf. Gen 12:3) and subduing the seed of the serpent.
These afflictions result in Pharaoh realizing his error and coming to address Abram. In the Hebrew, Pharaoh asks Abram an identical question
to that which Yahweh asked to Eve in Gen 3:13: "what is this that you
have done?," with the added "to me" in Pharaoh's question (Gen 12:18).
Cain was also asked a similar question after killing his brother: "what
have you done?" The inclusion of this repeated question compounds the
indictment of Abram in his deception. It may be asked by Pharaoh rather
than Yahweh, but it needs to be remembered that it is the author who put
the question in his mouth within this crafted narrative.

After facing Yahweh's plagues on Egypt, Pharaoh then (4) sends
(שלח, *šlḥ*) Abram out of his land along with his wife and all of his possessions. The Pharaoh of Israel's Exodus also urges Israel out of Egypt
along with all their possessions after Yahweh brings about the plague of
the death of the firstborn (Ex 12:31–32) in response to Moses' continual
request to have Israel sent (שלח, *šlḥ*) out of Egypt (see for example Ex
5:1; 6:11; 7:16; 8:1). "So Abram went up from Egypt, he and his wife and
all that he had, and Lot," (Gen 13:1) whom we have already seen as the

---

1. There are multiple words often translated as "plague" throughout the Exodus
narrative due to their conceptual and contextual similarity. This particular word only
appears in Ex 11:1.

"mixed multitude" of Abram's exodus out of Haran. Again, Lot plays the same role within the exodus pattern, along with the male and female slaves Abram acquired in Gen 12:16. Abram once again reaches an Eden-ic place as he comes back to Bethel and Ai, "the place where his tent had been at the beginning." There Abram again "called upon the name of the Lord" (Gen 13:4). The author has nearly repeated the events of Gen 12:8, which have already been discussed as a priestly and garden-like conclu-sion to the previous exodus cycle. By bringing Abram's journey back to the same location and his "calling on the name of Yahweh," the author has concisely signaled to the reader that (6)(7) Abram is restored to his Edenic state. Abram has again been brought back to Yahweh's dwelling and worships and purifies those coming out of this new exodus.

Tension Over Land

The reader is then introduced to a new tension between Abram and Lot regarding the promised land. Yahweh has prospered Abram and Lot to the point that, while dwelling together, the shepherds began quarreling over resources. Abram and Lot now have the opportunity to continue the pattern of brotherly strife or to make peace. It is clear that Lot and Abram are not literally brothers, but this need not exclude them from the pattern of brotherly strife. It ought to be noted that in Gen 13:8, Abram refers to Lot and himself as brothers, often unclearly translated as "relatives" or "kinsman"[2]. If the author saw the nephew-uncle relationship of Lot and Abram as an obstacle to fitting them within the pattern of brotherly strife, this verse dispels that obstacle.

Rather than take this opportunity to assert dominance over his nephew who followed him to this land, Abram sacrifices his own inter-ests to maintain peace with his "brother." Abram breaks the pattern and passes the test, showing loyal love rather than enmity. Lot, on the other hand, has (8) his own fall narrative. Within the Biblical world, rather than conceiving of north as "up" and south as "down," north was conceived of as "left" and south as "right." This is because, similar to how moderns look at an aerial map with north at the top, Israelites considered the sunrise to be at their front when they took directions. Therefore, north is naturally to the left and south to the right. Abram, in telling Lot to go left or right,

---

2. It is common, within the Bible, to see distant relatives referred to as "brothers," highlighting their family relationship. However, to refer to Abram and Lot as brothers in this context may be to strengthen the motif of brotherly strife within the passage.

was instructing him to take either the north or south part of the promised land. Instead, Lot lifted up his eyes and saw the richness of the land in the east and chose that land. It is possible that Abram was simply using "left" and "right" to say that he would choose what Lot did not, unrelated to north and south, but in either case, Lot's choice leads him east.

This decision by Lot mirrors Eve's taking of the fruit, the Sons of God's taking of the women, and Pharaoh's taking of Sarai. We do not have the repeated words "saw," "good," and "took," but the conceptual pattern is present. Lot saw a land that was good in his own eyes, and took it. The eastward direction in which this decision leads Lot is also the direction of exile in the previous narratives. This pattern applied to Lot condemns his decision. It shows that he has lost trust in Yahweh's wisdom, which is to remain in Canaan and be part of the blessing that will be given to Abram. This decision then leads him to a self-imposed exile outside of Canaan (Gen 13:12), mirroring the eastward journeys of Adam, Eve, Cain, and the people of Babylon. The negative connotations are brought to the surface in Gen 13:13 when we are told that the people among whom Lot settled were "wicked," and "great sinners" against Yahweh. Lot chose a place which seemed to have the blessings of the Garden, but he only found uncleanness there since he relied on appearance rather than Yahweh's promises.

Just as Lot lifted up his eyes and saw goodness in his own eyes, Abram, having passed the test and sacrificed rather than propagated strife, is instructed by Yahweh to lift up his eyes and see goodness. After Abram loved his brother instead of hating him, (7) Yahweh reiterates and expounds the blessings of Gen 12:2, 7. Having been faithful in potential strife over the land, Yahweh reiterates his promise to multiply Abram's offspring and give them the land. Despite Abram's failure in going to Egypt, now that Yahweh has promised to bless the nations through blessing Abram, Abram is maintained as Yahweh's elect and Yahweh mercifully rescues him from his failure. The blessing to be fruitful and multiply is again given to Abram, reiterating and confirming his status as the elect.

After this promise is reiterated, Abram comes to the oaks of Mamre and builds an altar. The oaks of Mamre are meant to bring the reader's mind back to the oak of Moreh that Abram came to in Gen 12:6[3]. We

3. Garsiel has noted a likely wordplay between the name Mamre (מַמְרֵא, mmr') and the verb "to see" (ראה, r'h). The verb ראה (r'h) is seen in Gen 13:10, 14 and in 18:1–2 in close connection with the oaks of Mamre. This same wordplay with ראה (r'h) is seen in the names Moreh (מוֹרֶה, mwrh) (Gen 12:6–7) and Moriah (מֹרִיָּה, mryh) (Gen 22:2). This common name wordplay, along with their alliteration, link the connotations of these locations in Genesis. (Garsiel, Biblical Names, 192–194).

are to see this oak, with a similar name as the first, and Abram's similar action of building an altar and have in mind the Edenic conditions of Gen 12:6–8. Again the author has created links via words and concepts in order to import rich meaning into a story.

Abram has come out of his second exodus and has been faced with a test similar to that of Cain. Just as Cain is faced with the chance to create strife with his brother over the firstborn blessing, so Abram is faced with a chance to propagate strife with a brother over the land that is promised to him. This opportunity for a fall comes right on the heels of Abram's failure to trust Yahweh in the land as he journeys to Egypt. Here, Lot fails this test, not through creating strife, but through looking for goodness apart from Yahweh's promises. Abram, however, passes this test and this exodus cycle comes to a conclusion with Abram again (7) making a sacrifice in a (6) garden-like place, having had the blessings of fruitfulness and multiplication reiterated and escalated. Once again the narrative has taken the chosen one through an exodus and ends with the priest-king, blessed and dwelling in Yahweh's land.

It is worth noting here that the themes of land and kinship will appear often throughout the narrative of Genesis, as will the element of the promised seed. Loyalty to Yahweh and fellow man in these matters are continually points of character testing and narrative tension. For a complete resolution to the book of Genesis, and the Bible itself, one must pass tests of loyalty to Yahweh regarding all of these key narrative elements.

THE TWO-GOATS MOTIF: ABRAM AND LOT

The narrative of Lot's self-exile out of the land begins to place Lot within the Two-Goats pattern. His story will continue beyond this point with a few twists and turns but this and the rest of his narratives place him within this motif. Cain, the first in this motif, was (D) sent out from the land, (C) protected by Yahweh, (E) was enabled to be fruitful, built a city, and (F) became a violent people. All of this came after (B) his own failure when faced with the chance to let his jealousy over the firstborn blessing become hatred. Lot's failure did not come through increased strife with Abram, but we see Lot take similar steps as Cain throughout his story. In the present narrative, when faced with the potential for brotherly strife, rather than failing through hatred, Lot fails by trusting in what is good in his own eyes. He repeats the failure of Eve. He then (D) exiles himself out of the promised land of Canaan, which was linked to the blessings of Yahweh. In this eastward exile, Lot comes to settle near the land of Sodom. Similar to the goat which bears the sins of the Israelites into the wilderness, where sin and uncleanness are at home, Lot travels to a land characterized by the sin of its people.

Lot is not given Cain's mark of protection in Sodom, but much of Gen 19 is devoted to a narrative in which Yahweh (C) protects Lot from the destruction of Sodom. Lot then proceeds to (E) become the father of both the (F) Moabites and the Ammonites. Lot does not go on to build a city as we saw Cain do, but he is blessed, even through such scandalous means as the narrative depicts. Lot, like Cain, becomes the fruitful father of two nations, both of which will become an enemy to Israel. There is much more to say about how the rest of Lot's narrative fits into the motifs we are exploring, but for now, we will note that this act of mercy towards Lot is part of the goat-for-Azazel pattern. Lot is exiled to a place of sin, protected by Yahweh, and made to multiply into nations which become rebellious nations, hostile to Yahweh and his people. Thus, Lot fits the description of the goat-for-Azazel brother.

Abram, on the other hand, (G) remains in the land. Within Gen 13 he comes to some Edenic oaks, drawing nearer to Yahweh after his most recent exodus and maintaining his status as elect. Throughout the rest of the Abram narrative, he maintains his status as the elect and receives Yahweh's increasing blessings and covenants. While Lot leaves the land, Abram is brought into Yahweh's presence multiple times to either intercede or have the covenants reconfirmed. As the author applies the respective narrative features to Abram and Lot, he demonstrates to us that Abram fulfills the role of the goat for Yahweh while Lot fulfills that of the goat for Azazel. The Two-Goats motif continues in the brothers of the covenant family.

Table 5

Correspondences to Sarai's exodus from Egypt

	Babylon	Sarai in Egypt	Exodus
Famine		Gen 12:10	Gen 45:4–13
Prepared speech to secure well-being		Gen 12:11–13	Gen 46:31–34
(1) Oppressed by Pharaoh		Gen 12:15	Ex 1:8–14
(3) Pharaoh Afflicted		Gen 12:17	Ex 7–12
Pharaoh sends out		Gen 12:18–20	Ex 5:1; 12:31–32
(4) Come out with mixed multitude and possessions	Gen 12:5	Gen 12:16; 13:1–2	Ex 12:35–36, 38
(6) Rested at Yahweh's garden/ dwelling	~Gen 12:8	Gen 13:3, 18	Ex 15:17; Lev 26:11–12, Deut 11:8–12; Josh 21:44
(7) Blessing: fruitful, multiply	Gen 12:2	Gen 13:16	Lev 26:3–10; Deut 11:7–16
(7) Commissioned to subdue	Gen 12:3	Gen 13:15, 17	Lev 26:6–8; Deut 7:16; Josh 18:1
(7) Act as Priests	Gen 12:7–8	Gen 13:18	Ex 19:5–6
Marriage/covenant	Gen 12:1–3	Gen 12:19	Ex 19:5–8; Jer 31:32; Ezek 16:8
(8) Rebellion	Gen 12:10	Gen 13:10–13	Ex 32:1–8; 2 Kings 17:6–18, Micah 1
(8) Fruitfulness frustrated/Exile East	Gen 12:10, 15	Gen 13:10–11	Lev 26:14–27; Deut 28:15–68; 2 Kings 17:6–18; Micah 1

Lot Captured

THE NEXT NARRATIVE BEGINS with a list of kings who went to war with one another, the first of which is Amraphel, king of Shinar (Gen 14:1)[1]. The reader ought to remember that Shinar was last seen in Gen 11, where the city and tower of Babylon were built. The mention of Shinar should signal to the reader that they are about to read the story of a wicked alliance. It may be expected that a battle between the seed of the serpent and the seed of the woman is about to take place, but the author quickly signals that both sides of this battle are seeds of the serpent. This is seen in that the first nation in the opposing alliance is Sodom (Gen 14:2). Only verses ago, we were told of Sodom's wickedness and that they were enemies of Yahweh as Lot set out to live among them.

In the midst of this war narrative, we are quickly told that Chedorlaomer and his allies defeated Rephaim, Zuzim, Emim, and Horites. The former three peoples are said to be giants, and the Horites are mentioned alongside these giants (Deut 2:10–12, 20–22). The Horites may have been giants themselves, but it is not said explicitly. Duet 2:11 tells us that all these peoples are "reckoned as Anakim" who are also called Nephilim (Num 13:33). These people groups are the giant clans descended from the Sons of God in Gen 6 and they are enemies of Israel throughout the scriptural narrative (cf. Num 13:28–33; Deut 9:2; Josh 12:4; 15:14; 2 Sam 21:18, 20)[2]. Just as in Deut 2, here we see foreign nations, seeds of the serpent, being Yahweh's instruments for clearing the giant clans out of the land.

---

1. This list of kings is given again in Gen 14:9 with Chedorlaomer at the front, likely because he seems to be the leader of this confederation. The king of Shinar is likely fronted at the beginning of this narrative to import Shinar's previously acquired connotations onto this confederation of kings.

2. Heiser has shown that within the Biblical narrative, the giants are offspring of the Sons of God who are at enmity with Israel at many points in their history. They are also a large part of the reason for the conquest of Joshua. See Heiser, *The Unseen Realm*, 183–191, 202–215

After Chedorlamer's conquest of the giant clans, Sodom and their allies go out to battle Chedorlaomer's armies. Sodom and their allies are quickly defeated and flee through a field of tar pits. Here many translations read that Sodom's armies "fell" into the tar pits, but Hamilton points out that the word here often translated as "fell" (נפל, *npl*) can also mean to "voluntarily lower oneself" or "settle" (cf. Gen 24:64; 25:18; 1 Sam 29:3; Jer 38:19)[3]. Rather than falling into tar pits (בְּאֵר, *b'r*, often translated "well"), it is possible that the armies of Sodom were hiding in pits, wells, or caves (cf. 2 Sam 17:18–21). The idea of hiding in a pit or cave from an enemy nation recurs throughout scripture. In Judges 6:2, the people hide in caves from Midian; in 1 Sam 13:6, they hide in caves from the Philistines; in 1 Kgs 18:4, the prophets are hiding in a cave from Jezebel; in 1 Sam 22:1, David flees to a cave as he is on the run from Saul; the author of Hebrews speaks of the many others who were persecuted and fled to live in dens and caves as well (Heb 11:38). This idea also will emerge later in Lot's story as he flees the destruction of his home in Sodom. As he fears for his life, Lot and his daughter take refuge in a cave (Gen 19:30). This image is also repurposed by the prophets to represent the destruction and distress that will be on the enemies of Yahweh and his people (Isa 2:10–11; Ezek 33:27; Rev 6:15).

By the simple statement of Sodom's armies fleeing into pits, the armies of Chedorlaomer further take on connotations of a fierce and oppressive king with no care for righteousness, such as those kings who oppressed Israel. The significance of this narrative goes far beyond the narrative itself. As one reads of Chedorlaomer and his armies, one sees a representative of the oppressive kings of the world; the oppressive kings who trample Yahweh's people. In this confederation of kings, a biblically minded reader may see nations like Egypt, Midian, Philistia, Assyria, Babylon, or any other nation that has opposed Yahweh's kingdom. This narrative will then inform the hope of those loyal to Yahweh. In this story we will see the actions of Yahweh and his elect in light of the oppression of the people he is in relationship with. It would seem that Ps 76 is a meditation on exactly this. The Psalm is the only other place in the Hebrew Bible where the City of Salem (Ps 76:2; Gen 14:18) is mentioned and it is about Yahweh's destruction of enemies in war, the taking of their spoil, and Yahweh's rescue of the humble. The Psalm is likely a reflection on Abram's victory in Gen 14, which will be discussed momentarily.

3. Hamilton, *Genesis Chapters 1–17*, see comment on 14:10

Lot gets swept away in the defeat of Sodom and taken by the opposing confederacy of kings, similar to Sarai being taken by Pharaoh. Out of this defeat comes a survivor who finds Abram dwelling in an Edenic setting. We again find Abram dwelling at the Oaks of Mamre, which we have already discussed, which we now find out are owned by an Amorite, the brother of Eshcol and Aner. Adding to the garden imagery is the name of Eshcol. This name means "cluster of grapes" and is seen again in Num 13:23–24. Num 13 contains the story of the twelve spies going into Canaan, the garden-like land which Israel was promised. In this fruitful garden-like land, the spies find a large cluster of grapes which must be carried on a pole between two men, and they name the place where they found the grapes Eshcol. By including this name in Gen 14, the author reinforces the Edenic imagery that is present in the Oaks of Mamre.

In the ESV, the next clause tells us that "These were allies of Abram" (Gen 14:13), but the text literally reads that "they were owners of a covenant of Abram" [AT]. These Amorite inhabitants of the land of Canaan are not only Abram's friends, but they have solidified their loyalties to one another through a covenant. Later in Genesis, we will see gentiles make covenants with the chosen one because they can see Yahweh's blessing on them. We may guess that the author wants us to look back to Gen 14:13 and assume that the same has happened here. Abram, having been blessed by Yahweh after he and his wife have each undergone their own exodus', is dwelling in a place that resembles the Garden of Eden and is living at peace with the nations around him, when he receives news of his captured nephew.

THE EXODUS MOTIF: LOT FROM CAPTURE

Upon (2) hearing from a survivor of the battle that (1) Lot has been taken, Abram quickly gathers a small army, divides his forces by night and (3) defeats the confederation of armies. Given the significance wrapped up in this narrative, as was discussed, it makes a great deal of sense that this pattern of events is replayed elsewhere in the biblical narrative, importing the significance of this narrative and developing the hope that this narrative creates[4]. Interestingly, the first time this series of events is seen again is in the story of Gideon, which begins with Israel cowering

---

4. Hamilton points out and discusses typological correspondences between this narrative and Judg 6–8; 1 Sam 30; and Ps 110. Hamilton, *Typology*, 166–171

in caves before the oppression of Midian (see Judg 6–7) as the armies of Sodom and Gomorrah may be doing here.

Through Abram's defeat of Chedorlaomer's forces, (4) Lot is given exodus from this oppressive army and comes out with "his possessions, and the women and the people" (Gen 14:16). This again reminds us of Israel's coming out with a mixed multitude and great possessions after the defeat of Egypt. At this point Lot disappears from the present narrative and the story follows Abram back to the land of Canaan. There he is met by Melchizedek, the king of Salem, carrying bread and wine in order to commune with Abram. As was mentioned before, Salem appears again in Ps 76:2, and by way of parallelism, we are told that Salem is Jerusalem, where Yahweh chose to dwell. So, once again, Abram, after enacting an exodus on behalf of a member of the elect family, (6) comes back to Yahweh's dwelling and (7) receives a blessing relating to Yahweh subduing Abrams' enemies. Now we may expect here that Lot should receive the blessing given the previous pattern, but throughout Genesis, when an exodus occurs for someone who is not the elect one, the elect one is typically the instrument through which the exodus comes. The elect one is then given the blessing and the one who was given exodus is blessed by being under the protection and care of the elect one. Abram has enacted an exodus and is now being blessed that he may be a blessing to all the families of the earth, as he has been to Lot.

It is interesting that the blessing comes from Melchizedek this time, rather than from Yahweh himself. Throughout Genesis, only a few characters give blessings other than Yahweh; Noah blesses his sons (Gen 9:26), Melchizedek blesses Abram (Gen 14:19), Abram's servant blesses Yahweh (Gen 24:27), Isaac blesses Esau and Jacob (Gen 27:23, 38–41), and Jacob blesses Pharaoh (Gen 47:7) and his sons (Gen 48–49). Each case of blessing not done by Yahweh or Melchizedek is either a blessing from fathers to sons, a praise of Yahweh, or Jacob blessing the head of another nation. All other blessings, including all other blessings given to Abram, are from Yahweh.

As we progress through the book of Genesis, we will run into several characters who, upon close examination, are seen to be Yahweh, although we are never told that explicitly. Melchizedek may be one of these characters. A convincing argument has been put forward by

David Mitchell that Melchizedek is pre-incarnate Jesus[5], the Angel of Yahweh[6]. Though the argument for the Exodus motif in this narrative does not rest on this point, it is worth noting as we seek to understand Genesis. Neither does the blessing of Abram hinge on this point, as, even if Melchizedek is simply a typologically significant man, he still conveys Yahweh's blessing as a priest.

After paying tithe to Melchizedek, Abram is faced with another test. He has the opportunity to become rich from the spoils which belonged to Sodom. By accepting this gift, Abram would increase in possessions, but he would also become united to Sodom and be expected to reciprocate the favor bestowed on him per the customs of ANE culture. At the beginning of this narrative, Abram was in covenant with Amorites who dwelled with him in an Edenic setting. However, these Amorites seem to be faithful covenant partners, while Sodom is explicitly wicked. Abram will not permit that his honor come from Sodom or that he be coerced to show loyalty to Sodom as the king of Sodom recalls that "I made Abram rich" (Gen 14:23). Abram only takes what was needed in order to carry out the battle and to see that his allies get their share. Abram passes the test by entrusting Yahweh with his inheritance. He has also passed a test of loyalty to his brethren once again by rescuing Lot. When his kinsman has been captured, he quickly rallies an army and rescues him. We are not given many details about Abram's thoughts or Yahweh's actions, but Melchizedek informs us that Yahweh was the one to give Abram the victory (Gen 14:20). Presumably trusting in Yahweh's promises to prosper him and not abandoning his kinsman, Abram puts his own household on the line and rescues him; another act of sacrificial loyalty to Lot.

5. He examines not only our current narrative but appearances and references to Melchizedek throughout the canon. Most notably he examines the translation of Ps 110:4 and its references in Heb 7, as well as how the author of Hebrews speaks about Melchizedek in light of typical Hellenistic references to divinity. Mitchell, *Jesus*, 51–90

6. Foreman and Van Dorn have done a book-length study on the Angel of the Lord, which will be referenced throughout this study. They show how various characters and names are references to someone who is Yahweh, yet also distinct from Yahweh. This same-yet-distinct character is traced through the canon and shown to, in fact, be pre-incarnate Jesus. In Appendix V, points for and against Melchizedek as Yahweh are listed. Even their list, which Mitchell's work surpasses, shows that a majority of the evidence points toward Melchizedek being the Angel of Yahweh. However, the evidence falls short of certainty in either direction. (Foreman and Van Dorn, *Angel of the Lord*)

Yahweh Comes to Abram

After passing these tests of loyalty on the battlefield and trust in Yahweh as the source of blessing, the scene changes and we are brought to a vision of the Word of Yahweh (Gen 15:1). Abram is told that Yahweh is his shield and that he shall have a reward. This scene seemingly comes in direct response to Abram's recent displays of fidelity to kin and God. This scene of promise and covenant is directly linked to the previous narrative and will be counted as part of the same exodus pattern for our purposes.

In light of the previous mention of characters who are Yahweh, yet distinct from Yahweh, take note that it is the *Word* of Yahweh that comes to Abram, not audibly, but in a *vision.* The *Word,* in many contexts, is a person that can be seen, not a statement to be heard. As Abram speaks to the Word, he calls him Yahweh (Gen 15:2). Anyone familiar with the beginning of John's gospel should immediately recognize this language. As the two begin their conversation, the narrative tension is heightened. Yahweh has promised Abram fruitfulness in the form of a son and promised him land. In Gen 15:3, 8, Abram questions both of these promises since he still has nothing to show for them. Yahweh reiterates his promise to make Abram into a great nation, and Abram, perhaps contemplating the power and loyalty he has already seen from Yahweh, counts Yahweh as reliable and firm. Abram in turn is counted as being right with Yahweh (Gen 15:6). However, Abram still wants further confirmation that he will indeed possess the land (Gen15:8). In response to this request, Yahweh makes a covenant with him, strengthening the connection between Abram's possession of the land and Yahweh's honor and trustworthiness. Yahweh (7) vows to give the land to Abram's many descendants after bringing them through an exodus; the exodus of Israel. As the sun goes down[7], he describes that exodus in terms that should be familiar to us by this point. See Table 6.

7. Hamilton notes this as a chronological issue since the stars were already visible (Hamilton, *Genesis Chapters 1–17*, comment on 15:17). Given this fact and our previous discussion about darkness, and the fact that Israel came through the waters before the sunrise, this comment likely is primarily symbolically significant.

Table 6

Israel's exodus foretold

	Israel's Exodus Foretold	Exodus
(1) Oppressed by King	Gen 15:13	Ex 1:8–14
(3) Kings Afflicted	Gen 15:14	Ex 7–12
(4) Come out with mixed multitude and possessions	Gen 15:14	Ex 12:35–36, 38
(6) Rested at Yahweh's garden/ dwelling	Gen 15:16	Ex 15:17; Lev 26:11–12, Deut 11:8–12; Josh 21:44
(7) Commissioned to subdue	Gen 15:16, 19	Lev 26:6–8; Deut 7:16; Josh 18:1

The exodus of Abram's offspring is characterized by (1) oppression under a foreign people, (3) the affliction of that people, (4) their coming out with possessions, and (6) being brought to Canaan. It is implied that Abrams' offspring will also have to take the land from the Canaanites, (7) subduing their enemies. Embedded within the covenant portion of this exodus cycle is an explicit reference to Israel's exodus out of Egypt in very familiar terms. Another element of this scene which adds to its allusions to Israel's exodus is the means by which the covenant was ratified. Yahweh commits to the promise he made by manifesting himself, or the Angel of Yahweh (cf. Ex 14:19, 24), as a cloud of smoke and fire. This strongly resembles the pillar of cloud and fire which passed through the Sea of Reeds with the people.

Within this covenant scene, there are also allusions to Abram's priestly status. By doing the priestly work of preparing the sacrificial animals he fulfills a duty that would typically be carried out by the priest[8] and by defending the animals and the place where Yahweh will pass by, he is fulfilling the guarding duty of the Levite[9].

Despite the great promises which are given in this scene, the narrative continues from this high place to (8) another fall narrative. Sarai and Abram begin to doubt that she is the means by which the promise of seed will be fulfilled. After all, that she is the mother of Abram's seed has not been made explicit by Yahweh, although she has been the subject of an

---

8. In Leviticus, the bringer of the offering may be involved in the slaughter of the animal, but the ordering of the parts of the animals was a priestly duty.

9. Schrock, "Priesthood and Covenant," 77

exodus which culminates in her reunification with Abram. As readers, we should be expecting her to be the mother of the promised seed by token of her exodus. This point is reinforced by the author as he paints Abram and Sarai's decision to use Hagar as a failure to trust Yahweh. When Sarai makes the suggestion to take Hagar, Abram "listened to the voice of Sarai" (Gen 16:2), echoing Yahweh's indictment of Adam in Gen 3:17, "Because you have listened to the voice of your wife . . ." Sarai then *took* Hagar and *gave* her to Abram just as the woman *took* the fruit and *gave* it to her husband (Gen 3:6). Hagar then has her own rebellion in that she looked down on Sarai, giving opportunity for Sarai to further this fall. Sarai does what is "good in [her] eyes" (Gen 16:6) and forces Hagar into her own exile.

Table 7

Correspondences to Lot's exodus from capture

	Sarai in Egypt	Lot Captured	Exodus
(1) Oppressed by King	Gen 12:15	Gen 14:12	Ex 1:8–14
(3) Kings Afflicted	Gen 12:17	Gen 14:15	Ex 7–12
(4) Come out with mixed multitude and possessions	Gen 12:16; 13:1–2	Gen 14:16	Ex 12:35–36, 38
(6) Rested at Yahweh's garden/ dwelling	Gen 13:3, 18	Gen 14:18	Ex 15:17; Lev 26:11–12, Deut 11:8–12; Josh 21:44
(7) Blessing: fruitful, multiply	Gen 13:16	Gen 14:19; 15:5, 13	Lev 26:3–10; Deut 11:7–16
(7) Commissioned to subdue	Gen 13:15, 17	Gen 14:20; Gen 15:14, 17–21	Lev 26:6–8; Deut 7:16; Josh 18:1
(7) Act as Priests	Gen 13:18	Gen 15:7–11	Ex 19:5–6
Marriage/covenant	Gen 12:19	Gen 15:18	Ex 19:5–8; Jer 31:32; Ezek 16:8
(8) Rebellion	Gen 13:10–13	Gen 16:2–4	Ex 32:1–8; 2 Kings 17:6–18, Micah 1
Fruitfulness frustrated/Exile East	Gen 13:10–11	Gen 16:5–6	Lev 26:14–27; Deut 28:15–68; 2 Kings 17:6–18; Micah 1

Hagar

THE EXODUS MOTIF: HAGAR

AFTER THE FALL OF Abram and Sarai and the beginning of Gen 16, Hagar becomes pregnant with Abram's child and she looks with contempt on Sarai (literally Sarai is small in her eyes). As the slave becomes a rival to her master, the relationship between Sarai and Hagar becomes one of sibling rivalry. These two now strive for dominance over one another, leading to the exile of one. Both the fruits and status of this rivalrous relationship will be inherited by the child of each woman respectively. In a very ironic turn of events, Sarai also (8) plays the role of the oppressive Pharaoh and Hagar the Egyptian becomes (1) the oppressed. This word translated as "dealt harshly" in Gen 16:6 is the Hebrew word ענה ('nh), which is used multiple times in the story of Israel's exodus to refer to their treatment under Pharaoh[1]. The word was also used only a few verses ago (15:13, translated as "afflicted") when referring to Israel's future oppressions under Egypt.

Hagar decides to (4) flee (ברח, brḥ) from Sarai's oppression (Gen 16:6), as the Israelites will flee (ברח, brḥ) from Egypt (Ex 14:5), and is found by the Angel of Yahweh at a spring in the wilderness on the way to Shur. There are several things to unpack in Gen 16:7. Let's begin with the fact that Hagar is in the wilderness on the way to Shur. It is significant that this is the place where she is found. In Ex 15:22, the people of Israel leave the Sea of Reeds and immediately come to the wilderness of Shur. By reading of Hagar in this location immediately after reading of her flight, the story is linked to the exodus and Israel. To strengthen this link, she is found by a spring in this location. The people of Israel wandered

---

1. See Ex 1:11, 12; the same root is also used in Ex 3:7, 17; 4:21

in Shur for three days until they found bitter waters which Yahweh made sweet for them. Now Hagar is visited by the Angel of Yahweh at a source of water. This spring may also bear Edenic symbolism as a link back to the spring in Gen 2:6 by means of the exodus pattern. More sources of water will be seen as key points in exodus cycles, such that they become an occasional part of the pattern. The inclusion of life-giving springs becomes part of Yahweh's provision in exile or as one is brought through an exodus. Hagar is in the wilderness, on the way to Shur, and by a life-giving spring in the midst of her own exodus.

Something must be said about the Angel of Yahweh as well. We have briefly discussed this character already, but this narrative is where the reader meets him and first learns of his identity. There are points within this narrative that make it very difficult to see this character as just another angel. He takes on the prerogatives of Yahweh in that he blesses Hagar. When giving Hagar the blessing of fruitfulness and multiplication, the Angel of Yahweh says that he himself will be the one to multiply her and give her children. Most significantly, once their conversation has concluded, Hagar "called the name of [Yahweh] who spoke to her, 'you are a God of seeing'" (Gen 16:13). The one speaking to her was the Angel of Yahweh. Suddenly the author just calls this character Yahweh and records that Hagar calls him a *God of seeing*. Very similar words are again applied to Yahweh in Gen 22:14. In this way, the narrative subtly overlaps the Angel of Yahweh and Yahweh, making them the same character, although they will be shown to have a level of distinction as well later in Genesis[2].

When the Angel of Yahweh blesses Hagar in Gen 16:11 he says that (2) Yahweh has "listened to" or heard her affliction, and when she names him, she declares that he is "a God of seeing." Both of these statements are echoed in the narrative of the exodus of Israel as Yahweh sees his people and hears their cries in Ex 2:25 and 3:7. He tells her to return and submit to Sarai, reestablishing Sarai as the "firstborn," so to speak, in this rivalry. In telling her to return, Hagar is also (6) placed within the household of his elect, the place we may have wished Lot would have remained. Yahweh then continues to, surprisingly, give Hagar (7) the blessing of fruitfulness and multiplication. At this point in the narrative, it would seem that Ishmael is Abraham's seed from Yahweh. Ishmael is Abram's son and he is part of a promise to be fruitful and multiply. The author has set up the reader to expect Ishmael to be the promised child at this point.

2. Foreman and Van Dorn, *Angel of the Lord*, see 23–33 for a development of the points made.

Ishmael is also shown to be a (5) new humanity; the beginning of the creation of a new nation. As Yahweh gives this blessing about Ishmael, Yahweh names him and describes his character within the world. He is a new person, and nation, who has been separated out, given a function, and named.

Hagar's part in this narrative quickly comes to an end as she bears this son to Abram. The author does not record her return but simply moves on with the narrative with Hagar in Abram's household. This is inferred by the fact that Abraham is the one who names Ishmael. The exodus cycle concludes in a similar way as Sarai's exodus out of Egypt. The bride (or in this case, concubine) of the elect is returned to her husband. Hagar's exodus has largely been an inversion of Sarai's exodus out of Egypt, and this point in the narrative follows suit. Her exodus is not from the oppression of a captor but from the hostile relationship she has created through her contempt and from her own flight from the elect family.

Hagar and Ishmael's story will continue, but for now, his blessing is to be found within Abram's household. One may assume that Hagar was heading to the wilderness of Shur to find her way back to Egypt. If this is true, this is indeed a very ironic exodus. Hagar finds exodus from the elect by being forced to go into exile in the wilderness, perhaps in hopes of reaching Egypt. Yahweh instructs Hagar to remain with Abram and Sarai in their Edenic dwelling at Mamre (Gen 16:9; 18:1). If we were first-time readers, it would seem that Yahweh has kept the supposed chosen seed, Ishmael, from being disconnected from Abram. The focus then shifts back to Abram and the covenants and promises made to him.

THE COVENANT OF CIRCUMCISION AND THE PROMISE OF ISAAC

The next covenant scene with Abram is neatly separated from the narrative of Hagar's exodus through the closing of the Hagar narrative with Abram's age and the opening of the next section with Abram's more advanced age. Even with the intentional separation, the two scenes share the same plot tension: where is the chosen seed coming from? Now that Hagar has returned to Abram and borne Ishmael, it would seem that Abram has his elected son. But in the next scene, the covenant between Abram and Yahweh is deepened and another son is promised to Abram in place of Ishmael.

Yahweh comes to Abram in a similar manner as in Gen 15, but this time, Abram believes he has received the son that Yahweh intended him to have. He believes he has seen the firstfruits of the divine promise, and therefore has no complaint to make, but rather trusts and bows when Yahweh comes to him to reestablish the covenant. The scene starts with Yahweh offering the *possibility* of the covenant to Abram on the condition that he maintains his loyalty to Yahweh (Gen 17:9). The mention of this condition may be due to Abram and Sarai's recent failure with Hagar. This failure causes a need for Yahweh to reevaluate his elect one and either deepen his covenant or declare it broken. After bowing, showing that his desire is to remain in covenant with Yahweh and receive his blessings, Yahweh is satisfied that Abram is blameless before him and reaffirms the covenant (Gen 17:2–4).

In this repetition of the covenant, Abram's re-creation as a new humanity is also repeated. Abram is renamed "Abraham" and Yahweh's purpose for him is reaffirmed: to make him a multitude of nations and kings, and to give his offspring the land of Canaan (Gen 17:6–8). Yahweh then adds to the stipulations of this covenant by requiring all males of the covenant to be circumcised (Gen 17:10). If they refuse circumcision, they refuse the covenant. But why circumcision as the sign of the covenant? It has been argued that the concept of circumcision likely came to Israel from Egypt, where priests were circumcised as a sign of their devotion to their respective deity[3]. Therefore, this sign intimates that Abraham's children, and any who take part in this covenant are going to be priests. The nation that comes from Abraham's elect seed is going to bless the nations just as Yahweh has blessed them. They will act as mediator between Yahweh and humanity. Each elect human that we have met thus far has had priestly qualities in that they make purification for humanity and that they represent Yahweh. Now the entire elect nation is to be a nation of priests (cf. Ex 19:5–6) who will fill both of these priestly functions. Any who would not take on the sign of priest and dedicate themselves to Yahweh have no part in the covenant and are to be cut off from the nation of priests. Abraham and his household adhere to this covenant and pass this test of faithfulness (Gen 17:23–27).

Yahweh's promises continue and the act of re-creation is extended to Sarai. Given that she has undergone her own exodus, we may have expected as much. She is renamed "Sarah" and given a purpose in Yahweh's

---

3. Meade, "The Meaning of Circumcision"

plans to bless Abraham. She is to be the queen, alongside Abraham, of a nation that will come from her own son. She will be the one to give birth to the promised kings and multitude. Abraham begins to be in disbelief and wishes that Ishmael may receive the promises instead, but Yahweh has decided to use Sarah (Gen 17:18–19). The resolution of the story of Abraham's firstborn remains in tension.

Although Yahweh has chosen Sarah over Hagar, he has still blessed Ishmael in an extremely similar way as he will bless Sarah's son (Gen 17:20). Ishmael is also to prosper into a great nation with twelve princes, mimicking the twelve tribal patriarchs that will be met later in the narrative. This similarity between Ishmael and Isaac shows Yahweh's love for the nonelect. The goal of election, after all, is to have one who can bring the many back to Yahweh; the whole plan is for the reconciliation of the non-elect. Ishmael is not made a blessing to the nations nor a priest to them, but he is given the fruitfulness which Yahweh intended humanity to have before their rebellion. This will not be the last time that Yahweh's love for the non-elect is displayed through his blessings.

Table 8

Correspondences to Hagar's exodus

	Creation	Hagar	Exodus
(1) Oppressed by King		Gen 16:6	Ex 1:8–14
Fled		Gen 16:6	Ex 14:5
To wilderness of Shur		Gen 16:7	Ex 15:22
Springs/well	Gen 2:6	Gen 16:7, 14	Ex 15:27; 17:6
(2) Angel of Yahweh/seeing		Gen 16:7, 9, 11,13–14	Ex 2:25, 3:7
(6) Rested at Yahweh's garden/ dwelling	Gen 2:15	Gen 16:9; 18:1	Ex 15:17; Lev 26:11– 12, Deut 11:8–12; Josh 21:44
(7) Blessing: fruitful, multiply	Gen 1:28	Gen 16:10	Lev 26:3–10; Deut 11:7–16
(5) New Humanity	Gen 1:26; 2:7	Gen 16:10–12	Ex 19:4–5; Isa 43:1

Lot in Sodom

THE EXODUS MOTIF: LOT OUT OF SODOM

THE NARRATIVE OF LOT's exodus from Sodom begins with Abraham at his Edenic trees (Gen 18:1, 4) when he is met by three men. Throughout Gen 18, the one speaking among the men is referred to as Yahweh and the narrator makes clear that Yahweh is one of these men by showing that Yahweh is in close physical proximity with the men who are visiting Abraham (Gen 18:1, 13, 17, 20, 22, 26, 33). Notice as well that Yahweh also refers to Yahweh in the third person, a phenomenon that will occur with the Angel of Yahweh as well, either making for awkward speech or showing a distinction between this man who is Yahweh and someone else who is Yahweh yet outside of this person.

Abraham urges these three men to rest[1] under his Edenic tree and receive a meal from him (Gen 18:4). Just as the Israelites would have to prepare the Passover meal while being prepared to make a hasty flight out of the land, Abraham hastily has a meal prepared for the men who have visited him. He also has three seahs of flour made into bread, far more bread than they could eat. Abraham's haste in preparing such a luxurious feast shows the gravity with which he receives his king into his dwelling.

As the men ate, Yahweh gives some specificity to his promise of a son through Sarah which Abraham was recently given. In the next year, Yahweh will return and Sarah will have a son. Her response is much like that of Abraham in Gen 17:17, she laughs and questions the promise on account of her age. Though it would appear that her question was not simply a question of how the promise will come about, but a lack of

---

1. The word translated "rest" in Gen 18:4 is not the word נוח (*nwḥ*) as we have seen often occurs, but the conceptual framework of resting in a garden is perhaps present through Abraham's request that these men recline with him at the Oaks of Mamre.

belief in Yahweh's ability, for which Yahweh calmly calls her out before going on his way.

The men leave and Yahweh discusses with them if he should reveal his current plan to Abraham (Gen 18:17). Abraham is the head of the nation that all other nations will be blessed through. Abraham is the father of the nation that will rule the nations, bringing them to Yahweh. Therefore Yahweh reveals his intentions to Abraham. Yahweh reveals that there is an "outcry (זעק, z'q)" and a "cry of distress (צעק, ṣ'q)" in the oppressive cities of Sodom and Gomorrah, elements which are seen in the exodus of Israel[2] as well as in other exodus cycles that we have examined. Yahweh is (2) going to go down to the cities in order to know whether or not these cries are legitimate (Gen 18:21), just as he will do in Ex 2:25. However, Abraham has a concern with Yahweh's plan and makes intercession for the cities.

Abraham likely knows that (1) his nephew's family resides in So- dom, so it would be natural for him to have concern for the city, but the reason that Abraham gives is his concern for the unfair destruction of the righteous. He ultimately asks Yahweh if he will spare the entire city if he finds ten righteous people in the city. If Yahweh's people are the salt of the earth, are ten pieces of salt sufficient for the preservation of Sodom and Gomorrah? Yahweh replies that he would indeed refrain from destroying the city if he found but ten righteous people in the city. However, we know how the story goes. Only three people are brought out alive as a mercy to Lot alone, and the city is swept away.

As Abraham and Yahweh finish conversing, the men who left Yah- weh enter Sodom at the end of the day. There Lot finds them as he sits in the gate of the city. Often, the gate of the city is the place of the judges and elders of the town. The fact that we find Lot here may very well point to his righteousness. This sojourner has become a judge within the town; he has become one responsible for keeping order and righteousness within Sodom. This thought may be behind the Sodomites' statement in Gen 19:9. Lot's being in the gate, however, may also be simply a necessity of the plot. Lot may be placed at the entrance of the city to facilitate his meeting with the messengers of Yahweh as they enter the city.

Lot greets the approaching men in much the same way as they were met by Abraham. Lot bows down, calls them "lords," and urges them to stay with him in order that their feet may be washed and they may rise

2. The root זעק (z'q) is seen in Ex 2:23 and צעק (ṣ'q) is seen in Ex 3:7, 9; 5:8, 15; 8:12; 11:16; 12:30; 14:10, and 15 in the exodus narrative.

and go their way in the morning (Gen 19:2). Lot then, also like Abraham, prepares them a meal, although Lot's offering is far less lavish. On
the eve of his flight out of the wicked city, he offers the men unleavened
bread (Gen 19:3), just as the Israelites ate on the eve of their exodus (Ex
12:8). After eating, all the people of the city came to Lot's home to rape
the newcomers (Gen 19:4). That all the people of the city came out is
emphasized in light of Abraham and Yahweh's recent conversation. Not
ten righteous were found. Only Lot has displayed righteousness and love
to these strangers. Just as Noah was shut into the ark to protect him from
the oncoming chaos, so righteous Lot shuts his guests into his home to
protect them from the people of the city (Gen 19:6). Yahweh will protect
the Israelites in the same way by "covering over"[3] them as the destroyer
goes through Egypt (Ex 12:13). Lot's actions are very commendable, and
thus far in this narrative, he has been a righteous character. Despite Lot's
deep flaws, such as his choice of Sodom and offering up of his daughter
for the men of Sodom to rape, he has shown loyalty shown to Yahweh's
messengers. Because of this loyalty to Yahweh and his servants he is separated from the men of Sodom and given exodus out of their destruction.

After Yahweh's messengers have seen Lot's defense on their behalf,
they begin to take action. Just as Lot *shut* (סגר, *sgr*) them in to protect
them, the messengers bring Lot into the house and *shut* (סגר, *sgr*) him in
(Gen 19:10). The men then (3) *strike* (נכה, *nkh*) the men of the city just as
Yahweh will repeatedly *strike* (נכה, *nkh*) Egypt in the process of delivering
Israel (see Table 9 for references). They offer to Lot the chance to bring all
in his household out of the city before they (3) *destroy* (שחת, *šht*) it (Gen
19:12–13; cf. Ex 8:24; 12:13, 23). As dawn comes, so does the time for the
destruction of the city and for Lot's exodus; another parallel with Israel's
exodus (Ex 14:24, 27). But Lot, perhaps discouraged by the disbelief of
his sons-in-law, lingers in the wicked city. This is in sharp contrast to
his former zeal towards the men and in contrast to Abraham's continued
haste in showing hospitality to Yahweh and those with him.

The word here for lingered (מהה, *mhh*) is only used in the Torah
here, in Gen 43:10, and in Ex 12:39. In Ex 12, we are told that the Israelites "were thrust out of Egypt and could not wait (מהה, *mhh*)." Lot's
lack of action is set in sharp contrast against the backdrop of Abraham's
haste and the Israelites' inability to linger. He is not displaying a fervent
trust in the word of Yahweh's messengers. He is displaying the character

3. See the earlier discussion on the Passover under heading "The Exodus Motif:
The Flood".

of his Sodomite sons-in-law or the Egyptians who did not take Yahweh's warnings seriously. He would have been left in the city, and subsequently so would have his wife and daughters, if not for Yahweh's merciful desire to bring him out.

Lot is instructed to (4) take his family and escape "to the hills" lest they be swept away (Gen 19:17). Herein lies another potential link to Israel's exodus, which shows Lot displaying a similar fear as that which Israel displays in the presence of Yahweh. The word translated as "hills" in the ESV is the word הר (*hr*), which also means "mountain"[4]. Interestingly, here the word is not plural as it is often translated, but singular. The men are instructing Lot to flee to *the mountain*. To this point in the narrative we have seen a handful of mountains, and we also know that there is a mountain range that runs through Canaan. So it is difficult to determine which mountain *the* mountain is. This could be an obscure reference to the nearest mountain to Sodom, but the reason for the reference to the singular mountain is possibly to strengthen the other links to the story of Sinai, where Sinai is often referred to as "the mountain"[5]. Lot, again not trusting that Yahweh has actually saved his life and the lives of his family, fears to go to the mountain "lest the disaster overtake [him] and [he] die" (Gen 19:19). This statement is mirrored by the Israelites statement in Ex 20:19. Seeing the great display of Yahweh's presence on the mountain they were "afraid and trembled." They say to Moses:

> You speak to us, and we will listen; but do not let God speak to us, *lest we die.*

The Israelites stand far off from the mountain in fear for their lives just as Lot fears for his life as he is told to go to the mountain. Moses goes on to explain that Yahweh's presence is a test which will teach the people to fear Yahweh and not transgress their covenant with him. This fear is not to cause them to flee the mountain, as Lot did, but to be loyal to Yahweh. This same event is recounted in Deut 5:23–39, where Yahweh explains that the people are correct in their statement, but he laments that this fear will not produce lasting obedience. Neither Israel nor Lot were meant to fear and flee, but seeing the fire of Yahweh raining down on Sodom and resting on Sinai should have inspired both to understand the end of Yahweh's enemies and remain loyal to him, to fear him. This is especially true

---

4. This same point was made in the discussion of Gen 12:8 under heading "The Exodus Motif: Abram Out of Babylon".

5. Through Ex 20 and 24 for instance.

in light of seeing the great loyalty shown to them by Yahweh in bringing them through an exodus out of their oppressive dwellings.

In his fearful request, Lot makes an intercession for Zoar (Gen 19:20), similar to Abraham's intercession for Sodom. Abraham makes intercession out of concern for the potentially righteous inhabitants of the city. Lot, in contrast, pleads with Yahweh's messengers to not destroy the small town of Zoar out of fear for his own life alone. His intercession is successful and he is told to flee to the city of Zoar. As he enters the city, we are given the information that the sun had risen (Gen 19:23) and Yahweh began to rain fire and brimstone on Sodom and Gomorrah. Once again the sunrise serves as an image of the deliverance of Yahweh's people and the defeat of his enemies.

The term in Gen 19:24 for rain (מָטָר, *mtr*) is a rare word in Genesis. It only appears in Genesis in Gen 2:5 to refer to the lack of rain on the land, in Gen 7:4 to refer to the rains that contributed to the flood, and here in Gen 19:24. The word is not seen again until Ex 9, where it occurs four times (Ex 9:18, 23, 33, 34), referring to the raining of hail and *fire* on Egypt. The reservation of this word for destructive rain in these narratives causes another link to be drawn between the flood, the destruction of Sodom and Gomorrah, and Israel's exodus. Additionally, that Egypt and Sodom and Gomorrah each have *fire* rained down on them (and that this does not happen elsewhere in the Torah) shows clear lines being drawn between these narratives by the author.

This rain of fire on Sodom and Gomorrah destroys the inhabitants of the cities as well as "what grew on the ground" (Gen 19:25). Likewise we are told that the hail and fire that rained on Egypt destroyed "every plant of the field and broke every tree of the field" (Ex 9:25). There are no verbal links in these statements, but the author has drawn another conceptual link between the two narratives. Each contains fire rain which destroys the vegetation, and any semblance of garden-ness in these once Eden-like lands (Gen 13:10).

After the destruction, Abraham comes to look upon the destruction of Sodom and Gomorrah (Gen 19:28), just as the Israelites look on the dead bodies of the Egyptian army (Ex 14:30). The elect one/community, after an exodus has been performed on their behalf, look back on the destruction of Yahweh's enemies. The next statement makes explicitly clear that Lot's exodus out of Sodom and Gomorrah was on Abraham's behalf. Just as Yahweh remembered Noah (Gen 8:1), and will remember his covenant with Israel's fathers (Ex 2:24), Yahweh remembers Abraham and his nephew Lot (Gen 19:29), who came to Canaan with Abraham. As part of Abraham's community, and despite the fact that he left the land of promise, Lot is rescued and looked on with favor from Yahweh.

Lot's Final Fall

After Lot is (C) brought out of his final exodus event, he has another fall narrative which is never resolved. He fears Zoar and, therefore, takes his two surviving daughters to (D) live in a cave (Gen 19:30). This may signal to us that Zoar, having been condemned along with Sodom and Gomorrah until Lot's intercession, is just as oppressive as Chedorlaomer's alliance or Israel's future oppressors[6]. Lot may have made a poor choice in his intercession. After all, he was not concerned with what was right or trusting Yahweh, but only with what he deemed safe in his eyes.

In this cave, Lot's daughters conspire to get children because of their belief that there are no men left in the land. As part of his daughters' conspiracy, Lot (8) becomes drunk and vulnerable to sexual exploitation (Gen 19:33). This setting should bring the reader back to Noah, lying drunk and uncovered (though this is used euphemistically in Noah's narrative) in his tent, poised for Ham's sexual violation. Now, rather than offering his daughters for rape, his daughters rape him in order to secure offspring. By setting this on analogy to Noah's fall, as if the circumstances themselves weren't enough, the author conveys that this is a fall. However, Lot's story ends here and he gets no redemption in the near future. In this narrative, Lot has become (E) two great nations through his daughters. His future hope lies in the coming seed of Abraham who will bless the nations.

Lot's becoming two nations has already been discussed in connection with the Two-Goats motif present in his and Abraham's relationship[7]. Within this narrative, Lot has been (D) self-exiled from his hand-picked dwelling after (C) receiving protection from Yahweh and has now (E) become two nations. These two nations, the Moabites and the Ammonites, (F) become enemies of Israel, seeds of the serpent, later in the Hebrew Bible. This sequence of events completes the Two-Goats pattern for Lot, placing him in the slot of the Goat for Azazel. Regarding

---

6. See the discussion of oppressive nations forcing people to hide in caves in "Lot Captured."

7. See section "The Two-Goats Motif: Abram and Lot" for explanation.

the Moabites and Ammonites as acts of new creation, having been involved in the separation of a family and designation as a new people, it would be reasonable to conclude that the two nations that come from Lot are (5) new creations within his exodus cycle. This may be strengthened by the fact that each child/nation receives a name that describes their function/character and by the fact that Ishmael, another Goat-for-Azazel character, has received a new creation pronouncement as well in Yahweh's blessing to Hagar (Gen 16:10–12). Lot's new sons have the markers of new creation and it is not unexpected that a Goat-for-Azazel character could be associated with new creation.

Just as Cain falls, is exiled, becomes a nation, and disappears from the story, so does Lot. This incestuous story of Lot beginning two nations is the last that he is spoken of in the Hebrew Bible except in reference to the nations that came from him. He has shown trust in Yahweh through his story. Lot came out of Canaan with Abraham, displayed loyalty to Yahweh's servants, and advocated for righteousness in a city bent on violence. However, after coming with Abraham through his exodus out of Ur, he voluntarily exiles himself to Sodom, going after what was right in his own eyes. This put Lot in a position to need an exodus of his own when an oppressive nation swept him away. This mixed bag of a character is then saved by his family ties with the elect of Yahweh. Lot again requires exodus from his wicked dwelling in Sodom, which again he receives because of the favor with which Yahweh has looked on Abraham. In Lot, we see the benefits of having ties to Yahweh's elect. Even a deeply flawed character who maintains loyalty to Yahweh's elect will be brought through the exodus that the elect one enacts or asks for from Yahweh. This is even (or particularly) true of the one who plays the role of the Goat-for-Azazel. The hope of the exiled nation, cast out to bear their sins, finds their hope in the deliverance and blessings of the elect one of Yahweh.

Table 9

Correspondences to Lot's exodus from Sodom

	Flood	Lot in Sodom	Exodus
(1) Violent city/ people	Gen 4:17, 23–24; 6:2–5	Gen 18:20	Ex 1:8–22
(2) Yahweh remembers/sees/ knows	Gen 8:1	Gen 18:21; 19:29	Ex 2:24–25
Cries against violence	Gen 4:10	Gen 18:21; 19:13	Ex 2:23; 3:7, 9
Unleavened bread in the evening		Gen 19:1, 3	Ex 12:18
Protected/shut behind door	Gen 7:16	Gen 19:6, 10	Ex 12:22–23
(3) Inhabitants struck		Gen 19:11	Ex 3:20; 7:25; 9:15, 25, 31; 12:12, 13, 29
(3) Destruction	Gen 6:13, 17	Gen 19:13, 14, 29	Ex 8:24; 12:13, 23
(3) Sea/sea monster/ enemies defeated/ restrained	Gen 7:21–23; 8:2	Gen 19:25	Ex 14:21, 26–28; 15:1–12; Ps 74:12–17
Rain (fire)	Gen 7:4, 12; 8:2	Gen 19:24	Ex 9:18, 23–24, 33–34
Fear to go to the mountain		Gen 19:19	Ex 20:18–21
Salvation at morning		Gen 19:23, 27	Ex 14:24, 27
(8) Rebellion	Gen 9:22	Gen 19:30–38	Ex 32:1–8; 2 Kings 17:6–18; Micah 1
(5) New Humanity	~Gen 8:15–16	Gen 19:37–38	Ex 19:4–5; Isa 43:1

Sarah and Abimelech

THE EXODUS MOTIF: SARAH FROM ABIMELECH

In Gen 20, Sarah is taken by Abimelech, king of Gerar. This is the second time that Sarah is taken by a king, and it is easily recognizable that this narrative and that of Sarai's exodus in Gen 12 closely parallel one another. The two narratives also depict Sarah's being taken and released in similar exodus terms.

To begin, both narratives begin with a journey through the Negev (Gen 12:9; 20:1) and a prepared speech that is intended to jeopardize Sarah for Abraham's safety. In both of these speeches, the half-truth that Sarah is only Abraham's sister is told (Gen 12:11–13; 20:2, 13). As discussed in the chapter, "Abram and Sarai in Egypt," his prepared speech parallels the speech prepared by Joseph and given to his brothers so that they may secure a good dwelling from Pharaoh (Gen 46:31–34). After she is introduced as Abraham's sister, she is (1) taken by the king (Gen 20:2) as she was by Pharaoh and as Israel will be taken as slaves by the Pharaoh of their day. The oppressive king is then (3) afflicted by Yahweh (Gen 20:3) as the Pharaohs of Gen 12 and the book of Exodus are, although in this narrative we are not told what the affliction is until the end of the story.

King Abimelech, when confronted by Yahweh in a dream, defends his innocence. We learn that Yahweh has kept him from sleeping with Sarah and he is now giving Abimelech the chance to right his wrong against Sarah and Abraham (Gen 20:6). Because Abimelech has been kept from sleeping with Sarah, there is opportunity for Abimelech to return her and create a "no harm no foul" situation. Also, Yahweh's promise of a chosen seed from Abraham is not threatened by the possibility that

Sarah's child is Abimelech's. Until Abimelech does make amends for his unintentional sin, Yahweh gives Abimelech's house a temporary, but tangible, affliction, warning them and allowing them to feel the effects of the wrong that is in the community. It is interesting that on the heels of the narrative of the destruction of Sodom and Gomorrah, Abimelech is concerned with Yahweh's treatment of the righteous[1] just as Abraham was in Gen 18. Abimelech asks Yahweh, "will you kill an innocent people?" (Gen 20:4). Yahweh responds with the information that he has kept Abimelech from sin and with the opportunity to right the taking of Sarah. Therefore, Yahweh's answer is implicitly, "no, I have no desire to kill a people righteous at heart, only that the situation be rectified." This same answer can be felt behind Abraham's discussion with Yahweh in Gen 18.

After waking from his dream, Abimelech confronts Abraham and asks him a question that has been heard several times at this point (Gen 20:9, cf. Gen 3:13; 4:10; 12:18): *"What have you done* to us?" This repetition again adds to the gravity of the accusation against Abraham. Abraham then (4) acquires great possessions and slaves by the hand of Abimelech and Sarah is reunited with her elect husband (Gen 20:14). This, also, not only mirrors Sarah's exodus out of Egypt but also Israel's as each acquire possessions, are sent out with a mixed multitude, and are brought to their respective covenant partners.

Now that the wrong has been righted, and Abimelech has shown faith to Abraham in the matter of his wife, Abraham intercedes for Abimelech and the women in his house (Gen 20:17) according to what Yahweh has said in Gen 20:7. In interceding for Abimelech, again Abraham displays priestly qualities as an intercessor. Abraham here intercedes for a man who has unwittingly sinned but maintains a heart of loyalty to Yahweh's elect and is able to secure forgiveness and blessing for him.

In Gen 20:18 we are given the information that the affliction that was on Abimelech's house was the closing up of all the wombs therein. By healing Abimelech's house, Yahweh gave all the women in his house the ability to bear children again. We have read of Yahweh's promise to give Abraham a son through his barren wife in Gen 17 and have been held in suspense since. The suspense has been heightened by Abraham's and Sarah's respective doubts that Yahweh could give such an old couple

---

1. The ESV translates the word צַדִּיק (*ṣdyk*) as "innocent," losing the connection to Abraham's concern for the righteous in Gen 18. "Innocent" is a valid translation but the word is also the typical word for "righteous." Abimelech is maintaining that he has kept a right-relationship with Yahweh's elect.

a child. We are not given the resolution to the promise in the narrative of Sarah's exodus from Abimlech's house, but by the healing of the women in Abimelech's house, the reader is shown that Yahweh does in fact have power over the womb; he can both take and give fertility. The question of the promise no longer involves Yahweh's ability to fulfill it, that has been demonstrated. The question that now remains is: *when* will Yahweh give Sarah the son?

Sarah has passed through her second exodus, both of which were required because of the cowardice of her husband. If the promised child is to come from Abraham and Sarah, then Yahweh will not allow them to be killed in Gerar, and Abraham should have trusted that fact. But Yahweh is faithful to the bride of the elect, once again giving her exodus out of the house of an oppressive king and bringing her back to her husband. After their reunion, and after Yahweh is shown to have power over the womb, Yahweh immediately (in narrative time) (7) fulfills his promise to make Abraham fruitful and multiplied by giving Sarah the (A) promised son (Gen 21:1–2). Abraham gives his son, Isaac, the priestly covenant sign of circumcision, and Sarah celebrates this new son from Yahweh. But once again, Sarah's exodus involves strife between her and Hagar and their sons.

HAGAR AND ISHMAEL SENT OUT (EXODUS MOTIF CONTINUED)

At the feast meant to commemorate Isaac's weaning, Sarah catches Ishmael (B) making sport of Isaac (Gen 21:9). She is enraged and demands that Abraham cast out Hagar and Ishmael. Abraham is troubled by this demand because of his love for Ishmael. It would seem that we are on the brink of another fall narrative as Abraham wrestles with whether or not to listen to the voice of his wife again. However, Yahweh comes to Abraham and reassures him (Gen 21:12). Isaac is the elect firstborn son and is to have all the inheritance. Ishmael is not to be around to receive part of Isaac's particular inheritance. Yahweh also intends Ishmael's exile into the wilderness to be the means by which he fulfills his words to Hagar in Gen 16 (Gen 21:13). With this knowledge, Abraham is no longer abandoning his son and concubine, but rather acting in accordance with Yahweh's blessing for them. Hagar and Ishmael are simultaneously being exiled from the elect family and given exodus to their own dwelling as they are

(4)(D) sent out (שלח, *šlḥ*) to their own place of blessing (Gen 21:14). This sending out continues the Exodus motif attached to Hagar in Gen 16.

By placing provisions on Hagar's shoulder, he places a burden on her before sending her out[2] (Gen 21:14). This burden is perhaps that of Abraham's mistake in having a child with Sarah's slave, but the text does not give any explicit reasoning. Hagar and Ishmael are then sent wandering in the wilderness. When Hagar and Ishmael run out of water, the author notes that "she lifted up her voice and wept. And God heard the voice (lit. sound) of the boy" (Gen 21:16–17). Though there are no oppressors in this narrative, Hagar and Ishmael cry out as Abel's blood cried out because of Cain's violence (Gen 4:10) and as Israel will cry out because of their slavery (Ex 2:23). In the present passage, the word for "wept" is בכה (*bkh*) and for "cry" is קול (*kwl*), more literally translated "noise" or "voice," rather than the words זעק (*z'q*) and a צעק (*ṣ'q*) used previously in Genesis. However, this noise coming from Ishmael is due to his distress and is heard by Yahweh as he hears the cries of the oppressed (Gen 21:17).

Yahweh hears their cries just as he hears the Israelites. He then reaffirms his (7)(C) promise to Hagar to make Ishmael into (5)(E) a great nation and reveals a well of life-giving water. The narrative has Exodus elements running throughout. However, this narrative does not begin or end as our other exodus stories, with oppressors and a resting in a garden-like place or reunion with a husband, respectively. Rather, this exile narrative is part of the Two-Goats motif as the culmination of the strife between Sarah and Hagar and their sons. This narrative section is also the culmination of Hagar's inverted exodus away from the elect family. The strife between these two sons will be discussed further after Isaac's role in the Two-Goats motif is explored.

As Ishmael's story comes to a close, we are told that "he lived in the wilderness and became an expert with the bow." This may very well be a subtle link to the mighty hunter we read about in Gen 10. Both Ishmael and Nimrod (and Esau, whom we will look at shortly) are hunters who build fruitful and great nations that (F) become enemies of Israel. If this link is intended by the author, then it strengthens Ishmael's placement within the pattern of (oppressive) nation-builder.

After these events, we do not hear of Ishmael again, except in reference to his descendants, as was true of Lot. He has been exiled to the

---

2. See note 13 in chapter "Noah."

wilderness and given his own blessing, but the narrative remains with the one through whom Yahweh will restore humanity to the Garden. However, Ishmael will still remain important to our discussion until we have examined the next couple chapters of Genesis.

Table 10

Correspondences to Sarah's exodus from Abimelech

	Sarai in Egypt	Sarah and Abimelech	Exodus
To Negeb	Gen 12:9	Gen 20:1	
Prepared speech to secure well-being	Gen 12:11–13	Gen 20:2, 13	Gen 46:31–34
(1) Oppressed by King	Gen 12:15	Gen 20:2	Ex 1:8–14
(3) King Afflicted	Gen 12:17	Gen 20:18	Ex 7–12
King sends out	Gen 12:18–20	Gen 20:14, 15	Ex 5:1; 12:31–32
(4) Come out with mixed multitude and possessions	Gen 12:16; 13:1–2	Gen 20:14–16	Ex 12:35–36, 38
(7) Act as Priests	Gen 13:18	Gen 20:17, 21:24	Ex 19:5–6
(7) Blessing: fruitful, multiply	Gen 13:16	Gen 21:1–2	Lev 26:3–10; Deut 11:7–16
Marriage/covenant	Gen 12:19	Gen 20:14	Ex 19:5–8; Jer 31:32; Ezek 16:8

The Climax of the Abraham Narrative

AFTER LEAVING ISHMAEL, AND before we pick up with Isaac again in chapter 22, we are given a brief narrative about Abraham, Abimelech, and Phicol. Abimelech sees that Abraham has been cared for by his God and he has seen Yahweh's strength. He has very recently witnessed Yahweh work on behalf of Abraham to bring his wife out of Abimelech's house. Naturally, Abimelech wants to make sure that he will not one day find himself as an enemy of Abraham and, subsequently, Yahweh. Abimelech desires that the men deal with one another in loyal-love (חסד, ḥsd; translated "kindly" by the ESV; Gen 21:23). Abraham agrees and now has peace with another inhabitant of the land as he did with Mamre, Eshcol, and Aner. Because of this oath, Abimelech and Abraham are to show loyalty to one another, as Abraham has shown to Lot, so long as one party does not violate their relationship. However, shortly after they make an oath together, strife arises.

The servants of Abimelech have taken a well from Abraham and his household (Gen 21:25). Again we see servants striving over resources, which causes the heads of each household to discuss a means of peace. This narrative resembles that of the strife of Lot's and Abraham's shepherds in Gen 13. However, this narrative is an inversion of Lot's departure from Abraham. Rather than Abraham's family dwelling with him and then separating from him, in this narrative, one who is separated from him comes to Abraham and makes a covenant of familial loyalty.

When accused, Abimelech does not know that the servants had taken the well (Gen 21:26). He is innocent and was not part of this theft. Therefore, Abraham gives seven lambs to Abimelech as representation of his ownership of the well. Abimelech accepts and the wrong has been righted. Abraham has, again, been faced with an opportunity for brotherly hostility. He could foster enmity against Abimelech, his brother by oath, and continue the pattern of brotherly strife but, just as he did with

Lot, he pursues peace. The author again tells the reader that they made a covenant together, binding themselves to one another (Gen 21:27). Abraham then plants a tree and calls on the name of Yahweh, likely with a sacrifice (cf. Gen 12:8; 13:4; 26:25). The last time Abraham has communed with Yahweh in this way was in Gen 13:18, immediately after Lot departed from him for Sodom. Also, the reader should remember the Edenic imagery discussed that has surrounded the previous trees within Genesis. After making peace with one of the nations, Abraham again is in an Edenic setting much like that of Gen 14:13: among the trees and at peace with those of the surrounding nations. Just as in previous narratives, having come through an exodus and a test of loyalty, Abraham worships and draws near to Yahweh.

The current narrative and the narrative of Lot's separation are both framed by strife among the servants and by an offering to Yahweh, suggesting that we are to read these narratives in parallel. The placement of this may be to bring a greater resolution to the motif of brotherly strife before the climax of Abraham's story. Abraham shows loyalty to Lot in Gen 13 although Lot leaves him. Abraham has shown loyal-love, but Lot has little regard for the blessing that will come through Abraham and does not maintain unity with Abraham. The narrative escalates when Abraham shows greater loyalty to Lot by rescuing him from a foreign army. The narrative climaxes in meeting Melchizedek, the king of what will be Jerusalem. In our current narrative, Abimelech fills the role of Abraham's brother via covenant. Rather than being close, then seeing and taking a wicked land, Abimelech is actually far off and attaches himself to Abraham for the sake of Yahweh's blessing. (We should not read the failure of Lot's choice of Sodom into Abimelech's returning home (Gen 21:32) as the narrative does not have the same thematic markers of "seeing good" and "taking," and given that he is simply returning home. After all, Abraham is seen sojourning with Abimelech at the end of this scene (Gen 21:34)). In both narratives, Abraham maintains loyalty to his community, however in this case, that loyalty is returned. This outcome was foreshadowed in the covenant between Abraham, Mamre, Eshcol, and Aner, but here we see a king of the nations covenanting himself to Abraham such that they are a peaceful community enjoying the blessings of Yahweh that come through Abraham.

Significantly, immediately after this is the narrative of Isaac's binding, which is the climax of Abraham's story. As we will see, this climax takes place on Mount Moriah, which is also the future site of Jerusalem.

Twice we have tales of Abraham's loyalty to his community each climaxing in priestly motifs and blessings on top of Mount Zion.

THE BINDING OF ISAAC

As has been mentioned, this next narrative section is the climax of Abraham's story. It begins with God planning to test (נסה, *nsh*) Abraham. This word is one of two words translated as "test" in the Torah[1]. The word נסה (*nsh*) more specifically means "to reveal"; to test an object or person such that their qualities can be seen. (נסה, *nsh*) often occurs in contexts where Yahweh gives a command that is to be followed as a test and it is also paired with the words "to know (ידע, *yd*ʿ)"[2]. This suggests to us that this sort of testing is done in the pursuit of knowledge about its object. In this narrative, Yahweh *tests* Abraham in order that he may *know* Abraham's true loyalties (cf. Gen 22:12)[3].

Abraham is spoken to by Yahweh and called to go to another land with the command "you go (וְלֶךְ־לְךָ, *wlk-lk*)" (Gen 22:2), just as he is in Gen 12:1. This beginning sets this narrative in parallel with Abraham's initial call to Canaan, where he was also given a command which would result in blessing if it were kept. It may be that the author also intends us to read the testing paradigm of our current narrative back into other narratives that feature Yahweh's commands to his elect.

This test consists of Abraham offering his long-awaited firstborn son from Sarah as an offering. This test would likely bring about doubts about Yahweh's faithfulness to his covenants with Abraham. He has promised blessing through Isaac. How can he uphold that promise if Isaac is slaughtered at an offering? Is Yahweh so flippant as to make Abraham wait decades for this son of covenant and then so quickly violate his own covenant? One could doubt that Yaweh's word is even as firm as Abimelech's, who has striven to make and maintain a covenant with Abraham.

---

1. The other is בחן (*bḥn*), which is the only word for testing used in the Joseph narrative. The word בחן (*bḥn*) means "to authenticate"; to test an object or person to verify their supposed qualities. Smith, *Testing*, 6–30

2. Smith, *Testing*, 8–9. See also Gen 22:1–2; Exod 15:25–26; 16:4; 20:20; Num 14:22; Deut 6:16–17; 8:2 for a command from Yahweh in the context of a test and Gen 22:12; Deut 8:2; 13:3; Judg 3:4; 6:37, 39; 2 Chr 32:31 for (ידע, *yd*ʿ) in the context of testing.

3. Gen 22:12 tells us that Yahweh now knows that Abraham *fears* him, rather than speaking explicitly of loyalty. However it has been demonstrated that *fear* in the Hebrew Bible is often linked to loyalty and covenant adherence (Smith, *Testing*, 31–63).

Abraham is to go to the land of Moriah, to a mountain of Yahweh's choosing. We are told in 2 Chr 3:1 that this Mount Moriah is, in fact, in Jerusalem. It is the mountain on which Solomon built the temple. As was mentioned, this narrative climax takes place in Jerusalem just as the climax of the narrative of Lot's capture. Abraham there met Melchizedek, the king of Salem, which is also Jerusalem. It is interesting, as well, that Abraham is not going to be told which mountain he is to go to until he is in the land of Moriah (Gen 22:2). This may be the author's way of showing that Yahweh sent Abraham to a specific mountain without bogging the narrative down with geographical instruction. However, it does seem to further put this narrative in parallel with a previous Abrahamic narrative and with Israel's. In Gen 12:1, when Abraham was called he was told to go "the land that I will show you." This statement further links these two stories. Also, the Israelites were going to learn of the place in which Yahweh would "place his name" once they got into the land, rather than being told to go straight to Jerusalem to set up the Tabernacle (cf. Deut 12:5). They will take a similar journey of testing and faithfulness with Yahweh.

Now, the fact that this Mount Moriah is the mountain on which the temple sat should already be bringing Edenic imagery into the reader's mind. The Garden was the temple Yahweh created for himself and which the subsequent tabernacle and temples sought to emulate; as copies of the real thing (cf. Ex 25:40; Heb 8:5). Reinforcing this garden-temple imagery is the fact that the word Moriah (מֹרִיָּה, mryh) is spelled strikingly similarly to the names of a couple other Edenic spots in Abraham's story. Notice the similarities between Moreh (מוֹרֶה, mwrh) (Gen 12:6), Mamre (מַמְרֵא, mmr') (Gen 13:18; 14:13, 24; 18:1), and Moriah (מֹרִיָּה, mryh)[4]. The alliteration, and near rhyming, of these significant place names is the author's way of linking the connotations of these places together. Each of these places has its own significance related to the temple/garden. When we come to Abraham's climax and read of a third *m-r-h/ '* word with Edenic connotations, it exponentially increases the value of the garden-temple symbolism within the scene.

We have seen Abraham come through multiple exodus events that end with a sacrifice in a garden-like setting. We have seen this to be true of Noah as well. When Abraham was initially called to Canaan, he made sacrifices at Edenic trees and on a mountain (Gen 12:6–8). By linking

4. (Garsiel, *Biblical Names*, 192–194); see also note 3 in chapter "Abram and Sarai in Egypt."

this story to the story of Abraham's first call by the use of a similar call, a mountaintop sacrifice, and the use of a name that brings the reader back to previous Edenic trees, we are meant to read this as the ultimate and renewed mountaintop sacrifice of his first exodus out of Haran. This is the climax, not only of Abraham's story as a whole but also of his initial exodus where he determined to follow Yahweh. His loyalty will be tested in a similar and heightened way, now that he has been refined for chapters and years, and he will receive a renewed and elevated promise like that which he received in Gen 12.

Abraham, in the face of whatever doubts he had, decides to maintain loyalty to Yahweh through this command. Abraham must reckon that Yahweh will maintain loyalty to his covenants through this event and is trustworthy. But Abraham knows that Yahweh swore to bless him through Isaac. If Isaac is killed on Mount Moriah, then Abraham's act of obedience will prove Yahweh a liar. Unless, of course, one of two things happens. If Abraham is to follow through on the command he was given, Isaac must be resurrected in order for Yahweh to fulfill his promises. Otherwise, Abraham must be stopped by Yahweh before the act is committed. Obviously, the latter is the case, but the fact that Yahweh tells Abraham to offer up Isaac as a command ques the reader to see the necessity for resurrection; and even expect that it will take place. The author of Heb 11:17–19 reads Gen 22 in this exact way. There are also Rabbis who were reading this story as though Isaac had truly been offered and brought back to life[5]. Though it is not said explicitly within the text, it is important to recognize that the author has attempted to put "resurrection" into the minds of the readers. After all, the idea of "death-to-life" has already been hinted at through the closing and re-opening of the wombs of the women in Abimelech's house, if not by the act of initial creation and of re-creation after the flood as well.

On the third day, Mount Moriah is found and as Abraham and Isaac went up the mountain, Isaac asks his father a question: "Behold, the fire and the wood, but where is the lamb (שֶׂה, sh) for the burnt offering?" (Gen 22:7). The word שֶׂה (sh), here translated "lamb," and used in Gen 22:8 as well, is not the normal word for "lamb." Rather, this word more generally denotes small livestock, such as sheep or goats. This word is common, however, there is another place where the the word שֶׂה (sh) is used in concentration as the object of an offering. The word appears five times in Ex

---

5. See for example Taanit 16a:6; Pirkei DeRabbi Eiezer 31:10

12 in reference to the Passover sacrifice. In Gen 22, the reader will quickly learn that Isaac is meant to take the place of the שֶׂה (sh). The firstborn son, Isaac, who is later replaced by a ram, is thereby linked to the Passover. Similarly, during Passover, the firstborn sons of Israel are replaced by small livestock in order to protect the households from Yahweh's destruction of his enemies.[6] Through these links, the Passover will continue to develop the profile of the coming elected brother who will crush the serpent. It seems that the elected brother, an offering associated with the Goat for Yahweh, will give his blood as a sign of protection for Israel.

The fact that Isaac is substituted by a ram for the burnt offering is also significant. The terms "burnt offering (עֹלָה, 'lh)" and "saw (ראה, r'h)" appear six and five times, respectively. The second occurrence of ראה (r'h) in Gen 22:14 (here translated "provide") is in the Nifal (passive/reflexive) form, which is often used to denote an appearance of Yahweh, i.e. Yahweh lets himself be seen[7]. The words for "burnt offering" and "saw" (particularly in the Nifal form) only occur together with a ram as the object of the offering in two other places. The first is the series of sacrifices in Lev 8–9 in which the priests are consecrated and the people are cleansed. All this is in preparation for Yahweh's appearance. The second place is in Lev 16 at the Day of Atonement[8].

By these intertextual links, the author intends to portray Isaac as the שֶׂה (sh) which takes the place of the firstborn as a sacrifice and protects the household from Yahweh's flood of judgment. He is also seen as the sacrifices which consecrate priests, cleanse people for Yahweh's appearance, and which cleanse the community at the climax of the Torah to maintain Yahweh's presence in their camp. It has been mentioned that Ishmael functions as the Goat-for-Azazel in the Two-Goats motif present between Isaac and Ishmael, and that Isaac functions as the Goat-for-Yahweh. However, before we continue discussing the narrative at hand, it would be beneficial to explore how Isaac and Ishmael fall into their respective roles.

---

6. Walters, "Wood, Sand, and Stars," 308

7. Walters, "Wood, Sand, and Stars," 310; see for example Gen 12:7, 17:1, 18:1, 26:2, 24, 35:1, 9, 48:3; Ex 3:2, 16, 4:1, 5, 6:3.

8. Walters, "Wood, Sand, and Stars," 309

THE TWO-GOATS MOTIF: ISAAC AND ISHMAEL

Ishmael, like Cain and Lot, has been driven out of the dwelling of Yahweh's elect as a result of his sin. Cain murdered his brother so Yahweh banished him. Lot chose what was good in his eyes, rather than clinging to the elect, resulting in greater and greater degrees of self-inflicted exile. Ishmael has (B) mocked his brother, who (A) was to inherit the promise, and (D) has now been exiled by Abraham and Sarah with Yahweh's approval. Just as the Goat-for-Azazel does, Ishmael and his mother are seen wandering in the wilderness (Gen 21:14). The word here for "wandered" is not the word for "wanderer" or "fugitive" in Gen 4:14, but the conceptual links are clear. By way of the verbal and conceptual repetitions within his narrative, the author of Genesis has portrayed Ishmael as the Goat-for-Azazel within this motif.

Isaac becomes (H) a sacrifice of purgation and communion on (G) Mount Moriah at the climax of Abraham's narrative and exodus just as the goat for Yahweh at the Day of Atonement (or Purgation) is the purging sacrifice at the climax of Israel's narrative and exodus within the Torah. Other links between Isaac and the Day of Atonement have been discussed above. The author has made clear the way in which he sees Isaac functioning. He is a purifying near-sacrifice which would cover the people on the day that Yahweh wipes away his enemies. His sacrifice would allow for Yahweh to dwell within his cleansed nation of priests. Clearly, Isaac was not the one to truly bring this reality about, as the Angel of Yahweh stopped Abraham and gave him a substitute. But we have been given the expectation that the elect will accomplish these things through his sacrifice.

It is here that we should remember Abel. This is not the first time that sacrificial language has been attached to the elect one. Abel, through a play on his name and the word for "best" or "fat" (of the flock) was linked to his purification offering at the entrance of Yahweh's garden temple. He is portrayed as closely linked to a purification offering which would cleanse the offerer and make him or her fit for Yahweh's presence. For the author to portray the elect as a sacrifice that could cleanse/protect the people for the appearance/dwelling of Yahweh is by no means new territory in Gen 22. Shem should likewise be remembered in this narrative. Shem was not linked to an offering but he does bear the burden of covering sin. As Yahweh clothed Adam and Eve's nakedness as an act of redemption after their rebellion, Shem, along with Japheth, bore the burden of covering his father's nakedness after his own failure. As Isaac is offered as a sacrifice, which would, at least in part, cleanse Abraham, so previous goat-for-Yahweh characters have acted to cover over sin. By these repetitions and patterns, the author of Genesis is building an expectation of what the seed of the woman will do. He is building a typological profile of the elect one who will crush the leviathan while having his heel struck at the same time. The piece added to the profile here is that an expectation of resurrection is presented (though we have mentioned that Yahweh's past acts of bringing life from death have foreshadowed this). This theme will escalate as we continue.

Getting back to the narrative, as Abraham is about to slaughter his son, he is stopped by the Angel of Yahweh. We should quickly note that at the beginning of Gen 22, it was God who commanded Abraham to slaughter Isaac, yet it is the Angel of Yahweh who says "you have not withheld your son, your only son, from *me*" (Gen 22:12, italics added). In Gen 22:15–18 the Angel of Yahweh swears by himself. He makes clear that *he* will bless Abraham, and that *he* is the one who commanded Abraham. Once again we have this figure who is Yahweh, yet is distinct from Yahweh in the way he is presented and speaks.

The Angel of Yahweh says to Abraham that the boy is not to be harmed because now he knows that Abraham fears God (Gen 22:12). Abraham has passed the test. He has heard the command of Yahweh and trusted in his wisdom. He has proven himself loyal to Yahweh even when faced with a command that could result in the loss of the promised son and prove Yahweh to be working towards the violation of his own covenants (unless there is a resurrection). Despite the difficulties, he counts Yahweh as trustworthy and powerful and looks to Yahweh as the source of his exaltation and blessing.

THE TEST

In Genesis 22, Abraham is given a command which is a test from Yahweh. Abraham, here has the opportunity to obey and have his status as Yahweh's mediator of blessing to the nations reaffirmed, or fail and potentially face exile. If Abraham were exiled he may come through another exodus given the pattern of his narrative, but we do not need to concern ourselves with this thought experiment for our purposes. This pattern of events, which is explicitly called a "test" in Gen 22, is found throughout

Genesis, as well as throughout the rest of the Bible. While we will see this motif reappear in our study of Genesis, the presence of *the test* (נסה, *nsh*) in Gen 22 offers a suitable vantage point for us to look back at implicit testing narratives earlier in the book.

Following the pattern of the test (נסה, *nsh*) seen in Gen 22, Adam and Eve receive blessings along with a command from Yahweh. They have the chance to prove themselves loyal and be exalted, or fail and be exiled. With the temptation of the serpent, Adam and Eve fail the test and face exile. Likewise, Noah received favor from Yahweh as the sole righteous one in his generation. He is given a command to build the ark which will be a means of blessing for him and all those who are rescued on it. This command is given with the prospect of having Yahweh's covenant established with him. Noah passes the test by obeying the command. He then receives blessing and a covenant.

The same pattern appears when Abraham is called to Canaan. Yahweh calls him to the difficult task of leaving his family (his means of support) and coming to Canaan so that Yahweh could bless him, give him land, give him a name, and make him a great nation. If Abraham does not follow the command, then he will remain in the Babylonian exile. Abraham makes the choice to come to the land of promise, receives blessing and covenant, and proves himself righteous by his fear of (or loyalty to) Yahweh[9]. It is worth repeating that both Gen 12:1 and Gen 22:2 contain the phrase "you go," linking the narrative of Abraham's first calling and his climactic test by way of the same testing command.

There are other words for "test" in the Hebrew Bible with their own nuances, and the motif is nuanced as these various words are used. When נסה (*nsh*) appears in the Hebrew Bible, or a testing narrative that contains a command from Yahweh, the one who receives the command has the opportunity to show their loyalty or disloyalty. Once Yahweh has seen the outcome of the test or his command has been obeyed/disobeyed and he knows the heart of the testee, he accordingly gives blessing or exile/futility[10]. Since the presence of this motif is not always explicit, it is worthwhile to point out in order that we may have a fuller understanding of the motifs within a given narrative. This test/command motif will continue throughout the book of Genesis as well as the Torah (cf. Ex 20:20; Deut 8:2).

9. Smith, *Testing*, 87–89
10. Smith, *Testing*, 155–157

Once Isaac has been spared, Abraham finds a ram which may be used as a replacement for Isaac (Gen 22:13). It is now seen how fortunately ironic it was when Abraham told Isaac that Yahweh would "provide (lit. see) for himself the lamb." Due to Yahweh's provision of this ram, Abraham names the place "Yahweh will provide (lit. see)." The author then ties the statement to what is most likely Jerusalem as he says "as it is to this day, 'On the mount of the LORD is shall be provided" (Gen 22:14). The word "provided (ראה, rʾh)" in this statement is in the Nifal (passive/reflexive) form. Another way to translate this statement is, "On the mountain of Yahweh, he shall appear" [AT]. Within Gen 22, the word ראה (rʾh) has been used to denote provision and this specific instance of the word is associated with the ram which has been provided. We have also discussed that this passage is linked to other passages in Leviticus in which ראה (rʾh) appears in the Nifal to denote Yahweh appearing. While "appearing" and "providing" are two distinct ideas in English, we must remember that both ideas are communicated with one word in the examined passages. It is also true that Gen 22:14 is vague enough to support either ראה (rʾh) referring to the provision of the ram or to the appearance of Yahweh. The author likely intends a double meaning through the blurred use of ראה (rʾh). Yahweh did indeed provide the sacrifice, and there is indeed an expectation in the associated passages that Yahweh will appear at his dwelling. However, we must recognize that the inclusion of Yahweh's appearance as part of the intended meaning in Gen 22:14 relies not on the passage itself, since the Angel of Yahweh speaks from heaven rather than coming down to the mountain, but on the close association of this passage with others in which Yahweh does appear.

Having been tested and found loyal, the Angel of Yahweh reaffirms that Abraham will be (7) blessed and multiplied and that his offspring shall defeat their enemies and be a blessing to all the nations. Upon receiving this blessing Abraham travels back to his Edenic dwelling at Beersheba (cf. Gen 21:33). The author then gives us a brief genealogy of Abraham's brother before we transition to the narrative of Sarah's death. This genealogy introduces Abraham's great-niece, Rebekah, who will become very important in chapter 24.

THE DEATH OF SARAH

The following narrative is one that often puzzles readers. Why is so much detail given to Abraham's purchase of a plot of land and his burying of Sarah? Other burials or similarly significant events are covered in a single sentence in other places in Genesis. So why devote so much paper space to this narrative? This narrative picks up on some themes and loose ends that need to be addressed. Abraham's story would not be complete without this scene about burying Sarah and haggling over land prices. There is no complete Exodus motif in this narrative, but we will take the time to look at the narrative in order to come to a more complete understanding of the book of Genesis thus far.

After the death of the mother of the true firstborn son, Abraham goes to the Hittites in order to purchase a burial place. The Hittites immediately respond with recognition that Abraham is a "prince of God" (Gen 23:5) and give permission for him to freely take any one of their tombs. This is similar to Abimelech's previous recognition that God is with Abraham in all that he does. But why does this fact warrant that the Hittites offer their tombs to Abraham as a gift? Similar to the king of Sodom, the Hittites know that, by the conventions of honor-shame societies, Abraham will be beholden to them if he accepts a tomb from them as a gift. By accepting the gift, Abraham will then owe some form of honor, favor, and allegiance to the Hittites. Abimelech sees that Abraham is cared for by God and decides to make a covenant with him, making them family as long as they each act in righteousness toward one another. The Hittites, on the other hand, attempt to make Abraham into a vassal as the king of Sodom attempted to do, and Abraham is aware of this. He will only take the land after having paid for it.

After having persistently attempted to get Abraham to accept the gift, Ephron finally decides that he will sell the land to Abraham (Gen 23:15). The price that Ephron gives to Abraham shows the Hittites' true intentions: they want some benefit from Abraham. If they can't get Abraham's loyalty, they at least want to milk this property exchange for all that they can. Relative to other land purchases in the Hebrew Bible, 400 shekels is an expensive price for a plot of land. However, Abraham accepts with no dispute since he is able to get the property he needs without being beholden to any external party. Just as with the king of Sodom, Abraham has kept himself from owing allegiances to any other than Yahweh and has trusted Yahweh to be his source of blessing. Abraham will not get his reward from Sodom (cf. Gen 15:1) nor the land from the Hittites. He will wait to receive these things from Yahweh.

After the purchase, we are told that the land Abraham acquired is a field full of trees near Mamre (Gen 23:17). This would be an odd detail if it were not part of the Biblical narrative. Abraham acquires a lush and fruitful field within the garden-like land of Canaan. In particular, Abraham acquires a lush piece of land near his Edenic dwelling of Mamre. This land is the first of the fulfillment of Yahweh's promise that Abraham would possess the land, and this is where Sarah would lie until the resurrection.

The Bride of Isaac

THE EXODUS MOTIF: REBEKAH OUT OF THE CITY OF NAHOR

TWICE WE HAVE SEEN the wife of the elect given exodus from the house of an oppressor back to her husband. We have also noted the significance of the exodus of the wife given that Israel is seen as the wife of Yahweh throughout the Hebrew Bible. Gen 24 is another exodus of the wife of the elect but with some very significant differences in the series of events and characters.

This narrative section begins with an old Abraham who has been blessed in all things by Yahweh (Gen 24:1). This makes Abraham look like an ideal character as he continues in the ideal Edenic state in which we saw him at the end of Gen 22. This is fitting since Abraham has now passed his ultimate test and had an ultimate reaffirmation of the blessings to him, and since this current narrative serves as a transition between Abraham and Isaac. The main actor in this narrative section will actually be Abraham's greatest servant. This servant is the oldest servant of Abraham's house who had charge of all that he had (Gen 24:2). The author leaves this man nameless and only refers to him as the servant, perhaps intending to bring other exodus-leading servants to mind, such as Moses.

The servant is commanded to go out to the place from which Abraham was given exodus, to the city of Nahor (Gen 24:10); to the nations where the bride is kept. This is similar to Yahweh's commissioning of Moses, whom he calls his servant (Ex 14:31; Num 12:7–8; Deut 34:5). Moses is commissioned to return to the nation from which he was previously given exodus, Egypt, to bring out Yahweh's bride. Also similar to Moses, the servant offers a potential issue with the proposed plan. The servant says, "Perhaps the woman may not be willing to follow me" (Gen 24:5), while Moses says, "But behold, they will not believe me or listen to my voice." Both question the belief of the bride, but the servant appears to make only an observation about a problematic scenario while Moses is trying to excuse himself from his calling. Once Abraham's servant receives an answer to his following question, he is satisfied and goes on with his mission. Moses on the other hand continues offering questions as a form of protest, never satisfied with the answers he receives (Ex 3–4). Abraham's servant seems to be better suited for an exodus mission out of the two. The question of the servant gives Abraham an opportunity to express his trust in Yahweh's promise that he will receive the land. It also allows his understanding that the promises are tied to the land to be mentioned (Gen 24:7). A wife must be taken from his own family and she will have to cut ties as he did; thus Isaac would not be united to another family through the union. This is the thrust of much of this narrative; if Isaac married a Canaanite, he would then be in familial bond with them. A marriage to a Canaanite would tie Isaac to a Canaanite family and their culture.

In Abraham's instructions, we also learn something else that links this narrative to Israel's exodus. He tells his servant that Yahweh will send his angel before him (Gen 24:7). Yahweh's angel, likewise, goes before the people of Israel to prepare their way in Ex 14:19; 23:20; 33:2. Additionally, the "presence (lit. face)" of Yahweh has been shown to be another way to refer to the Angel of Yahweh in many passages[1], including in Ex 33:14, where Yahweh says that his Presence (or Face) will go with Israel to give them rest. The Angel of Yahweh is not seen "going before" anyone again until the exodus of Israel, making this a strong connection.

Earlier in the same verse, Abraham says to his servant that the God of heaven took him from his father's house and land in order to give him the land of Canaan. This description of Abraham's exodus journey will be paradigmatic for the journey of the bride within this narrative. The servant's mission is to bring her on this journey, from her father's house to Canaan, if she is willing. He sets off towards (1)[2] Haran and comes to a well (Gen 24:11, called a spring in Gen 24:42–43). This is the second time

---

1. Foreman & Van Dorn, *Angel of the Lord*, 71–83; see also Isa 63:8–9.

2. Haran is not a place of oppressors but it is the place from which Abraham was called out of the Babylonian exile. The servant effectively goes out to bring Rebekah out of exile as Yahweh did with Abraham. Because of the lack of oppressors (though Rebekah's family will attempt to stall her exodus), elements (2) and (3) are absent. The links to Abraham's exodus may suggest that the elements (2) and (3) for the current narrative occurred in the Tower of Babylon episode.

that our main character has come to a well as part of an exodus cycle, soon after leaving their original location. The first was Hagar in Gen 16. In the discussion of that chapter, links to Israel's coming to a well after their exodus in Ex 15:25–27 and Ex 17:6 were noted. (Hagar also came to a well in Gen 21; as did Abraham in the same chapter during his strife with Abimelech. However, neither of these sections in Gen 21 contained their own exodus cycles, and therefore will not be included in the exodus pattern). The current well-scene in Gen 24, while part of the exodus pattern, also fits into a more particular pattern known as the "betrothal journey" pattern. These patterned narratives consist of twelve elements, which are at times deviated from by the biblical authors depending on what they intend to communicate in a given passage. Those twelve elements are:

1. The groom-to-be travels to a foreign country, either in flight from or commissioned by his kin.

2. He meets a young woman or young women at a well.

3. Someone draws water.

4. A gift is given or a service is performed that ingratiates the suitor with the woman and/or her family.

5. The suitor reveals his identity.

6. The young woman/women rush home with news of his arrival.

7. Someone from the family returns to greet and/or invite the suitor.

8. A betrothal is arranged, usually in connection with a meal.

9. The suitor resides with his bride's kin, sometimes begetting children.

10. The suitor returns, usually commissioned by the bride's kin.

11. The suitor is received by his kin at the end of his journey.

12. The suitor resides with his kin, sometimes begetting children.[3]

Within the Torah we see three betrothal journey narratives, each of them within an exodus cycle. The first is the current narrative in Gen 24, as mentioned, and the others are in the stories of Jacob and Moses. Each will be discussed as we come to them. Within this narrative, each of the twelve elements of the betrothal journey narrative are present and in order, but carried out by the servant rather than by Isaac himself. This may

---

3. The list has been reproduced from Martin, "Betrothal Journey Narratives," 508–509.

be due to Isaac's passivity within his narratives or due to the importance that he dwell in Canaan. Through the use of this narrative pattern, the author can easily communicate the nuances of a character or narrative through variations in the pattern. But in each instance of this pattern within the Torah, we see the elect, or the servant as a surrogate for the elect, who is in some form of exile. The elect then finds a well which becomes the catalyst for him receiving his bride.

As the servant sits at the well, he prays for a sign that he may know who the girl is that Yahweh has chosen for Isaac. Before he is finished speaking, the sign begins to take place, being performed by Rebekah, whom the author introduced in the genealogy at the end of chapter 22. The author quickly tells us that she is Abraham's kin, and therefore suitable for Isaac. The reader is made to see Yahweh's providence at work as the servant is held in suspense. Once the servant observed that Yahweh gave the sign through this girl, he adorned her with a gold ring and bracelets (Gen 24:22). When it is later settled that she is to go back to Canaan to marry Isaac, the servant further adorns her in Gen 24:53.

Now, there is no narrative in Israel's exodus of Yahweh adorning Israel with jewelry, but there is a correspondence that we should take note of between the adorning and the giving of the law. In Ezek 16:8–14, a passage that was discussed earlier, Yahweh is describing Israel's exodus in terms of marriage. Once the people have been brought out of Egypt and given a covenant with Yahweh (Ezek 16:8), he begins to adorn her with fine clothes and jewelry. Due to this adornment she "grew exceedingly beautiful and advanced to royalty" (Ezek 16:13) and her beauty gave Israel renown among the nations. One might guess that the adornment which Yahweh gives is the law at Sinai, and if we compare this passage to Deut 4:5–8 this seems to be confirmed. In Deut 4:5–8, Moses tells the people that they ought to adhere to the law because it will be their wisdom which will result in renown from the nations. The law given to Israel was given through Moses, Yahweh's servant who was sent to bring the people to Yahweh. So, just as Yahweh's bride was adorned through his servant Moses, Isaac's bride is adorned by the servant sent on his behalf.

After the servant reveals himself to Rebekah and thanks Yahweh for his providence, Rebekah runs to her relatives and the reader is introduced to her brother Laban (Gen 24:29). He will become a significant part of Jacob's story, but his character is set up for the reader now. We are told in Gen 24:30–31 that he gives an eager welcome to Abraham's servant but does so as a response to seeing the rich adornment which he has given to his sister. Wealth is Laban's sole motivator for his hospitality. The servant, on the other hand, would not eat the meal set before him until he had made his mission known. He recounts Yahweh's blessing of Abraham and retells the events of this chapter up to this point (Gen 24:33–49). He retells the story fairly precisely; perhaps emphasizing Yahweh's providence in his mission in order to convince Rebekah's family to let her go with him.

At the end of the speech, Rebekah's family recognizes that Yahweh has provided Rebekah for Isaac and provided success in the servant's mission. They tell the servant "take and go" (Gen 24:51, AT). This exact Hebrew phrase, "take and go" has been used as Pharaoh gave Sarah back to Abraham in Gen 12:19. These words "take" and "go" are also used in close proximity in Ex 12:32. The verse reads, "also your flock and your herd, *take* as you said *and go* and bless me also" [AT]. As Pharaoh urges Moses and the rest of Israel out of Egypt, he also tells them to "take and go." The morning after, the servant requests to take his leave, saying, "send me away" (Gen 24:54). The word "send (שלח, šlḥ)" will be repeated in Gen 24:56 and Gen 24:59 when the bride is sent out. We have also seen this word used in other exoduses already. Sarah is sent out of Pharaoh's house, she is sent out of Abimelech's house, and Moses tells his Pharaoh to "send my people away."

Rather than allowing the servant to go back to his master and complete his mission Laban and his mother try to detain the bride. They ask the servant "may the girl dwell with us days or ten, after, you go" [AT] (Gen 24:55). The phrase "days or ten" is an ambiguous phrase that likely represents an indefinite, and possibly endless, amount of time. Much like Pharaoh will do, Laban and his mother, after giving their word to send out the bride with Yahweh's servant, attempt to keep the bride. The servant must then, again, assert Yahweh's will and providence through the recent events, and again request to be sent out (שלח, šlḥ) (Gen 24:56). With this request and the willingness of the bride to go to her husband (a heart required by both Abraham and Israel), Rebekah and the servant are finally sent out (שלח, šlḥ) (Gen 24:59).

As Laban and his mother send out Rebekah, (7) they give Rebekah a blessing that sounds extremely similar to that belonging to Abraham. Compare Abraham's blessing in Gen 22:17 to Rebekah's blessing here in Gen 24:60.

I will surely bless you, and I will surely multiply your offspring
as the stars of heaven and as the sand that is on the seashore.
And your offspring shall possess the gate of his enemies.
—Gen 22:17

Our sister, may you become
    thousands of ten thousands,
and may your offspring possess
    the gate of those who hate him!
—Gen 24:60

In both, not only is multiplication of offspring mentioned but also victory over enemies in terms of possessing their gates. We have seen this promise of victory show up throughout the blessings of Abraham (Gen 12:3; 15:1). This promise of victory elevates this particular blessing beyond the blessing of fruitfulness that Ishmael receives and that is seen manifest in the many offspring of Cain, Ham, and Lot. The promise of victory causes this blessing to be read in line with the blessing of the elect one. This promise of victory has only been given to the elect offspring, beginning with the promise of the seed of the woman and continuing into the blessings on Abraham's seed. We ought to keep in mind here that the author of Genesis has crafted the book to make very intentional points, and the recording of this blessing on the lips of Rebekah's family is not to be read as a historical coincidence. By the giving of this blessing in the midst of her exodus from Nahor, we see that Rebekah, with Isaac, will be in the line of the serpent-crushing seed that has been promised through Abraham. She will be the mother of Yahweh's elect one, through whom a new nation will be formed that blesses all nations.

Rebekah, now adorned, (4) comes out of Nahor with a multitude of people. With her are the servant, his men, her nurse (Gen 24:59), and her young women (Gen 24:61). Rebekah and this mixed multitude come back to Canaan and they come to Isaac wandering in the Negeb. No conversation takes place between Rebekah and Isaac, but rather the servant speaks to them. This also may be an intentional foreshadowing of Moses by the author as Moses served as an intermediary between Yahweh and Israel. As is customary, the bride puts on her veil, she is brought to her husband, and to his tent. Having come through an exodus out of Mesopotamia, like Abraham before her, she has now been willingly brought by the servant to Yahweh's elect in order to become his bride. She then takes the place of Sarah as the bride of Yahweh's elect and mother to the promised seed that will crush the enemies of Yahweh and his people.

As the story transitions from the generation of Isaac to his children, we are given the genealogy of Abraham and Ishmael. The author tells us that Abraham took another wife and had more sons and grandsons, some of which become nations that will be seen again later in Genesis. However, Abraham gives these sons gifts and, just as he did with Ishmael, exiles them from the land of promise. With a provision from their father in hand, these sons are sent east (Gen 25:6), which we have already seen as a typical direction of exile in the biblical narrative. Just as with Ishmael, we may presume that Abraham's reasoning is that he will not have any sons besides Yahweh's elect, from Abraham's chosen wife, inheriting the land tied to Yahweh's promises. This is an act of trust in Yahweh in order to ensure that the land is available for the elect seed, when he comes, and not filled with relatives and allies whom the elect would be wrong to dispossess. Abraham then dies in a good, old age and is buried in his Edenic tomb with his wife (Gen 25:9–10), his bones dwelling in the land until he is given full possession of it.

Table 11

Correspondences to Rebekah's exodus from the city of Nahor

	Sarai in Egypt	Isaac's Bride	Exodus
Highest servant sent		Gen 24:2	Ex 14:31; Num 12:7–8; Deut 34:5
Angel of Yahweh sent ahead		Gen 24:7	Ex 14:19; 23:20; 33:2
(1) Servant goes to nations		Gen 24:10	Ex 4:20
Spring/well		Gen 24:11, 20, 62	Ex 15:25–27; 17:6
Must leave father's house		Gen 24:4, 7, 38, 40	
Bride adorned		Gen 24:22, 53	Deut 4:5–8; Ezek 16:8–14
"take and go"	Gen 12:19	Gen 24:51	Ex 12:32
Request to be sent		Gen 24:54	Ex 5:1
Bride detained		Gen 24:55	Ex 5:1–2; 8:8, 15, 28–32; 9:27–28, 34–35; 10:16–20; 12:31–32; 14:8–9
Bride sent out	Gen 12:18–19	Gen 24:51, 59	Ex 12:31–32
(4) Come out with mixed multitude and possessions	Gen 12:16; 13:1–2	Gen 24:22, 53, 59, 61	Ex 12:35–36, 38
(7) Blessing: fruitful, multiply	Gen 13:16	Gen 24:60	Lev 26:3–10; Deut 11:7–16
(7) Commissioned to subdue	Gen 13:15, 17	Gen 24:60	Lev 26:6–8; Deut 7:16; Josh 18:1
Marriage/covenant	Gen 12:19	Gen 24:67	Ex 19:5–8; Jer 31:32; Ezek 16:8

Jacob and Esau

THE TWO-GOATS MOTIF: JACOB AND ESAU

THE STORY OF JACOB and Esau begins in Gen 25 with the wife of the elect again being barren (Gen 25:21). This time, the reader is not left in suspense for long as Isaac asks Yahweh to open her womb and he does. The author is developing a pattern of Yahweh giving life to the dead womb in the line of the seed of the woman. Once she conceives, we learn that there will be strife between these brothers from before they exit the womb. Yahweh tells Rebekah that the twins will be divided (דרפ, *prd*) peoples from birth (Gen 25:23). The word "divided (דרפ, *prd*)" is only used nine times in the Torah and the last occurrences were in Gen 13:9, 11, and 14. The word is used, and concentrated, in Gen 13 to describe Lot's division from Abraham. The brotherly strife and division pronounced in the current narrative should signal to the reader that the Two-Goats motif may be about to appear.

When Esau is born, the author tells us that he is hairy (שער, *ś'r*) such that he appears to be wearing a cloak (Gen 25:25). That Esau is שער (*ś'r*) is reiterated in Gen 27:11, 23. This becomes a wordplay with Esau's future place of dwelling, Seir (שֵׂעִיר, *ś'yr*)[1], which is built off of the same Hebrew root. The word "Seir (שֵׂעִיר, *ś'yr*)" also shares consonants with one of the Hebrew words for goat (שָׂעִיר, *ś'yr*). Interestingly, this word for "goat" is concentrated in Lev 16, appearing fourteen times. The fact that the consonants of שעיר (*ś'yr*) are found throughout the Esau narrative and concentrated in the Day of Atonement instructions should connect Esau and the Day of Atonement in the mind of the reader. The fact that he is hairy (שער, *ś'r*) like a goat and that the narrative has thus far built

---

1. See, for example, Gen 33:14, 16; 36:8, 9, 20, 21, 30

116

the pattern that striving brothers are compared to the goats of the Day of Atonement shows that the author intends for the reader to see Esau as one of the two goats in the Two-Goats motif. The author immediately gives hints as to which goat Esau is as well.

Not only is Esau the eldest, showing that he will (A) be a servant to Jacob based on Gen 25:23, but he is also a skillful hunter. This should remind the reader of Ishmael, who grew up to become skilled with the bow (Gen 21:20) in the wilderness. Since Ishmael fits within the Two-Goats motif as the goat for Azazel, this comparison is the author hinting that Esau will play the role of the goat for Azazel. Adding to this hint is the fact the word here translated "hunter (צוד, ṣwd)" only appears in reference to Esau and to Nimrod (Gen 10:9). By comparing Esau to the rebellious builder of wicked cities and to Ishmael, it becomes further insinuated that Esau may fit into the pattern of the goat for Azazel by becoming an exiled city builder. The narrative of Jacob and Esau is full of unexpected inversions but the narrative will bear out that these intimations were not an inversion, as Esau will indeed (B) show hostility to the elect, (D) leave the land of Canaan, go to Seir, and (E)(F) become a hostile people. Meanwhile, Jacob will be brought through an exodus and (G) brought into Yahweh's presence. The presence of these elements will be noted throughout the narrative.

JACOB GAINS THE BIRTHRIGHT

One of the inversions of the Jacob narrative is that, though he is the elect, Jacob's name, יַעֲקֹב (yʿkb), characterizes him as a betrayer; a supplanter; literally, a heel-grabber (cf. Gen 27:36)[2]. Jacob's name is actually spelled with the same letters as the word for "heel (עקב, ʿkb)" found in Gen 3:15, as well as in Gen 25:26, with the addition of the beginning yod (י). By depicting Jacob as a betrayer who "grabs the heel," the author has portrayed Jacob in a way that mimics the serpent of Gen 3. Going forward we would expect him to be the seed of the serpent and the goat for Azazel. However, before Jacob was born and named, Yahweh (A) chose the younger to carry the blessing that would bless the nations (Gen 25:23). Jacob will, indeed, behave like the seed of the serpent, like a deceiver, for much of

2. There are other proposed derivations for Jacob's name, but the wordplay found within the narrative links him to the heel (עֲקֹב, ʿkb) of Esau which he grabbed (Gen 25:26) and the word עקב (ʿkb, meaning to betray or grab by the heel), which Esau uses in reference to him (Gen 27:36). See Garsiel, *Biblical Names*, 21

his life and Yahweh will use the results of his actions in order to continue his plan to redeem humanity. This is displayed in the way by which Jacob acquires the birthright.

As Abraham gave the role of firstborn to Isaac over Ishmael at Yahweh's instruction, so should Isaac and Rebekah have given the birthright to Jacob due to Yahweh's proclamation in Gen 25:23. But Isaac, the man of prayer, seems to have weakened in his trust in Yahweh as he is now head of a household that is divided by favoritism; Isaac's for Esau and Rebekah's for Jacob (Gen 25:28). Isaac seems to have allowed his stomach to discern what is good rather than Yahweh's words. So, now Yahweh must see to it that his elect, Jacob, carries Abraham's blessing and becomes the firstborn of the elect family. Yahweh must see to this in the face of the lack of loyalty from Isaac; from the elect one of the previous generation.

What is surprising is that we do not see Yahweh intervene in the story, but rather Jacob's snake-like character is allowed to manifest. In birth, Jacob piggybacked off of his brother in order to come out of the womb, and again he will use Esau for his own benefit. Esau, like his father, allows his stomach to decide what is good. A quick meal becomes good to him and he despises the birthright of Yahweh's elect (Gen 25:34). Jacob takes advantage of his brother's ill discernment and trades him a bowl of stew for the birthright. No one in this narrative displays the loyalty or trust expected of elect one. Yahweh does not even seem to come to anyone's mind. However, this will not be the last time, nor has it been the first, that Yahweh will use the bad intentions of his own people to elevate the elect one such that he can be a blessing to the nations. The story of Jacob's acquisition of the firstborn and blessing continues in Gen 27, but first, the author takes us through another exodus of the wife of the elect.

Rebekah and Abimelech

THE EXODUS MOTIF: REBEKAH FROM ABIMELECH

GEN 26 BEGINS IN much the same way as Sarah's first exodus narrative, in Gen 12, and Israel's exodus (see Gen 45:4–13). There is a famine in the land that forces the elect family to migrate. However, unlike Abraham and Israel, Isaac is warned not to go down to Egypt. The author does not give the exact reasoning as to why Isaac has to stay in the region of Canaan, but it seems that Yahweh has determined to bless Isaac's seed and promise them the land, as he did Abraham, contingent on his staying in the land (Gen 26:3–4). Isaac has the opportunity to go to Egypt and forfeit the promise for his current household to be blessed.

Isaac remains in the land, per Yahweh's instructions, and settles in Gerar. Isaac then tells the Philistines that his wife is his sister because he fears for his life, thinking that the people of the land may kill him and take her (Gen 26:6–7). This is a near repetition of Abraham's actions in Gen 12:11–13 and in Gen 20:1–2. Though Rebekah was not taken as Sarah was and Yahweh did not intervene, Isaac has come to a foreign land and lied out of fear for his safety, as in previous narratives. In time Abimelech uncovers this lie by observing Isaac's relationship with Rebekah (Gen 26:8). Abimelech confronts Isaac on his lie about his wife, just as he and Pharaoh had done to Abraham. Abimelech once again asks the question that we have seen throughout Genesis, "What is this you have done to us?" (Gen 3:13; 4:10; 12:18; 20:9). He then turns to the people and tells them, "whoever touches (נגע, ngʿ) this man or his wife shall surely be put to death (מוֹת יוּמָת, mwt ywmt)." Abimelech protects Rebekah and Isaac, still displaying loyalty to the chosen family and his righteousness, despite the deceptions that he has undergone.

119

Abimelech's proclamation of protection over Isaac and Rebekah actually echoes Yahweh's warning about the Tree of the Knowledge of Good
and Evil in Gen 2:17, and Eve's repetition of the command to the snake in
Gen 3:3. In Gen 2:17, Yahweh warns Adam not to eat of the tree "for in the
day that you eat of it you shall surely die (מוֹת תָּמוּת, *mwt tmwt*). Eve also
relays this instruction to the snake, adding "neither shall you touch (נגע,
ngʿ) it." Yahweh's command is later echoed in Gen 20:7, when he warns
Abimelech to return Sarah lest he die (מוֹת יוּמָת, *mwt ywmt*). Through
this statement, Abimelech's character as one who is loyal and righteous
is enhanced. Just as Sarah and the fruit of the Garden were "seen" and
"taken," so Rebekah is at risk of being wrongfully taken. Now Abimelech
has played the role of Yahweh by keeping this forbidden woman from
the people and giving a warning of death to any who may *see* her as *good*
and *take* her. By learning from the command that he heard from Yahweh
and by maintaining loyalty to the elect, Abimelech has become an effec-
tive instrument of protection for the elect and removed the necessity for
Yahweh's intervention.

Despite Isaac's failure in the land of Gerar, Yahweh is true to his
promise to bless Isaac if he stayed in the land. In this same year of famine, Yahweh miraculously provided a crop of a hundredfold and made
him wealthier in all the ways in which he made Abraham wealthy (Gen
26:12–14). Yahweh (4) made Isaac wealthy and into a multitude of people
in Gerar. Despite his breach of trust, Isaac was allowed to remain in the
land of Gerar by Abimelech. However, as Isaac increased, Abimelech sent
him out because the size of his household was too mighty (Gen 26:16).
The word עצם (*ʿṣm*), here translated as "mightier" by the ESV, is not used
again in the Torah except in Ex 1:7 and 20 to describe how "strong" and
numerous the Israelites had become in Egypt. Pharaoh sees the great-
ness of Israel and oppresses them so that they would not leave Egypt.
Abimelech, on the other hand, is contrasted to the wicked Pharaoh.
Seeing that Isaac has become great and that there has become tension
between Isaac and the Philistines (Gen 26:15), Abimelech asks him to
depart (Gen 26:16). Presumably, Isaac's house became great enough that
the land could not support both Isaac and Abimelech. Abimelech could
have oppressed the elect as Pharaoh would, but he sees separation as the
solution, echoing faithful Abraham's request for Lot to depart from him
(Gen 13:9). For now, Isaac interprets this request as an act of hatred (Gen
26:27).

In Gen 26:14–15 this great increase in wealth and servants had made the Philistines envious of him. This envy leads to the Philistines attacking and quarreling (ריב, *ryb*) over Isaac's wells, forcing Isaac to move until he finds a place where he can live peacefully. Through these narrative points, the reader's mind should be brought back to the narrative of Lot's separation in Gen 13. Lot and Abraham had both become large households and they occupied too small of a territory to support themselves. This led to quarreling (ריב, *ryb*) between their servants and the need to separate. In Gen 13, Abraham generously offers Lot his choice of the land, showing kindness to Lot and trusting Yahweh for his promised land.

The current narrative also shares elements with the story of Abraham and Abimelech's covenant in Gen 20 and 21. After Sarah had received exodus in Gerar and subsequently been blessed with a son, Abraham complained to Abimelech over the theft of one of his wells (Gen 21:25). Abimelech professes innocence in this theft and Abraham then keeps peace by offering a pledge of his ownership of the well rather than retaking the well by force. Once again, in Gen 26, after the elect's wife has been given exodus in Gerar and the elect has been blessed (Gen 26:24), the Philistines have attacked the wells of the elect one. Isaac then, while letting the stolen wells go, complains to Abimelech about his hatred towards him in sending him out (Gen 26:27). Abimelech continues to be shown as a righteous character when he proposes a covenant (Gen 26:28). He sees the blessings of Yahweh on Isaac and desires to pursue peace. Through his declaration the reader also learns that Abimelech sent Isaac away in peace rather than in hatred (Gen 26:29). In both narratives, the elect's wife is given exodus in Gerar, the elect is blessed, there is contention over wells, the elect complains to Abimelech, and peace is made through covenant on account of Yahweh's blessings. In these repetitions, this narrative displays Abimilech's growth between narratives, the pattern of peace with the nations, and the provision of Yahweh.

Up to Gen 26:24, Isaac has faced tests of his trust in Yahweh and love of fellow man. Ultimately he passes this test as he has remained in the land as Yahweh had instructed at the beginning of this narrative. Isaac gave up his wells instead of taking them back by force, and he trusted Yahweh for his provision (Gen 26:22). Just as with Abraham and Sarah in Gen 12 and 13, after the bride has come through an exodus and the elect one has passed a test of brotherly loyalty, Yahweh comes to Isaac and (7) affirms his blessing and covenant (Gen 26:24). Again, the elect one builds an altar and calls upon the name of Yahweh (Gen 26:25). This sacrifice is Isaac's mountaintop purification and communion with Yahweh. While there is no mountaintop or tree mentioned explicitly in this narrative, Isaac is in Beersheba (Gen 26:23), where Abraham previously planted a tree and called upon the name of Yahweh after he had made a covenant with Abimelech (Gen 21:33). Beersheba, with its previously established garden-like connotations, is significant as the location of the climax of this narrative. Isaac, like Abraham, goes through an exodus and brotherly strife narrative, both involving the Philistines, and ends in the same garden-like location.

When Abimelech comes to Isaac to request a covenant of peace, Isaac agrees to this and the two men part ways in peace (Gen 26:31). The author tells the reader that Isaac's servants then dig a well in Beersheba (Gen 26:32). The finding of this well after Isaac's covenant with Abimelech serves as the grounds for the reestablishment of Beersheba. Beerhsheba has again been established in the context of the elect one's acquisition of a well and an oath with Abimelech. By these events, the author is linking the end of this story with the end of chapter 21. Abraham had a dispute with Abimelech over a well, made a covenant, established Beersheba, planted a tree, and made an offering. As was previously discussed, chapter 21 was a high point in Abraham's story in that after he had been through his own exoduses he had been loyal to Yahweh and had dwelt in peace with the nations in an Eden-like state by his tree and offering. Isaac does not mirror Abraham's planting of a tree (perhaps because one is already there), but we do have an Isaac who has been blessed by Yahweh, offering sacrifices and at peace with the nations in the same location as faithful Abraham. In order to strengthen the image of Isaac as the faithful elect one in an Edenic state in chapter 26, the author establishes significant links between the climax of the present narrative and that of Abraham's covenant with Abimelech.

Though this narrative lacks oppressors that take Rebekah, this narrative still bears the marks of an exodus of the elect's wife. There are close parallels between the current narrative and that of Sarah's previous exoduses, as well as the presence of narrative elements which link it to Israel's exodus (see Table 12). Therefore, while this narrative is a variation on the motif, it still fits well within the Exodus motif framework. In this variation, the narrative displays an exodus cycle in which the formerly oppressive king has learned loyalty towards Yahweh and his elect. Isaac's wife has been brought through an exodus out of the threat of being taken into a king's house, just as Sarai had been in Gen 12 and

20, but Abimelech plays the role of both potential threat and deliverer. After this deliverance, Isaac faces brotherly strife just as Abraham did in Gen 13 and 21. Isaac acts faithfully in the midst of this strife, as Abraham did, and Abimelech once again reciprocates this loyalty. In this chapter, the author ends this narrative section with Isaac portrayed as loyal to Yahweh, loyal to brothers/covenant partners, and in an Edenic dwelling. This generation of the elect has been brought to a climax and resolution so that the narrative focus can pass to the next generation.

Table 12

Correspondences to Rebekah's exodus from Abimelech

	Sarah and Abimelech	Rebekah and Abimelech	Exodus
Famine		Gen 26:1	Gen 45:4–13
Prepared speech to secure well-being	Gen 20:2, 13	Gen 26:7	Gen 46:31–34
King sends out	Gen 20:15	Gen 26:16	Ex 5:1; 12:31–32
Too numerous		Gen 26:16	Ex 1:9, 16
(4) Come out with mixed multitude and possessions	Gen 20:14–16	Gen 26:13–14, 17	Ex 12:35–36, 38
(7) Act as Priests/ Purification	Gen 20:17	Gen 26:25	Ex 19:5–6
Spring/well	Gen 21:24, 30	Gen 26:22, 25, 32	Ex 15:25–27; 17:6
(7) Blessing: fruitful, multiply	Gen 21:1–2	Gen 26:3–4, 12–14, 24	Lev 26:3–10; Deut 11:7–16

Jacob in Paddan-Aram

AT THE END OF Gen 26, the narrative returns to Isaac's two sons. In Gen 26:34, Esau takes wives at the same age at which Isaac takes Rebekah, drawing a comparison between the two. Whereas Isaac took a daughter of his kinsman, who had been brought through an exodus by his father's greatest servant, Esau took Hittites (one of the residents of Canaan). These Hittite women caused "bitterness (מָרָה, *mrh*) of spirit" for Isaac and Rebekah (Gen 26:35) as the Egyptians would later make life bitter (מרר, *mrr*) for the Israelites (Ex 1:14). Through this poor choice of wives, it seems the author has created the expectation that Esau will not be one who is concerned with Yahweh's blessings and that he would not receive his parents' favor. It seems that it would not be difficult for the younger son to gain favor over the older. It seems that Esau would indeed serve Jacob. It is much to the reader's surprise then that he is Isaac's favored son and that Isaac intends to bless him (Gen 27:4), even with a blessing of lordship over his brothers (Gen 27:9).

It is interesting that Yahweh's pronouncement that "the older shall serve the younger" (Gen 25:23) is not brought up in Gen 27. This pronouncement would have been grounds for Rebekah to make an appeal to Isaac that he bless Jacob, rather than Esau. However, she instead resorts to deception in order to make sure that Jacob is blessed rather than Esau. Rather than looking to Yahweh's promise for Jacob's blessing, she instead acts out of favoritism for her younger son, as does Isaac for his eldest (Gen 25:28). In her selfishness, Rebekah has used the means of the serpent to secure her favorite son's blessing.

Rebekah clothes (לבש, *lbš*) Jacob in the skins (עוֹר, *'wr*) of goats (Gen 27:16) just as Yahweh clothed (לבש, *lbš*) Adam and Eve with skins (עוֹר, *'wr*) as they were expelled from the garden (Gen 3:21). This action, rather than restoring Jacob, may signify that Jacob has been commissioned by Rebekah to fulfill her plan or it may be a foreshadowing of his exile from the land through the connection to Adam and Eve's exile. In either case, Jacob uses these hairy (שֵׂעָר, śʿr) skins to obtain the Abrahamic blessing through deception and disloyalty. By acting as a seed of the serpent, Jacob obtains a blessing of abundance, victory over enemies, and of blessing for those who bless him (Gen 27:27–29; cf. Gen 12:2–3). Once Isaac and Esau learn of the deception, Esau is caused to cry out (צָעַק, ṣʿk), just as Abel's blood (Gen 4:10) and those oppressed by Sodom did (Gen 18:21; 19:13), and as the Israelites will do in Egypt (Ex 2:23). By way of Esau's cry, Jacob is likened to the oppressors; the seeds of the serpent that appear throughout the Biblical narrative.

Jacob now carries the Abrahamic birthright and blessing through his own efforts, rather than by waiting on Yahweh. He is much like Abraham and Sarah who used Hagar to advance Yahweh's purposes rather than waiting on Yahweh to enact his plan. Despite using the means of the serpent, and though he ought to have looked to Yahweh, Jacob does put himself in the place of the elect as Yahweh intended. Meanwhile, Esau is left only with the hope that one day he will be able to free himself from his brother's oppression.

To this point, this narrative section is a confusing one for the attentive reader. Thus far in the book of Genesis, the elect of Yahweh have been flawed but faithful individuals who trust Yahweh to fulfill his promises. This narrative contains two brothers as the others do, but neither seems to be "elect material." One is characterized as a Nimrod, a goat for Azazel, and has taken foreign wives. The other has taken his place as the firstborn by conniving and manipulation. He bears more resemblance to the serpent than he does to any of his faithful forefathers.

THE EXODUS MOTIF: JACOB FROM PADDAN-ARAM.

The (now self-inflicted) brotherly strife that Jacob receives from Esau results in (1) Jacob's exile from the land of promise. Once Rebekah hears that Esau plans to kill Jacob for his deceptions (Gen 27:41), she formulates a plan to have him sent to Paddan-Aram until Esau's anger subsides. She tells Jacob that she will send and bring Jacob from there (Gen 27:45); that she will enact Jacob's exodus, when Esau has cooled off. After formulating this plan and promising Jacob an exodus (a bold claim within the biblical narrative), she disappears from the biblical narrative except for passing references. This woman who has followed in the footsteps of Abraham and Sarah in her own exodus events, has become a seed of the serpent and become insignificant to the story of Yahweh rescuing his elect.

Isaac, ironically, "sends" Jacob out (Gen 28:5) to Paddan-Aram with the same instructions that Abraham's servant received when he was sent to Mesopotamia. Neither Isaac nor Jacob are to take a wife from the Canaanites but are to take them from Abraham's kin (Gen 28:1–2). This unlikely firstborn then receives the full blessing of Abraham (Gen 28:3–4) and sets off on the same journey as Abraham's servant as he goes to find a wife within Bethuel's household. By recording similar instruction and a similar journey to that of Abraham's servant, the reader ought to expect more similarities between their journeys, including the occurrence of another exodus event in the coming chapters. Meanwhile, Esau resorts to further polygamy in what may be a desperate attempt to gain a greater blessing from his father (Gen 27:8–9).

Jacob's Journey

As Jacob goes along on his exilic journey, he stops to rest and dreams of a stairway that went from the land and "reached the heavens" (Gen 28:12). This sounds much like the ziggurat "with its top in the heavens" that was seen in Gen 11. In Gen 11 humanity attempted to reach the heavens with the tower of "Babylon," which in the Babylonian language means "gate of god."[1] Meanwhile, Yahweh has revealed to Jacob the true "gate of heaven" (Gen 28:17). Here Yahweh blesses Jacob with the Abrahamic blessing; land, fruitfulness, and the subduing and blessing of the nations (Gen 28:13–14). Yahweh also promises that he will give Jacob exodus out of Paddan-Aram and will bring him back into Canaan (Gen 28:15). Jacob returns the promise that if Yahweh will uphold his promise, he will set up Yahweh's house at Bethel and will give a tenth of all Yahweh gives to him (Gen 28:22). This is the second time that a tithe has come up, the first being Abraham's tithe to Melchizedek in Gen 14:20.

Jacob continues on eastward, having the promises and blessings of Yahweh with him, and comes to a well. Just as with Abraham's servant, this well is where he finds his bride, beginning another betrothal journey narrative[1]. (Jacob's journey contains eleven out of the twelve elements of the betrothal narrative pattern, omitting the twelfth element[2]). Also

1. Martin, "Betrothal Journey Narratives," 510–511
2. See discussion and list in chapter "The Bride of Isaac"

similar to the servant, upon meeting his bride, Jacob is brought to Laban and invited to stay. Despite their familial connection, which both Laban and the author make much of (Gen 29:13–14), Laban (1) reduces Jacob to a servant by discussing his wages (Gen 29:15). Laban's character doesn't seem to have developed from chapter 24. Though he puts on a grand show of affection towards his kinsman, he takes the first opportunity to profit from his arrival.

Jacob offers to work for Laban for seven years for Rachel, perhaps because he is in no hurry to return to Esau or perhaps the author is highlighting that Jacob worked in increments of seven for his bride to communicate the significance of the marriage of the elect. Whatever the reason may be, when the time comes for Jacob to take his bride, he does get her but is again wronged by Laban and deceived into taking Leah as a wife before taking Rachel. Ironically, Jacob asks Laban, "Why then have you deceived (רמה, *rmh*) me?" (Gen 29:25), echoing Jacob's "deceit (רמה, *rmh*)" of Isaac in Gen 27:35. Jacob now faces oppression in his exile in similar ways in which he acted as the serpent towards his own family.

Despite the deception and oppression through which it came, Yahweh has given Jacob a bride, two, in fact, in the midst of his exile from his land. Yahweh has promised to provide for him and bring him back to Canaan, but he will do much more than Jacob has asked by giving him wives and children, that the line of the seed of the woman may continue.

The Exodus motif: The Birth of Jacob's Children

The narrative of the birth of Jacob's children is filled with exodus imagery as well, though it is seated within a narrative of sisterly strife. The section begins with Leah suffering affliction (ענה, *'nh*; Gen 29:32), just as Israel suffered affliction (ענה, *'nh*) in Egypt (Ex 1:11–12; 3:7, 17; 4:31). Her affliction is the distaste that Jacob has for her, and through bearing children, she seeks to win his love. Yahweh begins to give her children as he sees and hears her affliction (Gen 29:32–33), just as he sees and hears the afflictions of Israel (Ex 2:24–25). With her third child, Leah is convinced that her husband will be attached to her. It seems that this continues to be Leah's hope throughout the birthing narrative (cf. Gen 30:20), indicating that her hope was not met with her third child. However, her fourth child, Judah, brings her to praise Yahweh (Gen 29:35). Whether this is because she has received some affection from her husband or not, she has shifted her focus to the praise of Yahweh for her children.

It would here be beneficial to note that exoduses of the bride of the elect have taken place multiple times. The author may be creating the expectation that Leah and Rachel ought to have their own exodus events just as the other wives of the elect have had. It may be that the author, while not giving Leah or Rachel explicit exodus narratives as the reader may now expect, gives the birthing narrative instead. Through the features of this narrative, each of these women becomes part of the Exodus motif, though with its own reversals and irregularities, as with many elements of the Jacob narrative. Rather than being brought out of the oppressor's house and back to their husband, these women are oppressing one another in their competition for children. Leah hopes to gain the affections of her husband who, rather than longing for her from afar, is displeased with her. Despite these things, Yahweh does see, hear, and 'deliver' them within this situation through conception.

Seeing Leah's fruitfulness, Rachel becomes jealous of her sister. She desires Leah's blessings and status, as other siblings have done throughout Genesis. This brings her to demand children from her husband (Gen 30:1). Jacob finds himself with a barren wife, as Isaac did, but shown in sharp contrast to him. Whereas Isaac prayed for his barren wife, Jacob berates Rachel and follows Abraham's failure in taking her servant as another wife. Through this servant, Rachel gets her first child. In response to this child, Rachel recognizes that God has judged her by closing her womb, but has also *heard* her and given her a child (Gen 30:6) as he had done for Leah. The second child brings Rachel to proclaim that in these "wrestlings" with her sister, she has prevailed (Gen 30:8). Through these first two sons, Rachel seems to share the character of Jacob. She acts out of desire for the blessings of her sibling, she is judged yet also rescued, and she continues to prevail in obtaining blessing by her own efforts. This similarity of character will become more evident later. Meanwhile, Leah has been a more humble character. She has been hated and afflicted, she has awaited Yahweh's help and received it, and is brought to praise him.

Despite her more noble character, seeing that she ceased bearing children and that her sister began having children through her servant, Leah joins in the contest by giving her servant to Jacob (Gen 30:9). She counts these children as blessings and good fortune, but the use of these servants are the women's schemes for seed rather than Yahweh's provision. Yahweh is said to have opened the wombs of Leah and Rachel (Gen

29:31, 30:22), but the opening of wombs is not recorded for the servants. Leah and Rachel are now using servants as mechanisms for getting children as they act out the pattern of sibling rivalry that has been seen throughout Genesis. This pattern of rivalry and scheming for blessing continues as Rachel sells a night with her husband for Reuben's mandrakes (Gen 30:14).

As Jacob will later rely on magic to affect the color of the lambs being bred, so now Rachel relies on mandrakes to increase her fertility. In Rachel's exchange with Leah for these mandrakes, Leah seems to make clear that Rachel still holds Jacob's affection while Leah gets none. Leah "hires (שׂכר, śkr)" Jacob with mandrakes (Gen 30:16) just as Laban hires and oppresses Jacob through wages (שׂכר, śkr) (Gen 29:15; 31:7). This is a subtle nod to the fact that Jacob has become an object within the sister's competition. He is even being oppressed by the oppressed sister. Despite Leah's affliction of Jacob, Yahweh hears her complaint and sees that she has given up her mandrakes in an attempt to become impregnated by Jacob again. In seeing and hearing these things, Yahweh gives Leah two more sons and one daughter. She honors Yahweh's gift to her in their names and is again convinced that these children will win her husband over to her (Gen 30:20). Again, we are not told if this hope is ever met, but Yahweh has indeed established her name as a fruitful mother within the elect family.

Leah's last three children come between Rachel's acquiring of mandrakes and her first birth. It is possible that Yahweh has worked in tandem with Rachel's beliefs about the mandrakes, but the distance that the author has put between her getting mandrakes and Rachel's giving birth is likely to signal to the reader that they were of no effect. Apart from her own striving, Yahweh finally remembers and hears Rachel (Gen 30:22, cf. Ex 2:24). Rachel's first son is named Joseph (יוסף, ysp), which is a wordplay on the word "add (יסף, ysp)" (Gen 30:23), as well as, ironically, on the word for "taken away (אסף, 'sp)" in Gen 30:23. Rachel celebrates and wishes for another son through the naming of Joseph, but through this naming, the author gives a subtle foreshadowing of Joseph's future. Contributing to the Exodus motif within this passage, the line "God has taken away my reproach" may be a subtle allusion to the ideas present in Josh 5:9, where Yahweh rolls "away the reproach of Egypt." In Josh 5, the people had just come into the promised land and were being recircumcised. Though this is not the context of Gen 30, Rachel is put into the Exodus motif through Yahweh's *remembering* and *hearing*, and when she is 'delivered' her reproach is taken away by Yahweh. Similarly, when Israel is delivered into the land, Yahweh removes their reproach.

The narrative of the birth of Jacob's children contains no complete exodus cycle, but up to this point, the author has created the expectation that the bride of the elect will pass through an exodus. Though the author does not do that with Rachel and Leah, this narrative about the birthing of their children contains elements that are part of the Exodus motif. These women have come through this creation of new lives, having each gone from some form of affliction to a state of praise to Yahweh. However, the Jacob narrative is full of inverted expectations. This family is not oppressed from the outside within this narrative, then delivered as a whole. Rather this family is oppressed from within, by one another. Our chosen family is full of those acting like the seed of the serpent and oppressors. However, Yahweh is committed to this family and blesses them through this experience, continually removing affliction and reproach. Rather than standing far off from the complicated oppressive relationships within this family, he continues to deliver each member of the family despite their failures.

Jacob Flees Laban

Once Jacob has been given wives and children in the land of his exile, he requests to be sent away (שלח, šlḥ) (Gen 30:25), as Abraham's servant has done and Moses will do for Israel. Laban, seeing that he has prospered by employing Yahweh's chosen, seeks to keep Jacob as his servant as he sought to keep Rebekah. He presses Jacob to name his wage until Jacob offers to only take the speckled, spotted, and black of the flock as his wage, which would allow Laban to pay Jacob very little. However, the reader is soon to find out that this proposal is part of Jacob's latest deceit. Jacob continues to strive for his blessing through trickery, rather than waiting on Yahweh.

In Gen 31:12 Jacob knows that his success in breeding spotted lambs came from Yahweh, but the reader is not told that Jacob's method was given as instruction from Yahweh. Throughout his narrative, Jacob has only had to wait on Yahweh to fulfill his promises, but he continually relies on himself to bring about blessing before Yahweh gives it. Given Jacob's character up to this point, as well as later in the narrative, Jacob has likely supplemented Yahweh's promised deliverance from Laban and power over the womb with his own magical attempt to bring about speckled and spotted sheep. However, through Jacob's actions, Yahweh increased Jacob's flocks and (3) decreased Laban's. Again, Jacob's deceit brings about the fruition of Yahweh's intentions. In Gen 30:43, we are told not only that Jacob's flocks were increased, but that his servants and other livestock increased as well, which have not been part of the narrative up to this point. This seemingly awkward placement of information is meant to signal that Yahweh has increased Jacob into a rich mixed multitude in the same way that he had increased his fathers in their own exoduses, with male and female servants and multiple species of livestock (cf. Gen 12:16; 14:16; 20:14).

Now that Yahweh had increased Jacob with (4) possessions and a family in the midst of his exile, Yahweh announces that it is time for Jacob's exodus back to Canaan (Gen 31:3). Once this announcement is made, the author records a conversation between Jacob and his wives, where Yahweh's provision is recounted. In this conversation, the reader learns that in this time of exile, Jacob's oppressor has not been allowed to harm him because of Yahweh (Gen 31:7). This is similar to the way in which Sarah was protected from Abimelech (Gen 20:6). The reader is also reminded of Jacob's prosperity which Yahweh gave him and of Jacob's vow at Bethel (Gen 31:13). As Jacob prepares for his exodus, the mention of Bethel brings to mind the place where his exile began and where, through Yahweh's promises, his exile is to end.

Jacob fled (ברח, brḥ) from Laban (Gen 31:21) as instructed, but was pursued (רדף, rdp) by his oppressor and overtaken (נשׂג, nsg) (Gen 31:25). The same language is used to describe Pharaoh's pursuing (רדף, rdp) and overtaking (נשׂג, nsg) of Israel during their flight (ברח, brḥ) (Ex 14:5–9). Before Laben catches Jacob, Yahweh continues to protect Jacob by warning Laban in a dream not to harm Jacob. Once Laban overtakes Jacob, he does heed Yahweh's warning but accuses Jacob of stealing his family, property, and gods. However, Jacob did not flee because he had wronged Laban; he did not flee for fear of justice being brought on him. Jacob fled because he feared for his wives (Gen 31:31). Instead of selling out his wives for fear of his own life as Abraham and Isaac had done, leading to their wives being taken by their oppressors, Jacob fears that his wives will be taken by his oppressor and acts to prevent it. Yahweh has seen Jacob's affliction at the hands of Laban[3] and rebuked his oppressor (Gen 31:42). Yahweh has even taken the riches of the oppressor and made them plunder for Jacob (Gen 31:9). It is also likely intended that the oppressors' gods are to be seen as shamed and defeated, as Yahweh will do to Egypts gods, as Rachel sits on them (Gen 31:34) and they are subsequently buried (Gen 35:4).

After Jacob is protected from and vindicated to Laban, the two men make a covenant of peace and share a meal (similar to the events of Abraham's covenant with Abimelech in Gen 26). In preparation for this peace meal (7), "Jacob offered a sacrifice in the hill country" (Gen 31:54), or more literally "on the mountain." By this, the author brings to mind the post-exodus offerings of Jacob's fathers, by which they purified the new-creation family and communed with Yahweh on mountains that echo Yahweh's mountain-garden dwelling in Eden. Jacob then continues his journey toward Canaan and is met by angels as (6) he comes into "God's camp," perhaps hinting at the Cherubim that guard the way into Yahweh's garden-dwelling[4]. Though not quite in Canaan, he has been brought safely back out of Laban's house, with his multitude, and back to Yahweh.

Though Jacob's exodus journey is not entirely over, because he has not been brought back to Bethel, Jacob has been sent into oppression in Mesopotamia, made fruitful and rich from his oppressor, sent out, and made to experience the defeat of his enemy's gods. Upon his final vindication before his oppressor, and truce with him, Jacob enjoys a meal of peace with another people and offers sacrifice to Yahweh on a mountain. Jacob is then brought to make camp at Yahweh's camp; Yahweh's dwelling. Jacob will be instructed to return to Bethel before his story is complete, but this exodus cycle is neatly closed for the moment as a new cycle begins.

---

3. In Gen 21:37–42, Jacob details ways in which, compared to the local norms of the relationship between livestock owners and herdsmen, Laban has mistreated him. See Morrison, "Jacob and Laban," 156–160.

4. As Sailhamer agrees (Sailhamer, *Pentateuch as Narrative*, 197)

Table 13

Correspondences to Jacob's exodus from Paddan-Aram

	Isaac's Bride	Jacob in Paddan-Aram	Exodus
Servant goes to nations	Gen 24:10	Gen 28:2, 5	Ex 4:20
Spring/well	Gen 24:11, 20, 62	Gen 29:2, 10	Ex 15:25–27; 17:6
Must leave father's house	Gen 24:4, 7, 38, 40	Gen 28:2, 5	
Exile		Gen 29:1	Lev 26:14–27; Deut 28:15–68; 2 Kings 17:6–18; Micah 1
(1) Elect detained	Gen 24:55	Gen 29:15; 30:27	Ex 5:1–2; 8:8, 15, 28–32; 9:27–28, 34–35; 10:16–20; 12:31–32; 14:8–9
(1) Oppressed		Gen 31:5–7, 14–16, 38–41	Ex 1:8–14
Request to be sent	Gen 24:54	Gen 30:25	Ex 5:1
(3) King Afflicted		Gen 31:9	Ex 7–12
Fled		Gen 27:43; 31:20–22	Ex 14:5
Pursuit and overtaking		Gen 31:25	Ex 14:5–9
(2) Angel of Yahweh/ seeing		Gen 31:11–12, 42	Ex 3:2–4
Bride/elect sent out	Gen 24:51, 59	Gen 30:25; 31:42	Ex 5:1; 12:31–32
(4) Come out with mixed multitude and possessions	Gen 24:22, 53, 59, 61	Gen 30:26; 31:16–18; 32:10	Ex 12:35–36, 38
(6) Rested at Yahweh's garden/dwelling		Gen 32:1–2	Ex 15:17; Lev 26:11–12, Deut 11:8–12; Josh 21:44
(7) Act as Priests		Gen 31:54	Ex 19:5–6
(7) Blessing: fruitful, multiply	Gen 24:60	Gen 28:3, 14–15; 29:31; 30:24, 27–28, 43; 32:12	Lev 26:3–10; Deut 11:7–16
(7) Commissioned to subdue	Gen 24:60	Gen 28:4	Lev 26:6–8; Deut 7:16; Josh 18:1
Marriage/covenant	Gen 24:67	Gen 29:23, 28	Ex 19:5–8; Jer 31:32; Ezek 16:8

Jacob Wrestles

THE EXODUS MOTIF: JACOB FROM THE ARMY AND THE WRESTLER

In the Face of Esau's Army

NOW THAT JACOB HAS been given exodus out of Laban's house and been brought to the edge of Canaan, he must again face his brother Esau. Last that Jacob had seen Esau, Esau was plotting to kill him. Before meeting with Esau, Jacob will send messengers to attempt to work his own deliverance (Gen 32:3). Just as Yahweh's messenger was sent before Abraham's servant (Gen 24:7) and Israel (Ex 14:19; 23:20, 23; 33:2) to enact exodus, so Jacob sends his messengers to deliver himself. He, unlike the faithful elect ones elsewhere within this pattern, continues to rely on his own schemes through the sending of his messengers. He continues to "strive with men" to obtain blessing.

Upon learning from his messengers that (1) Esau has what appears to be an army, he likely assumes that his plans will not work and turns to ask Yahweh for deliverance on the basis of his promises (Gen 32:11–12). Now, rather than fearing for his family in that Laban may take them, Jacob fears for his family in that Esau may "attack" them and become another oppressor. He needs exodus from the "hand" of Esau (Gen 32:11) as Israel will be given exodus from the "hand" of the Egyptians (Ex 3:8, 18:9–10). Jacob remembers that Yahweh had promised him that he would become a people, so Jacob calls on Yahweh to rescue his family and not undo the beginning fulfillment of that promise. The reader will later find out that Jacob could have stopped here, trusting that Yahweh is trustworthy, but he continues.

After offering supplication to Yahweh, he then prepares a "present (מִנְחָה, *mnḥh*)" for Esau (Gen 32:13). מִנְחָה (*mnḥh*) can simply mean present or gift, but more often it is used to denote offerings to Yahweh[1]. That this word is often used to refer to offerings is significant because the purpose of this gift is to "appease (כפר, *kpr*)," or to purge his guilt before Esau. Jacob hopes that with this gift, "Perhaps he will accept me," or more literally "lift my face" (Gen 32:20). After Cain's poor offering, his face falls and Yahweh encourages him to do well. This will bring about a lifting up of Cain's fallen face. Jacob is facing the consequences of his past failures and, unlike Cain, humbles himself before his brother and seeks peace so that Esau may lift his face. Ironically, this humility is driven by fear and seems to come from a lack of trust in Yahweh for deliverance. After Jacob's offering of prayer to Yahweh for deliverance, he makes an offering to Esau for purgation of guilt and the lifting of his face, rather than to Yahweh. Jacob acts out a parody of his priestly role. Though Yahweh has promised him that he will become a multitude (which here means his family's survival), Jacob relies on his own means for deliverance. The actions which follow further reveal Jacob's true character.

After sending his messengers with the gifts, the next step of Jacob's plan is to send everything he owns and every member of his family across the river which separates him and Esau. Jacob's cowardice escalates here as he places his family closer to what he presumes is an attacking army, while he remains behind a geographical barrier. Jacob's first plan was to split his household into two camps so that one may escape if the other is attacked (Gen 32:7–8). Now it seems his plan is to allow his family and servants to be slaughtered while he watches from afar and escapes. Safely on the side of the river farthest from Esau is precisely where (1) another man comes and attacks Jacob.

Wrestling with God

As this man (1) attacks Jacob, Jacob realizes that he is more than just a man. At the end of this wrestling match, Jacob makes clear who he believes this man to be by naming the place "the face of God" and saying that he has "seen God face to face" (Gen 32:30). Jacob believes, just like

---

1. Most often the מִנְחָה (*mnḥh*) is the grain offering, which is not directly associated with purgation. However, it does refer to offerings more broadly throughout the canon. In the context of Genesis, Abel's sacrificial offering, which was likely a purification offering, is referred to as a מִנְחָה (*mnḥh*) (Gen 4:4).

Abraham had (Gen 18), that he has seen Yahweh come to him in the form of a man. Hosea confirms this interpretation in Hos 12:3–5:

> In the womb he took his brother by the heel,
>   and in his manhood he strove with God.
> He strove with the angel and prevailed;
>   he wept and sought his favor.
> He met God at Bethel, and there God spoke with us—
>   the Lord, the God of hosts,the Lord is his memorial name:

The god that met Jacob at Bethel and wrestled him at the Jabbok bears the name Yahweh. Jacob realizes this in the middle of their fight. This is why he demands blessing from his attacker and the attacker is able to give it (Gen 32:29). Within this narrative, Jacob has ironically exhibited characteristics of the seed of the serpent and oppressors. Therefore, rather than there being another oppressor who is struck within this narrative, (3) Jacob is the one who is struck (נגע, *ngʿ*; Gen 32:25) as the Egyptians are.

Along with (7) blessing, Jacob also (5) receives a name change which is associated with new creation, as has been discussed. Yahweh describes a functional characteristic of Jacob and renames him accordingly (Gen 32:28). Jacob has continually used his own craftiness in his dealings with Yahweh and with man to get what he wanted. Despite his craftiness, Yahweh has brought this deceiver through an exodus and blessed him according to his promises. Yahweh has remade him into a delivered nation and changed the name of the head of this nation from "heel-grabber" to "strives-with-God;" Israel. By the renaming of Jacob and description of Jacob's function within the world, the author places Jacob into the new-creation motif.

Before this hand-to-hand encounter with Yahweh, Jacob feared seeing Esau face-to-face. In Gen 32:20 Jacob attempts to use his gift to "appease [Esau's] *face*" with the present that goes before his "*face*." Afterward, Jacob would see Esau's "*face*" and perhaps have his "*face*" lifted. In this chapter, the word face (פָּנֶה, *pnh*) is a keyword, occurring eight times by Gen 32:21 and four times in Gen 32:20 alone. The author highlights Jacob is in need of deliverance from the face of his brother. Therefore, when Jacob says in Gen 32:30 that he has "seen God face to face" and that his "life has been delivered," he understands that he received the deliverance that he had asked for, not only from before Yahweh but from before the face of Esau as well. Jacob later reiterates this understanding as he says "I have seen your face, which is like seeing the face of God, and you have accepted me" (Gen 33:10)[2]. It is not that Jacob sees Esau as visually comparable to Yahweh in this verse, but by means of verbal repetition, the reader is brought back to Gen 32:30, in which Jacob realized, through his encounter and blessing from Yahweh, that he had received the deliverance for which he asked.

Remembering that enemy armies are often depicted as the serpent in scripture, Israel was delivered from the serpent in that the Egyptian army was crushed under the sea, and Jacob was delivered from a potential serpent in that Yahweh delivered Jacob from the army that he feared. Having been assured of his deliverance, the sun rises on Jacob (Gen 32:31) as it did on delivered Israel (Ex 14:27).

After this we see a marked difference in Jacob's actions. While he clearly shows favoritism and still some fear of danger in the ordering of his wives (Gen 33:1–2), Jacob, rather than using his family as fodder for Esau's army, leads them as they go toward Esau. Trusting in Yahweh, Jacob now takes his rightful place at the front of the line rather than cowering in the distance. When he comes to his brother, he is met with Esau's forgiving embrace. Esau even attempts to reject Jacob's gift, showing that there was no need for it. All this time, Jacob had only to trust that Yahweh would make his family into a great nation, rather than allowing them to be killed through Esau's army. Esau even offers to assist in the care of Jacob's flock until they come to Seir (Gen 33:16). Again, perhaps still fearing Esau, (8) Jacob deceives him. Jacob says that he will travel behind Esau until they also reach Seir (Gen 33:14), but as soon as Esau begins his journey home, Jacob turns to go to Succoth. It is here that Esau disappears from the narrative except for passing and genealogical references as has been true of the other goat-for-Azazel characters.

That Jacob comes out of his deliverances from Laban and Esau and goes to Succoth (Gen 33:17) is likely significant within Jacob's journey. It appears that Jacob was at this location for some time, given that he built booths for his livestock, but within the narrative, the location is only given a brief mention. The author likely included this location because as the Israelites began their journey to the Sea of Reeds their first stop was a place bearing the name Succoth (Ex 12:37; 13:20). These two Succoths are in different regions, but by mentioning the name as a first stop within

2. The term here translated "accepted (רצה, rṣh)" is used only here in Genesis and is not used again until Leviticus, where it is used of the acceptance of offerings (Lev 1:4; 7:18; 19:7; 22:23, 25, 27).

two exodus narratives, a plausible link is drawn between them. Jacob's journey to Shechem, in Gen 33:18, is significant for the same reason except it is not a link to Israel's exodus, but rather to Abraham's. When Abraham was brought to Canaan, he first came to Shechem (Gen 12:6). This is where Abraham came to the Oak of Moreh, had Yahweh's promise reiterated to him, and built an altar. As Jacob comes to the end of his exodus out of Paddan-Aram and his deliverance from Esau, the mention of this city imports connotations of being rested in Yahweh's dwelling. It was discussed that this site bore connections to the garden of Eden in Gen 12, and now Jacob has finished his exodus journey in the same location. Jacob has even acquired a piece of this land (Gen 33:19) just as Abraham acquired a field from the Hittites; each has obtained a firstfruits of Yahweh's promise of land. Mirroring Abraham's action in Gen 12, Jacob also built an altar in Shechem (Gen 33:20), where he presumably offered sacrifices of purification and communion with Yahweh. In this, he would act as a priest, just as the previous elect ones had done.

At the end of this deliverance narrative, Jacob has been rested in Yahweh's promised land (owning a part of it), he is fruitful and blessed, and has built a place of worship for Yahweh. Jacob seems to be situated very well in this section, with the only tension being that he has not yet returned to Bethel. In Gen 28:22, Jacob set up a stone which was to be Yahweh's house if he was brought back from Paddan-Aram. Yahweh has fulfilled this promise and yet (8) Jacob has not set out for this site to establish it or to give tithe at Yahweh's house. This neglect, despite the positive picture at the end of Gen 33, will prove to be a mistake. It will be corrected, but first Israel will be oppressed, once again, in Shechem.

Table 14

Correspondences to Jacob's exodus from Esau's army/the wrestler

	Babylon	Jacob Wrestles	Exodus
Angel sent ahead		Gen 32:3	Ex 14:19; 23:20; 33:2
(3) Inhabitants Struck		Gen 32:(8, 11), 25	Ex 3:20; 7:25; 9:15, 25, 31; 12:12, 13, 29
Rescue (from the hand)		Gen 32:11, 30	Ex 3:8; 6:6; 12:27; 18:9–10
(7) Act as Priests/ Purification	Gen 12:7–8	Gen 32:20	Ex 19:5–6
(5) New humanity	Gen 12:2	Gen 32:28	Ex 19:4–5; Isa 43:1
(7) Blessing: fruitful, multiply	Gen 12:2	Gen 32:12, 29	Lev 26:3–10; Deut 11:7–16
Salvation at morning		Gen 32:31	Ex 14:24, 27
(6) Rested at Yahweh's garden/ dwelling	~Gen 12:8	Gen 33:18	Ex 15:17; Lev 26:11–12, Deut 11:8–12; Josh 21:44
Succoth		Gen 33:17	Ex 12:37; 13:20
Shechem	Gen 12:6	Gen 33:18, 19	
(8) Rebellion	Gen 12:10	Gen 33:14, 17, 18; cf. 28:20–22	Ex 32:1–8; 2 Kings 17:6–18; Micah 1

Dinah

THE EXODUS MOTIF: DINAH FROM SHECHEM

JACOB IS NOW LIVING in Shechem, having neglected to go back to Bethel as he had promised to do when Yahweh first came to him (Gen 28:22). The narrative of Shechem primarily focuses on Dinah, Jacob's only daughter. She goes out to "see the women of the land" and she quickly becomes a forbidden fruit to Prince Shechem. The author describes their interaction with the same formulaic "saw and took" language seen in Gen 3:6, 6:2, 12:15, 16:3, 20:2, and 30:9. (1) Shechem "saw her" and "seized (or took, לקח, *lkh*) her" (Gen 34:2). She has become a captive in the house of a foreign king just as happened to Sarah and Rebekah and will happen to Israel. Shechem keeps Dinah in his house, desiring that she be given to him as a wife, now that he has already had her. When this news reaches Israel, it seems that Jacob is rather passive about the abuse and capture of his daughter, while his sons are the ones who become rightfully angry (Gen 34:5, 7).

Hamor and Shechem come to Israel and ask that they give Dinah and allow marriages and trading to happen between their people (Gen 34:8–10). Hamor and Shechem are asking for a covenant that is similar to that between Abraham and Abimelech or Isaac and Abimelech, but different in that this covenant would make Israel and these Canaanites into one people. The previous covenants were for the purpose of peace between two people groups. They were also the result of the nations coming to the elect one because of how great they could see Yahweh to be. The covenant proposed by Shechem is the result of lust and would have the effect of the Israelite and Yahwistic identity being subsumed in the Canaanite identity. As Israel traded and made marriages with the Shechemites, they would "become one people" (Gen 34:16, 22), even to the point that their wealth would become Shechem's (Gen 34:23). Hamor and Shechem's intentions are for the gain of themselves and their families, similar to those of the king of Sodom and Ephron.

Here, Israel is at risk of losing their distinctive identity and taking on the identity of the Canaanites. When the children of Israel re-enter the land after their exodus out of Egypt, the same concern is present. Deut 7:2–5 specifies that when Israel goes in to conquer the land, they are not to covenant or intermarry with the Canaanites lest they be turned to their gods. Rather they are to destroy their altars and idols and, as the ESV translates, "devote them to destruction (חרם, *ḥrm*)." It would be beneficial to note that חרם (*ḥrm*) is better understood as "to remove an identity from use," as opposed to "devoting to destruction."[1] In other words, Israel is to destroy the communal identity of the Canaanites such that their culture cannot be adopted by Israel. Incidentally, this involves the killing of many of the inhabitants[2]. Israel is to maintain a distinctive identity as Yahweh's nation of priests. In Gen 34, the family which is to be a blessing to the nations is about to covenant and intermarry with Canaan, which Deut 7 says will lead them to idolatry and destroy their Yahwistic identity. This tension may not be on the minds of Jacob's sons and is not explicit within the narrative, but the reader who knows the Torah is intended to catch the tension and foreshadowing within this story.

Besides the proposed peace between the two parties, this narrative also echoes previous narratives of strife and peace through the note that "the land is large enough for them" (Gen 34:21). Abraham and Lot's strife began with the land not being large enough to support them both and the fact that Isaac became too great for Abimelech encouraged strife between their shepherds. In those narratives, there was an elect one who wished to maintain peace with the people who were being blessed through him. They desired to maintain peace despite that people's failures. However, this narrative is an inversion of those previous strife narratives. There is an oppressive nation with abundant land that wishes for peace for its own benefit while the elect nation is amplifying strife to the point of executing the oppressors. The inverted link to these previous narratives may suggest that once the people grew to the point that land became sparse, conflict would ensue as it had in previous narratives. The link may also,

1. Walton, *Israelite Conquest*, 179–192

2. Although some of the Canaanites will forsake their Canaanite identity and take on that of Israel, such as the family of Rahab. In this case, the Canaanite identity is still destroyed while the people are not.

and more likely, be meant to strengthen the irony and condemnation of the elect family's violence in light of their forefathers' righteous pursuit for peace in the midst of conflict. This link brings insightful nuance to the story of Dinah's need for exodus. At this point, regardless of the solution of the brothers, Shechem has taken Dinah, as the Pharaoh and Abimelech had done to the elect wives, and the sons of Israel are left by their father to bring justice to the situation themselves.

The sons of Jacob resort to deception to deliver their sister (who we learn has been held in Shechem's house all this time in Gen 34:26). They do indeed covenant with the people of Shechem, but with every intention of breaking this covenant once Shechem's men are sore from circumcision. The sons of Jacob then, just as their descendants will do to the Canaanites, (3) kill many of the inhabitants of Shechem and plunder their city[3]. Once they have destroyed the oppressors, (4) they deliver Dinah out of Shechem's house (Gen 34:25–29).

Jacob's sons have acted deceptively in order to bring about Dinah's deliverance, making them look much like their father. They have used their own cunning to bring about that which Yahweh is in the habit of giving to those who trust him. If Jacob had gone to Bethel as he had promised, this abuse of his daughter would not have happened, but, in any case, Yahweh has shown that he consistently gives exodus to his people. Jacob's sons have used their own schemes to bring about an exodus for their sister and this has earned them a rebuke from their father who realizes that the surrounding peoples will know them as covenant breakers. This narrative will serve as the reason why Simeon and Levi are passed over for the firstborn blessing in Gen 49. However, Jacob does not shine in this story either due to his passivity; his sons allude to this notion in Gen 34:31.

Dinah, a daughter of Israel, has been given a deliverance expressed in exodus terms. She has been brought out of the house of her oppressors and they have been defeated, just as Israel will be brought out of the house of slavery and the armies of Pharaoh will be defeated. The sons of Israel also have come out with many possessions just as Israel will plunder Egypt and come out with many possessions (Ex 12:35–36, 38). In addition to this, as they have come back to the land from Paddan-Aram,

---

3. Particularly the males, as they would have comprised Shechem's warriors as well as carried the communal identity as heads of houses. If the women and children were taken into the houses of another people they would take on the identity of the head of that house.

the risks of Israel intermingling with the Canaanites have been foreshadowed, yet Israel's sons have preserved their identity as Yahweh's people. In this narrative, we have seen the first time that a group who can be called "the children of Israel" undergo an exodus event and subdue the land of Canaan to protect their household and, perhaps unknowingly, to maintain the priestly nature of their nation. These elements will appear again in the conquest of Canaan in the book of Joshua as Israel is rested in the land after their exodus.

Jacob's Journey to Bethel

After these events, Yahweh instructs Jacob to finally go to Bethel and make an altar (Gen 35:1). In this command, Yahweh reminds Jacob of his flight from Esau in order to remind him of his neglected promise to make the stone he had set up into Yahweh's house and give a tithe. He has learned loyalty and trust toward Yahweh more than he had at the beginning of his narrative, but he still shows a lack of full loyalty to Yahweh in this neglect. Yet, Yahweh continues to work with him and refine him.

Following Yahweh's command and reminder, Jacob seems to have developed a fervor for Yahweh and instructs his family to cleanse themselves for his presence. Rather than taking his children's rings and making an idol before Yahweh's dwelling as Aaron will do (Ex 32:2), Jacob takes the rings and the idols and puts them away. Jacob and the multitude that is with him (Gen 35:6) then travel to meet Yahweh. The previous narrative of Dinah's exodus created worry that the surrounding nations may act with hatred towards Israel, but a fear of God fell on the surrounding nations allowing them to travel safely (Gen 35:5; cf. Ex 15:13–16; Josh 2:9–11). (6) Upon reaching Bethel, Jacob finally builds an altar and renames the place "God-of-the-house-of-God" (Gen 35:7). He assigned name and function to this place as Yahweh's house as he had promised to do, completing his journey to Yahweh's house from Paddan-Aram.

The author follows Jacob's arrival at Bethel with a note about the death of Rebekah's nurse (Gen 35:8). This seems to be a random fact, but may be given due to the fact that, last we heard of Rebekah, she had claimed that she would bring Jacob out of Paddan-Aram in Gen 27:45. She had used deception to secure the blessing that was promised by Yahweh. She then said that she would give Jacob exodus out of Mesopotamia. Since Gen 27, she has faded from the story and apparently not been counted worthy of a proper burial within the narrative. While it may have been expected that her death is recounted at the climax of Jacob's narrative as Sarah's death is recounted after the climax of Abraham's narrative, she is only given a mention through the death of her nurse.

The narrative continues by reiterating that Jacob's coming to Bethel marks the end of his exodus out of Paddan-Aram (Gen 35:9). There (5) his name change is reiterated and he (7) again receives the Edenic and Abrahamic blessing (Gen 35:9–12). Jacob then erects the stone that he promised to make Yahweh's house and anoints it with oil as Moses will anoint the tabernacle (Ex 40:9). Though Jacob's exodus out of Paddan-Aram was previously concluded with his arrival at Shechem, tensions remained as he had promised to return to Bethel and did not. Now that he has returned to Bethel, the true end of his exodus journey has come. At Bethel, he has his new-creation status re-inaugurated, receives the blessing of Abraham's seed, and erects a house for Yahweh. All this as Israel will do at Sinai, once they have been brought out of their exodus and to Yahweh's presence.

The narrative of Isaac's children is coming to an end, but before it does, we are told that Rachel finally gets the second son she had hoped for in Gen 30:24, but it is also her death. As she is dying in labor, she names the son Ben-oni (Gen 35:18), meaning either "son of my strength" or "son of my sorrow." However, Jacob renames him Benjamin, meaning "son of good fortune" or "son of the right hand." Whichever meaning is correct, due to the name he gives him, it would seem that Jacob looks at the youngest son of his favorite wife as his favorite child. In the next narrative, we will see that Joseph is chosen, but this hint towards the favoritism of Benjamin will become significant during Joseph's test of his brothers. After Benjamin's birth and Rachel's death in the region of Bethlehem and Migdal Eder (or the Tower of the Flock) (Gen 35:19–21), the reader may be surprised that the favored wife is not buried in the tomb of Jacob's fathers; in the cave in the field of Machpelah. Rather, this favored wife, mother of favored sons is buried at Bethlehem, away from the family tomb. Although, she is given a pillar that her name may be remembered through the generations. The story of the birth of Jacob's children is finally concluded with Reuben's taking of his father's concubine[4] and a

---

4. This was discussed in conjunction with Ham's offense as an attempt to seize power within the family. Reuben has attempted to take on the firstborn right and leading role of the father by taking his father's concubine.

final list of all Jacob's children (Gen 35:22–26). The death of Isaac is then recorded, giving closure to the narrative of his children, Jacob and Esau.

Table 15

Correspondences to Dinah's exodus from Shechem

	Sarai in Egypt	Dinah	Exodus
(1) Oppressed	Gen 12:15	Gen 34:2, 23	Ex 1:8–14
(3) King Afflicted	Gen 12:17	Gen 34:25–26	Ex 7–12
Bride/elect comes out	Gen 12:18–19	Gen 34:25	Ex 5:1; 12:31–32
(4) Come out with mixed multitude and possessions	Gen 12:16; 13:1–2	Gen 34:27–29; 35:6	Ex 12:35–36, 38
(7) Act as Priests	Gen 13:18	Gen 35:7	Ex 19:5–6
(6) Rested at Yahweh's garden/ dwelling	Gen 13:3, 18	Gen 35:6	Ex 15:17; Lev 26:11–12, Deut 11:8–12; Josh 21:44
(5) New humanity		Gen 35:10	Ex 19:4–5; Isa 43:1
(7) Blessing: fruitful, multiply	Gen 13:16	Gen 35:11	Lev 26:3–10; Deut 11:7–16
(7) Commissioned to subdue	Gen 13:15, 17	Gen 35:12	Lev 26:6–8; Deut 7:16; Josh 18:1

Esau's Journey to Seir

THE EXODUS MOTIF: ESAU TO SEIR

BY THIS POINT, THE contours of the Exodus motif have been seen many times, and the author may expect the reader to catch references to the Exodus motif through more brief references. In the previous generations, both Lot and Ishmael (through Hagar) went through exodus events that led them to become their own nation. Lot was given exodus out of Sodom and became the father of the Moabites and Ammonites. Ishmael and Hagar are sent out to the wilderness by Abraham (Gen 21:14), completing Hagar's inverted exodus. It is in this wilderness that Yahweh would begin to fulfill his promise of multiplication for Ishmael (Gen 16:10).

In Gen 36, following the death of Isaac and as a transition from the narrative of Isaac's children to the narrative of Jacob's children, is a genealogy of Esau's family. In Gen 36:6, the author informs the reader that Esau had (4) acquired a multitude of people and possessions in Canaan. He then takes this mixed multitude and departs for Seir, where (D) (E) he would become the father of the Edomites (who (F) would attack Israel later in their history; see Obadiah for example). In this brief note about Esau coming out of Canaan with a mixed multitude to the land of his inheritance (cf. Deut 2:5), the author associates Esau with the Exodus motif. By itself, Gen 36:6 may not be enough to convince that the author is indeed employing the Exodus motif, but given that the mixed multitude and great possessions is one of the most used exodus characteristics and that the other non-elect brothers were associated with the Exodus motif, it seems plausible that the author has intended to apply the motif to Esau here. Yahweh indeed uses exodus-like events to bring the non-elect brothers to a place of fruitfulness, until they are blessed through

Abraham. Even the brother representing the goat for Azazel is given deliverance and blessing until they are given access to Yahweh through the brother representing the goat for Yahweh.

THE TWO-GOATS MOTIF: SHEM AND HAM

When the narrative of the flood was discussed, it was mentioned that the Two-Goats motif was present, but, due to its subtlety, it would best be discussed later. Now that the Two-Goats motif has been examined in the narrative of Cain and Abel, Abraham and Lot, and Jacob and Esau, the presence of the motif will be more readily noticed despite the subtlety of the markers. Due to the brevity of the narrative of Shem and Ham, it can be understood why overt markers of the Two-Goats motif are not present. The author has employed the motif with each brotherly pair throughout Genesis thus far, therefore in hindsight the reader would expect that the motif is present in the sons of Noah as well.

Neither Shem nor Ham bore direct links to the Day of Atonement goats but they and their descendants do bear the characteristics of the Two-Goats motif. Shem is (A) the elect brother, as demonstrated in Gen 9:26–27. Shem is not seen to be brought into Yahweh's land or presence, but he is given a significant blessing from Noah. Yahweh is Shem's god and Shem, as Abraham, is to be a blessing to other nations. This is seen in that Japheth is to "dwell in the tents of Shem." Ham, on the other hand, (B) makes an attempt at the right of the firstborn through the rape of Noah's wife, as has been discussed. Ham does not directly do violence toward Shem, but he does attempt to usurp his position out of jealousy. He does not go on to be protected and brought into the wilderness, but in the genealogy in chapter 10, his grandson Nimrod goes on to (E) become a great city builder (Gen 10:6–12). It is worth mentioning that Gen 11 depicts Babylon, which Nimrod established, as being built after an eastward journey, implying exile. Through his grandson Nimrod, Ham has indeed become fruitful and become a multitude of peoples. Most of these nations that come from Nimrod will also (F) become enemies of Israel later in the Biblical narrative.

While Shem does not bear connections to offerings as Cain and Isaac do, he does have significant connotations of atoning attached to him. After the failure of Adam and Eve, Yahweh clothed their nakedness in garments of skins, which have been discussed as a reinstatement to their priestly position. It has also been discussed that Shem and Japheths's covering of Noah's nakedness mirrors that action. Through Shem and Japheth's covering of Noah after his failure, Shem is portrayed as reinstating Noah as Yahweh's representative before he gives his blessings and curses to his sons. Through this narrative element, Shem is shown to be bringing about forgiveness for the elect family and the redemption of their role. Shem is not linked directly to a sacrifice, but he does play a role in working out atonement for the elect family after their failure.

The characteristics of the Two-Goats motif in the narrative of Shem and Ham are less pronounced than with other brothers due to the brevity of the story. However, when these characteristics are viewed in the context of the motif as employed with the other brotherly pairs, the author does seem to have intentionally employed the motif between Shem and Ham, with Shem playing the role of the goat for Yahweh and Ham, the goat for Azazel. Since this motif is seen in each brotherly pair thus far in Genesis, in the story of the next set of brothers, the author will use the motif more freely, with increased creativity as well as profundity.

Joseph

THE NARRATIVE OF ISRAEL'S sons (Gen 37:2) begins with details about his oldest son from his favorite wife. Joseph is presented in a manner that would cause most to sympathize with his brother's hatred of him. Joseph, being the second youngest, is rightfully working as a servant[1] to his older brothers as they shepherd their flocks. One would expect that the youngest sibling is to help and learn from the older brothers in their trade. However, Joseph has intentions to rule his brothers, rather than serve them. The ESV is representative of most modern translations in Gen 37:2:

> Joseph, being seventeen years old, was pasturing the flock with his brothers.

However, there is an alternate way to translate this verse, which may be more appropriate. In this passage the Hebrew את ('t) is applied to the brothers and ב (b) is applied to the flocks, where, simply put, את ('t) can either mark the direct object of the sentence or be translated as "with" and ב (b) is often translated as "to," "in," or "with." The ESV translates את ('t) as "with" here, meaning that Joseph was shepherding, or pasturing, [to] the flocks *with* his brothers. However, if את ('t) is the direct object marker, then Joseph was not shepherding the flocks, but rather his brothers. The verse would read as such:

> Joseph, being seventeen years old, was shepherding his brothers with the flock.[2] [AT]

---

1. Translated "boy" in the ESV (Gen 37:2), as the term literally means "boy" but is often used in reference to servants.

2. See also Emadi, *From Prisoner*, 54, n. 62; and Hamilton, *Genesis Chapters 18–50*, Comment on 37:2 for points favoring this translation.

This alternative translation has two primary supporting points. First, a similar usage of אֵת ('t) and בְ (b) is found only a few verses later, in Gen 37:12. In this verse, אֵת ('t) is clearly the direct object marker. Just as the brothers shepherd the (אֵת, 't) flocks in (בְ, b) Shechem, so perhaps Joseph shepherds the (אֵת, 't) brothers with (בְ, b) the flock. (Lest it seem too odd to say that Joseph is shepherding humans, it ought to be noted that it is common in the Hebrew Bible to refer to rulers as shepherds[3]). If This translation is correct, then it would work in conjunction with the negative picture of Joseph that the author is painting at the beginning of this narrative.

Joseph, while likely trying to boss his older brothers around, brings a bad report of them to Jacob. The author never tells the reader that this report is valid, only that Joseph has spoken negatively of his brothers to their father[4]. It would seem that Joseph is seeking to be in the place of firstborn as he takes command over his brothers and puts them down to his father. This is a common attitude of the non-firstborn brothers throughout Genesis, and similar actions have already been seen with Reuben (Gen 35:22). It would also seem that Joseph (A) is successful in his quest for the firstborn as Jacob gives him a long-sleeved robe. (Joseph may have been able to acquire the status of firstborn without his efforts since he is the oldest son of Jacob's favorite wife). By giving him this robe (Gen 37:3), Jacob has honored Joseph over all his brothers. It is also worth pointing out that the word here for robe (כְּתֹנֶת, ktnt) has not been used since Gen 3:21 to refer to Adam and Eve's priestly garments. The word is also only used eleven other times in the Torah after Gen 37 and only to the priest's robes[5]. Through this robe Joseph is not only exalted as firstborn, but as a priest.

This reading of the beginning of chapter 37 will likely cause the readers to sympathize with the brothers. All of Jacob's sons, besides Joseph and Benjamin (who does not feature in the current narrative section), have mothers of lower status in their father's eyes. They were birthed either by servants or the unfavored of Jacob's wives. This fact alone likely gives the brothers a distaste for Joseph and Benjamin and a sense of solidarity among themselves. To add insult to injury, Joseph then begins bossing them around, slanders them to their father, and is affirmed in

3. e.g. 2 Sam 5:2; 7:7; Jer 10:21; Zech 10:3; Ezek 34:2

4 The word used here for "report" (דִּבָּה, dbh) often denotes slander. See Ps 31:13; Prov 10:18; 25:10; Jer 20:10; Ezek 36:3.

5. Ex 28:4, 39, 40; 29:5, 8; 39:27; 40:14; Lev 8:7, 13; 10:5; 16:4

these actions. Just as the non-elect brothers throughout Genesis, the sons of Jacob become hostile the firstborn (cf. Gen 37:11).

This tone continues as Joseph recounts his dreams to his family. Joseph, perhaps despite better judgment, announces his first dream, which he and his brothers both interpret as pointing to Joseph's rule over them. Jacob only rebukes Joseph at the announcement of his next dream, in which Jacob and his wife seem to be bowing to Joseph as well. Given that throughout scripture, dreams are communication from Yahweh, (A) Joseph has been shown to be Yahweh's elect through these dreams. It would seem that Joseph is going to be much like his father in that despite his selfish and conniving character, Yahweh will place him over his brothers. At this point, no particular brother shines as righteous. All are represented as jealous schemers.

Joseph's character up to this point makes the brother's resentment of Joseph at the prospect of his divine leadership understandable. The author has constructed this narrative with such tension that violence toward Joseph is expected, even without consideration of the brotherly strife motif. Largely because of his own arrogance, Joseph will suffer violence at the hands of his brothers and be exiled out of Canaan.

THE EXODUS MOTIF: JOSEPH

Joseph's exile begins in Gen 37:14 when Jacob sends (שלח, *šlḥ*) Joseph to his brothers. This echoes the beginning of Jacob's exile, which began when he was sent (שלח, *šlḥ*) to Laban by his own father (Gen 28:5). Joseph is sent to gather a report on his brothers. This mission will likely not improve their opinion of him given the results of the last time Joseph gave a report of his brothers. Seeing him from afar, (1)(B) they plot to dispose of him and ultimately decide to (D) sell him as a slave, sending him to Egypt (Gen 37:27). However, the author finds it significant enough to include that the brothers first throw him into a pit (בּוֹר, *bwr*) (Gen 37:24). The word "pit (בּוֹר, *bwr*)" is worthy of note because it is used throughout scripture as a metaphor for death and Sheol. For example, Ps 30:3 says:

> O Lord, you have brought up my soul from Sheol;
>   you restored me to life from among those who go down to the pit.

And in Isa 38:18 we read:

> For Sheol does not thank you; death does not praise you;
>   those who go down to the pit do not hope for your faithfulness.

In these verses, as well as others[6], the pit is equated with death by way of parallelism. As Joseph is cast into a pit, the author intends for the reader to see Joseph as symbolically cast into death. The author intends to portray Joseph as descending alive into Sheol. As Joseph is brought out of the pit by his brothers, he is portrayed as coming out of Sheol and back to the land of the living. Joseph is literarily resurrected. Just as David is brought up from Sheol and restored to life from the pit in Ps 30, so Joseph is drawn out of the pit. This is one of several instances of the death-to-life motif present in the Joseph narrative, which will be explored further[7].

We had learned in Gen 37:22 that Reuben intended to rescue Joseph and restore him to his father. Rather than an act of altruism, this act may have been Reuben's means of getting the firstborn status that he coveted. Perhaps by restoring his favorite son, Jacob would honor Reuben and make him a leader within the family. This intention may be behind Reuben's self-concerned grief upon learning that Joseph had escaped in Gen 37:29–30. Having lost his opportunity, Reuben joins the brothers in their plans to deceive their father regarding Joseph's absence.

THE TWO-GOATS MOTIF: JOSEPH

Joseph's (B) arrogance towards his brothers in his pursuit of the firstborn status has brought him the hate of his brothers. This hatred grew until they sold him into slavery and (D) exiled him from Canaan. In order to cover their sin they "slaughter (שׁחט, šḥt)"[8] a goat and dip Joseph's robes in the blood. Through this action, (H) Joseph has been associated with a sacrificial goat whose blood is used to hide the sins of the sons of Israel; the goat for Yahweh. Interestingly, "blood" is not a common word in Genesis. it occurs in Gen 9:4–6, where Noah is commanded to not eat blood and is told that whoever sheds man's blood will have his blood shed by men. The only other place "blood" occurs before the Joseph narrative is in Gen 4:10–11, in reference to Abel's blood crying out from the ground.

6. eg. Ps 28:1; 88:3–7; 143:7; Prov 1:12; Isa 14:15, 19; Ezek 26:20; 31:14; 31:16; 32:18, 23–30

7. Pulse, *Figuring Resurrection*, "Chapter 5: The Death-and-Resurrection Motif in the Joseph Narratives"

8. It is worth noting that this word is used in the Hebrew Bible primarily to denote the slaughter of sacrificial animals.

It would seem natural to see a link between our present text and Gen 9:5–6, as the brothers intended to shed a man's blood, and they indeed will fear vengeance for that (Gen 42:22). The mention of blood also strengthens this text's commonality with Gen 4. In both texts, there is mention of brothers killing brothers, blood, and cultic language. Joseph's link to Abel through blood and the threat of murder further suggest the cultic significance of the violence done to Joseph. It has been discussed that Able was associated with his purification offering then his blood was spilled. In the current narrative, Joseph's brothers intended to spill his blood, but they instead slaughter a goat in his place and apply its blood to his robe. Abel and Joseph are not only linked by the spilling of blood but by their links to offerings.

In the Two-Goats motif, the expectation has been created that the brother in the slot of the Goat for Yahweh will be brought closer to Yahweh and his land. However, Joseph is exiled out of the land because of the sin of the sons of Israel. To add to this, there is no other brother that clearly takes the role of the Goat of Azazel. In this, Joseph has been associated with both the Goat for Yahweh and the Goat for Azazel as he is sent out of the land; a fact noticed by other commentators[9]. As the narrative continues, it will be seen that Joseph (C) is helped by Yahweh, and, through the literary conventions of this narrative, (G) is brought into Yahweh's presence and exalted. These details will be explored as we continue.

Upon hearing the brothers' lie, Jacob mourns bitterly for his son (Gen 37:33–35). Despite Jacob's belief that his son is dead, Joseph is being carried "down" to Egypt by traders. Throughout the Genesis narrative, when the patriarchs go to Egypt, they go "down" to Egypt and they return "up" to Canaan. However, Egypt is not geographically below Canaan. This language is not geographically rooted but rather is a feature of the narrative. Egypt is set on analogy with death and Sheol by the biblical author[10]. Joseph is carried along to become enslaved, and ultimately he will find himself there in another pit, which as has been discussed, can be a metaphor for Sheol. Joseph goes "down" to Egypt (Gen 37:25; 39:1), just as Jacob expects to go "down" to Sheol (Gen 37:35). This literary land of the dead is where Israel finds herself when Yahweh comes to rescue her and make her a new creation. In this journey, Joseph, once again, faces literary death.

9. Orlov, *The Atoning Dyad*, 36

10. Pulse, *Figuring Resurrection*, "Chapter 5: The Death-and-Resurrection Motif in the Joseph Narratives"

JUDAH AND TAMAR

The narrative of Judah and Tamar in Gen 38 lacks the explicit characteristics of the Exodus motif that have been seen thus far, so I have not
treated it as its own exodus event. However, in this narrative, the author
repeats many elements from the Joseph narrative, setting them in parallel[11]. Judah is not clearly given his own exodus through these verbal
links to Joseph's exodus narrative, but Judah's narrative does foreshadow
Joseph's as well as continue the theme of election.

Chapter 37 ended with Joseph having been brought "down" to Egypt
and sold. Chapter 38 begins with Judah going "down" from his brothers
(Gen 38:1), quickly linking these narratives together[12]. He takes a Canaanite wife and has three sons: Er, the firstborn, whose name is "bad"
(translated "wicked" in Gen 38:7) spelled backwards[13], Onan, whose
name is similar to the word for "sorrow" or "wickedness"[14], and Shelah[15].
Given that the author seems to have intentionally made wordplays with
the names of Judah's sons, it is interesting to note that the name of Er's
wife, Tamar, means "date palm"[16]. This woman will indeed be a fruitful
tree which propagates the means of Yahweh's blessing. Her husband,
however, was wicked in Yahweh's sight and was therefore killed. It was
then Onan's responsibility to father an heir for his firstborn brother, but
he avoided impregnating his brother's widow. This would allow him to
maintain Er's property while Er's name dies with him. In this, the reader
again sees a non-firstborn brother jealous of the firstborn. For his hatred
of his brother, Onan perished as well (Gen 38:10). The duty to raise up
offspring for the firstborn now falls to Shelah, and Judah is to give him to
Tamar when he comes of age. However, Judah, apparently seeing Tamar
as a bad omen, fails to give Shelah to Tamar (Gen 38:14). Tamar is owed
a son from Er's relatives to raise up in his name and to secure her own
future. Judah has put both his deceased son and his widow at risk by

11. For more in depth analysis, see Hamilton, *Genesis Chapters 18–50*, "Genesis
38:1–11"; Emadi, *From Prisoner*, 57–60; Waltke and Fredricks, *Genesis*, 507–509

12. So Alter, *Narrative*, 4–5

13. Kalimi, *Metathesis*, 31–32

14. Or "strength/power," but the context makes "sorrow/wickedness" more fitting.

15. Shelah's name may mean to "mislead" and work in conjunction with the fact
that the place he was born, Chezib, means "to deceive" (Garsiel, *Biblical Names*, 124).
This narrative serves as an excellent example of the way the Biblical authors utilize
wordplay to support the narrative throughout Genesis and elsewhere.

16. Köhler et al., *HALOT*, Entry 10213 תָּמָר

withholding his son. Having not been given to Shelah, Tamar takes matters into her own hands and deceives Jacob to secure her husband's heir.

When Judah had been consoled (Gen 38:12, note the contrast to
Jacob who refused comfort over his deceased son), he went to his sheep
shearers and Tamar seized her opportunity. She changed her clothes to
appear as a prostitute whom Judah pursues (Gen 38:16). (This will be
seen to contrast Judah with Joseph who flees the pursuing adulteress).
Similar to Judah's deception of Jacob by the goat's blood on Joseph's robe,
Judah is deceived by Tamar's veil and pledges a goat to her. Tamar then is
given what she needs; she conceives by a relative of her deceased husband
(Gen 38:18). Along with this provision, she receives Judah's signet, cord,
and staff, then changes back into her original garments (Gen 38:18–19).
This parallels Joseph's reception of Pharaoh's signet[17], a gold chain, and
new garments upon his vindication. When Tamar is accused of becoming
pregnant through immorality, these articles also serve as the means of
her vindication.

To this point, Judah has led the brothers in their violence against
Joseph, taken a Canaanite wife, begrudged his son to his daughter-in-
law, slept with a cult prostitute (which would likely be idolatry as well
as sexual immorality), and then hypocritically called for the burning
alive of his daughter-in-law for the same sin. Judah has become a natural
leader among his brothers but his character is one of the worst in the
book of Genesis. However, the present narrative serves to refine and test
Judah. When he is presented with his own belongings, proving that he is
the one who impregnated Tamar, he realizes that he has wronged her by
withholding Shelah and that her deception was used to right that wrong
(Gen 37:26). Judah openly confesses and turns from his wrongs, signal-
ing a change of character in this patriarch.

When Tamar gives birth, again there is another pair of brothers; she
gives birth to the second set of twins within Genesis (Gen 38:27). Immediately, the mention of twins ought to make the reader remember Jacob
and Esau. Links to Jacob and Esau's birth narrative continue as there is
strife between the brothers in their birth. Jacob and Esau struggled together in the womb (Gen 25:22) and Jacob came out by holding Esau's
heel (Gen 25:26). Perez came out by cutting in front of his firstborn
brother, associating him with Jacob, and Zerah was given a red thread

---

17. The Hebrew words for "signet" are different in each of these two instances, but
conceptually similar.

to denote his birth order, associating him with Esau's red hair[18]. Through these narrative links, the author is creating the expectation that these two brothers will have a very similar story to that of Jacob and Esau. Joseph held the firstborn status before his exile, but the reader now expects that Perez may be Yahweh's elect, striving with God and man until he is given the position of firstborn. The author does not give us any details of Perez's life, or even any explicit indication that he has become Yahweh's elect, but as the Biblical narrative continues, it becomes apparent that the author indeed intends to portray Perez as the one through whom Yahweh's promises continue (see Ruth 4:12; 18–22; Luke 3:33).

Many are puzzled by the placement of the Judah and Tamar narrative in the midst of the Joseph narrative. However, by examining the similarities that this story has with that of Joseph, one begins to see thoughtful intentionality in its arrangement. Judah, a man who by no means fears Yahweh, is placed into a very similar deception to that with which he deceived his own father. Through this experience, this man who led his brothers in oppression has been refined into a man who can lead in righteousness. In this narrative, another person who has been oppressed by Judah, Tamar, is presented to the reader. This oppressed woman involves herself and Judah in a deception which bears elements of Judah's deception of Jacob concerning Joseph. She has been oppressed, changed her garments, and worked a deception involving a goat. Likewise, Joseph has been oppressed, had his garments taken, and been the object of a deception involving a goat. As the Joseph narrative continues, the reader is to notice further similarities between Gen 38 and the rest of Joseph's story. The author has primed the reader to expect that Joseph will likewise put on his rightful garments again, be vindicated, and win Judah's repentance.

Tamar has not explicitly been given exodus in this narrative, but her story intentionally parallels the narrative of Joseph, which does contain an exodus. Through this, it is possible that the author wishes the reader to see Tamar as having been delivered in an exodus-like manner in parallel with Joseph.

---

18. Note that different words for "red" are used in these narratives (translated "red" and "scarlet," respectively, in the ESV). The author, as they often do, is using synonymous language to link narratives.

BACK TO JOSEPH AND HIS EXODUS

Returning to Joseph, he has been sold by the Ishmaelites to one of Pharaoh's officers. Yahweh shows loyal love to Joseph and (C) remains with him in the midst of his exile (cf. Gen 39:2, 21) as he had done for Abraham and Jacob. This love shown to the chosen one again brings favor from the nations. Potiphar sees Joseph's success from Yahweh and places him as second in command in his household (Gen 39:6). Yahweh has brought Joseph out of the pit and through his exile and has given him a measure of exaltation. Though this exaltation is relatively minor, given that Joseph is still the slave of a servant of the king, this pit-exile-exaltation movement becomes a pattern in the Joseph narrative.

Now that Joseph is at a high point in the pit-exile-exaltation pattern, the story is primed for something to go wrong. Potiphar's wife "cast her eyes on Joseph" (Gen 39:7). She saw that Joseph was good and attempted to take him[19], but it would seem that Joseph has changed through his experiences. Rather than elevating himself, he rebukes Potiphar's wife by stating his place within the household and affirming a fear of Yahweh (Gen 39:8–9). He knows that he has been given all things; all things except for one, and he will not take what is not his (if only Adam and Eve had offered the same words to the serpent; Joseph has passed the test that they did not).

Potiphar's wife persisted in these temptations to the point that she grabbed Joseph by his clothes to pull him in. Joseph flees the temptress and is once again stripped by an oppressor. Just as Joseph's brothers had done, (1) Potiphar's wife disrobes Joseph then uses his garment to deceive the head of the house (Gen 39:16–17). As part of this scene of deception, Joseph again finds himself in a pit (Gen 39:20; 40:15). In chapter 37 Joseph found himself stripped of his exalted position and in literary death (or the pit) due to his own arrogance towards his brothers. In chapter 39 Joseph finds himself stripped of his exalted position and in literary death though he was righteous in the face of the test. These two narrative sections closely mirror one another, but there is a marked difference in the character of Joseph. Yahweh has used this time to refine him, as Judah was refined by the events of chapter 38. And once again Yahweh shows faithfulness to his elect one as he is sent deeper into his exile. (C) Yahweh

---

19. The word motif of "seeing" something as "good" and "taking" is not present with Potiphar's wife, but her actions and the casting of her eyes on Joseph bear the sin/fall connotations that are found in the seeing/taking motif.

causes Joseph to prosper and once again, as the keeper of the prison no-
tices, he is relatively exalted to second in command of the prison in which
he resides (Gen 39:22).

While in prison, Joseph encounters another pair of dreams from
two of Pharaoh's servants (Gen 40:8). Yahweh gives Joseph the ability to
correctly interpret these dreams and tells them what will take place three
days from the time of the interpretation. One will be restored to his of-
fice as cupbearer and the other will be hanged. Given that he has done a
significant and God-supported service for the men, Joseph uses this opportunity to request that the cupbearer get him out of the pit (Gen 40:14).
He simply requests that the servant bring his case before Pharaoh so that
Pharaoh can give him justice. However, once the cupbearer is restored to
his position, (1) he forgets Joseph. This "forgetting" is not simply a lapse
of the mind but rather is a lapse of the cupbearers due loyalty to Joseph[20]
(cf. Deut 6:12; 8:11).

While the cupbearer was restored after three days, Joseph will have to
wait until the third year (Gen 41:1) until his skills become relevant enough
for him to be mentioned to Pharaoh. Pharaoh has two perplexing dreams
that the wise men and magicians were not able to interpret (Gen 41:8).
At this point the cupbearer mentions Joseph and Joseph is able to change
his clothes and come before Pharaoh. It is worth noting that, as Joseph's
disrobing coincides with his fall from exaltation, his changing of clothes
in Gen 41:14 signals the beginning of his exaltation. Indeed, it is signaled
that this will be a significant exaltation since Joseph has not donned new
clothes since he received the long-sleeved robe from his father.

Joseph also shaves himself in preparation to meet Pharaoh. Shaving
is not a common action in the Torah, but when it is done, it is done as an
act of cleansing (Lev 13:33; 14:8–9), at times in preparation for a Nazirite
vow (Num 6:9, 18–19). Joseph's shaving as an act of cleansing fits alongside his changing of garments as well, since the changing of garments,
while having great literary significance in this literary section, was also
done in Gen 35:2 as an act of cleansing in preparation to meet Yahweh.
Joseph is ritually purifying himself before his encounter with Pharaoh.
He is also associated with the Nazirite vow, which he will be associated
with again in Gen 49:26 by his being called a נָזִיר (*nzyr*), which is translit-
erated as "Nazarite" in Num 6.

---

20. Waltke and Fredricks, *Genesis*, 527

Joseph comes to Pharaoh and is again faced with a pair of dreams (Gen 41:14–15). (C)[21] God enables Joseph to know that the dreams tell of seven years of plenty followed by seven years of famine and to give wise advice on how to plan for the coming situation. This interpretation and wisdom are another instance of Yahweh being with Joseph and prospering him in the sight of the nations. Joseph's proposal pleased Pharaoh and his servants and caused the Spirit of Yahweh to be recognized as in him (Gen 41:37–38). For the third time while in his exile, Joseph is brought to be second in command, only this time (6)(G)[22] he is brought to be second in command of the entire kingdom of Egypt (Gen 41:40).

Joseph again has all of his master's charge under his command, with the exception of one thing (Gen 41:40). Just as Adam and Eve had charge of all things but were not to touch the Tree of the Knowledge of Good and Evil, Joseph is (7) given charge of all things except for the throne of Pharaoh. Adam and Eve were to rule with Yahweh's wisdom, not try to be Yahweh. Likewise, Joseph is to rule on behalf of Pharaoh, not as Pharaoh. When Joseph was in Potiphar's house, he was tested with a situation in which he had authority over all things except for one. He was faithful to his master and, therefore, proven worthy of his exaltation under Pharaoh.

As a sign of his exaltation, Pharaoh gave Joseph his signet ring, a garment of fine linen, and a golden chain as a necklace (Gen 41:42). In the discussion of the Judah and Tamar narrative, it was noted that a signet ring and a change of clothes were related to Tamar's vindication, which, based on the connections between that narrative and the Joseph narrative, should cause the reader to expect similar events in the Joseph narrative. Now it is seen that, like Tamar, a signet ring and new garment[23] are related to Joseph's vindication. The garment of fine linen and the gold chain on Joseph's neck have additional links to other Torah narrative sections that will be of interest.

In Ex 28, Moses is given instructions for the fabrication of the High Priest's garments. The author informs the reader that the ephod,

21. This instance of Yahweh's protection on the goat for Azazel falls in line with Yahweh's exaltation of the goat for Yahweh as well. However, this dream interpretation and recognition of the Spirit of Yahweh in Joseph falls in line with the pattern of Joseph's prosperity and wisdom being recognized by those whom he is under (i.e. Potiphar and the keeper of the prison).

22. The following pages will discuss the ways in which Pharaoh plays the role of Yahweh in this section. This is Joseph's exaltation as well as his coming into Yahweh's presence, literally.

23. Though these Hebrew words are different, the conceptual links are present.

breastpiece, coat, turban, and undergarments are made of "fine linen (שֵׁשׁ, *šš*)" (Ex 28:6, 8, 15, 39, 42). Just as the High Priest's garments are made of fine linen, so Joseph is given garment of "fine linen (שֵׁשׁ, *šš*)" when he is exalted (Gen 41:42). The High Priest is also given gold twisted chains which attach to the shoulder pieces and hold the breastpiece and ephod in place (Ex 28:22–27). While the Hebrew word for "chain" is different it is significant that Joseph is also given a gold chain. All of this priestly adornment is given to Joseph when he is 30 years old. This is the same age at which the Levites began to service the tabernacle (Num 4:3, 23, 30)[24]. These elements work together to strengthen the correlation of Joseph to (7) an Edenic, priestly figure.

Additionally, (5) Pharaoh renames Joseph (Gen 41:45). It has been discussed that renaming occurs as a signifier of re-creation. Therefore, the renaming of Joseph adds an explicit "new creation" element to his exaltation. At this climax of the description of Joseph's exaltation, Pharaoh also gives Joseph a wife. It has also been discussed that at the end of an exodus, a chosen one will often receive his wife. This was true for Adam, Abraham, Isaac, and Jacob[25]. Most significant is the added parallel with Adam. The other's received their wives from oppressors as their wives went through an exodus. Adam is brought through the creation-exodus and given his wife by God, as Joseph is given a wife by Pharaoh. This receiving of a wife adds another signal that Joseph's exodus has come to an end as he moves from slavery and death to vice-regent. It is also one of several elements that connect the current narrative with the Garden in Eden and, interestingly, puts this Pharaoh in the place of Yahweh.

Each of the following elements have been discussed, but it will be beneficial to reiterate them to show the ways in which the author portrays Pharaoh as in the place of Yahweh and Joseph as a new Adam. In both the story of the Garden and the story of Joseph, the elect one is given authority over all things except one; the Tree of the Knowledge of Good and Evil and Pharaoh's throne, respectively. The elect ones are also given names and brides by Yahweh and Pharaoh, respectively. Going beyond the Garden, there are a few more noteworthy correlations. Just as Jacob

24. While these ages are applied to the Levites and not the Levitical Priests explicitly, Joseph is still associated with Tabernacle service. The same association is made with *the* High Priest Jesus as it is noted that he began his ministry at 30 years of age (Luke 3:23).

25. Jacob received his wives *in* exile rather than after, then exodus themes were applied to their birthings. The receiving and conceptions of his wives are still given in the context of Yahweh's deliverance through exodus.

and his company changed their clothes to cleanse themselves for an encounter with Yahweh, Joseph changes his clothes to cleanse himself for an encounter with Pharaoh. Likewise, Joseph shaves himself, as would one who wishes to be ritually cleaned or to devote themselves to Yahweh by a Nazarite vow. The elect one is also clothed by Yahweh and Pharaoh, respectively. The author could have mentioned that Joseph simply prepared himself, or left these details out entirely and left the reader to infer that Joseph made himself presentable for Pharaoh, but they saw these details as significant enough to include in his narrative. Lastly, Joseph begins his service at the Levitical age of 30. But rather than entering into the service of Yahweh, he enters into the service of Pharaoh. Yahweh has been mentioned relatively few times in the Joseph narrative, but the author has crafted the narrative such that he is seen at work in Joseph's exodus. The author portrays Pharaoh performing actions similar to Yahweh's action at Adam's exodus out of the waters so that the reader would look at Joseph's exodus out of the pit to kingship as another instance of Yahweh bringing a chosen, tested priest-king out of ruin. Yahweh has providentially made a new Adam, in Joseph, through the wise choices of Pharaoh.

To this point in the Joseph narrative, Joseph has become the chosen firstborn, the goat for Yahweh, and the goat for Azazel. He has been betrayed, literarily and ritually slaughtered, and literarily through death. He has then been seen to possess the "Spirit of God" (Gen 41:38), which has not been explicitly referenced with the phrase "Spirit of God" since Yahweh created the world and the life within it in Gen 1. Joseph becomes a new creation like Adam, is exalted as a priest-king, given authority and a wife, and is thereby given exodus out of the death that he was exiled into. Joseph's narrative will continue as he remains in his exalted state and his brothers re-enter the picture. As the exalted elect one and both goats of the Two-Goats motif, it will be important to observe the actions and character of Joseph as his narrative continues. Through the remaining narrative, the author teaches the reader about the character of the seed of the woman.

Table 16

Correspondences to Joseph's exodus from his brothers/slavery

	Jacob in Paddan-Aram	Joseph	Exodus
(1) Exile	Gen 29:1	Gen 37:28	Lev 26:14–27; Deut 28:15–68; 2 Kings 17:6–18; Micah 1
(1) Oppressed	31:5–7, 14–16, 38–41	Gen 37:28; 39:1, 20	Ex 1:8–14
(5) New humanity	Gen 32:28	Gen 41:45	Ex 19:4–5; Isa 43:1
(6) Rested at Yahweh's garden/ dwelling	Gen 32:1–2	Gen 41:40	Ex 15:17; Lev 26:11–12, Deut 11:8–12; Josh 21:44
(7) Act as Priests	Gen 31:54	Gen 41:42, 46	Ex 19:5–6
(7) Blessing: fruitful, multiply	Gen 28:3, 14–15; 29:31; 30:24, 27–28, 43; 32:12	Gen 39:5, 23; 41:49	Lev 26:3–10; Deut 11:7–16
(7) Commissioned to subdue	Gen 28:4	Gen 41:40–44	Lev 26:6–8; Deut 7:16; Josh 18:1
Marriage/ covenant	Gen 29:23, 28	Gen 41:45	Ex 19:5–8; Jer 31:32; Ezek 16:8

Israel Comes to Egypt

JOSEPH AFTER EXALTATION

THE IMAGERY SURROUNDING JOSEPH during his exaltation has made him an Adamic figure that has been brought through death and seems to be living out the promises of Abraham. He is living as a king who is a father of nations (cf. Gen 45:8) and a blessing to the nations (Gen 41:57), empowered by the Spirit of God for his task. As the reader continues in his story, one of two things are to be expected. It is to be expected that this new Adam will replay the failure of the first, or that he will properly fulfill the role for which Yahweh made him. This plot tension will be at work in the narrative along with the preexisting plot tension of Joseph's broken relationship with his treacherous brothers, the children of Israel.

While Joseph was in Egypt selling grain to the nations as Pharaoh's vice-regent, Joseph's brothers were facing starvation in Canaan. There is another famine in the land just as in the days of Abraham (Gen 12:10; 41:54). Abraham's famine drove him to exile himself to Egypt, from which he was given exodus. The brothers are also driven into an Egyptian exile by the famine that they face, and this exile will not be resolved ultimately until the book of Exodus. Nevertheless, the brothers are forced into Egyptian exile, following in the footsteps of their great-grandfather. They are sent down to Egypt to purchase grain where they come face to face with Joseph (Gen 42:6). The author has artfully crafted the story of the brother's reunification with Joseph in such a way that the attentive reader is kept in a constant state of suspense. While the scope of the current project prevents a full analysis of the contours of this narrative[1],

---

1. Mier Sternberg has done an excellent analysis of this narrative in light of the plot tensions within Genesis and the literary conventions of the biblical authors, showing the cohesiveness and artistry of the narrative. (Sternberg, *Poetics*, 285–309)

several aspects will be highlighted in order to bring greater clarity to the role the elect one plays and to the larger narrative.

When Joseph recognizes his brothers, he remembers his dreams of lordship over them and treats them as hostile (Gen 42:8–9). At first, it would seem that Joseph is acting out a long carried grudge against his brothers. Upon further examination, it will be seen that Joseph is actually carrying out a necessary act of reconciliation.

The brothers tell Joseph that one of their brothers is no more and the youngest is at home with his father (Gen 42:13). This youngest is Benjamin, Joseph's only full brother, born by Jacob's favorite wife. It would be natural for the brothers to bear a similar resentment for Benjamin as they had for Joseph. So how does Joseph know that Benjamin is truly with his father? How does he know that his brothers have not killed or traded Benjamin as they did to him? Joseph sends his brothers home with their grain and money while keeping Simeon in prison, who, at this point, is next line for firstborn per the birth order (since Reuben has disqualified himself; cf. Gen 49:4). When they return with Benjamin, they will be proven honest and Simeon will be free. Twice it is said out of Joseph's own mouth that he is "testing (בחן, bḥn)" them to know whether or not they are telling the truth (Gen 42:14, 16). Joseph wishes to authenticate[2] his brother's claim that they have not killed Benjamin before trusting them. At this point the brothers begin to confess their guilt regarding Joseph. Reuben, again ineffectively attempting to be the leader, blames his brothers and falsely claims that he attempted to prevent their actions (Gen 42:22).

To amplify the test, Joseph creates a scenario similar to that of his own sale into slavery. The brothers have lost one brother but are able to return home with an abundance of silver. It would perhaps be tempting for them to pocket the money and abandon their would-be firstborn brother as they did to him. They may have lost another brother, but they have a great deal of money and would not have to confront the harsh Egyptian again.

When the brothers return home and Jacob sees that his son's sacks contain extra money, it seems that he has suspicions similar to those of Joseph. Upon seeing the money, he says, "You have bereaved me of my children" (Gen 42:36). Perhaps Jacob suspects treachery in the disappearance of Simeon as well as Joseph. In any case, he is hesitant to send the remaining son of his favorite wife with these treacherous brothers.

---

2. בחן (bḥn), though often translated as "testing," more precisely means to "authenticate" (Smith, *Testing*, 6–30).

Reuben again attempts to lead by offering Jacob the execution of his own grandsons if he were to not return with Benjamin (Gen 42:37). Reuben seems to dig his hole deeper with every attempt to lead. Jacob continues to refuse to allow Benjamin to go with the brothers until Judah offers, not his sons, but *himself* as a pledge of Benjamin's safety (Gen 43:9). Upon Judah's self-sacrificial pledge, Jacob again sends his sons to Egypt to buy food along with a gift to appease the harsh Egyptian.

When the brothers arrive, Joseph sees that they have returned with the money for the previous load of grain and have brought Benjamin (Gen 43:21). They have passed the test, but, while their words have been verified and they have not abandoned Simeon for money, their true loyalty to the second son of Rachel remains to be seen. Joseph continues his test by preparing a meal and giving Benjamin the largest portion. He gives the brothers reason to resent Benjamin, but they seem to rather only enjoy their feast (Gen 43:34). So Joseph carries this test a step further in order to finally see if the brothers will abandon another son of Rachel or if they will treat him as family. Joseph sends the brothers on their way back home with their grain, but he has framed Benjamin by planting a cup for divination among his belongings (Gen 44:2). Perhaps the brothers are meant to see Benjamin as attempting to take the role of firstborn through the use of divination. Similar to the story of Jacob and Laban, and the exodus of Israel, the brothers are pursued (רדף, *rdp*) and overtaken (נשג, *nsg*) by Joseph's servant under suspicion of theft (Gen 44:4). Once overtaken and accused, they pledge that the thief shall die. The servant, rather than agreeing to kill the thief, will take the guilty one to Egypt as a servant. Benjamin is found to be that one.

The brothers are now given the opportunity to leave this new favorite son and be rid of him, and by taking the opportunity they would show their true heart regarding Benjamin. However, all the brothers return to the city with the detained Benjamin (Gen 44:13) to find Joseph waiting for them. Judah, seeing this as retribution from God for their violence against Joseph, offers all the brothers to Joseph as servants (Gen 44:16). However, this would hardly serve as justice for a cup stolen by one man. While this offer does display solidarity with Benjamin, there is still a step further than one must go to display that Benjamin is loved as a brother.

Judah ventures to speak to Joseph again and gives a detailed confession that Benjamin is indeed the favored son out of the brothers (Gen 44:20, 30). But rather than this being a resentful statement, it is a statement full of concern for his father. He then makes known that he is a pledge for Judah's safety so it is his place to substitute Benjamin as prisoner and slave (Gen 44:32–33). Judah offers his life in place of Benjamin's and at this, Joseph is satisfied that his brothers, led by Judah, are changed and refined men. They show true loyalty to their family, even their favored brother. At this, Joseph reveals himself and is finally reunited with his brothers (Gen 45:3).

Joseph, as the exalted elect one, who has been tested and vindicated through his own exile and exodus, tests and refines his brothers in the midst of a famine. Through this time of exile, Joseph proves his brothers as righteous and establishes their brotherly bonds once again. This goat-for-Azazel brother who is also Yahweh's elect, does not go out to become fruitful and hostile to the elect family, but rather goes out to be fruitful and work reconciliation for the family. The elect brother goes out to bring his family to him and save them.

THE EXODUS MOTIF: ISRAEL TO EGYPT

The brothers are brought, along with the entire family, to Egypt and are delivered from (1) the famine. As mentioned, Israel's exile into Egypt will not be fully resolved until the book of Exodus, but the brothers do receive an exodus within their generation from the famine and exile that they face. As a family that has (4) become a multitude, the children of Israel come to Egypt with many possessions and are (7) blessed to be fruitful and multiply (Gen 46:3, 6). Once in Egypt, Joseph provides for all the needs of his family (Gen 45:18) and they receive land in which they become a greater multitude. To those with a knowledge of the narrative of the book of Exodus, or with a knowledge of the importance of staying within the land of Canaan throughout Genesis, this migration seems quite foreboding. However, this migration, though counterintuitive on some points, is blessed by Yahweh (Gen 46:3) and a means of deliverance from the current famine and back to the elect son. Therefore, the author has associated this migration to Egypt with (6)[3] Edenic blessing and the acquisition of a land (Gen 47:6; which is what was promised to Abraham regarding Canaan). This migration into Egypt, rather than being an act of rebellion and rejection of blessing, is associated with the Exodus motif.

---

3. In light of Pharaoh's portrayal as Yahweh in this narrative, as Israel comes into Egypt, they are, according to the literary conventions of this section, coming into Yahweh's land.

On the trip to Egypt, Jacob sends (שׁלח, *šlḥ*) Judah ahead of him to show the way (Gen 46:28). In Gen 37, Joseph was sent (שׁלח, *šlḥ*) to check up on his brothers, functioning as the firstborn. By sending him to lead, Jacob is now treating Judah as the firstborn in the same way he treated Joseph as the firstborn. Once in Egypt, Joseph instructs his brothers on how to address Pharaoh. Though this speech preparation is between Joseph, vice-regent of Egypt, and his brothers, it may be that this scene is meant to draw a conceptual link with the previous speech preparation in Gen 12:13. Abraham, fearing for his life, plans for Sarah to tell Pharaoh that she is Abraham's sister, in order that it may go well with him. In the current passage, Joseph plans for his brothers to tell Pharaoh that they are "keepers of livestock" (Gen 46:34), and not explicitly shepherds, in order that they may dwell in Goshen. In each instance, the chosen one devises a half-truth for his dependents to tell Pharaoh for the well-being of the family. The brother's blatant disregard for Joseph's instructions (Gen 47:3) perhaps points to Yahweh's provision and the foolishness of relying on deceit for security in light of Yahweh's promises. Finally, Jacob comes to Pharaoh and (7) blesses him, showing himself to be greater than Pharaoh and showing himself to be fulfilling the call of Israel to bless the nations (Gen 47:7).

Though relatively few of the Exodus motif markers are present, and though the migration will bring Israel into slavery, within the current narrative the author has displayed a few markers of the Exodus motif in Israel's migration to Egypt. This is in order to display the deliverance that the exalted elect one has worked for his family, and which he passed through before them. Though the family of Israel will soon need exodus out of Egypt, Yahweh has given them exodus into Egypt, out of famine, into the protection of Yahweh's elect.

As Joseph continues his role as Yahweh's pit-redeemed firstborn, he is a blessing to the nations as well as his family. In the time of famine, he sells food to Egypt and allows them to live. As the Egyptians run out of things to sell for food, they willingly sell themselves to Pharaoh through Joseph as servants[4] (Gen 47:25). By Joseph's life-saving wisdom, the

---

4. In a modern western cultural context, it is worth noting that the tendency may be to harbor disgust toward Joseph for buying all the Egyptians property to the point that they sold themselves into slavery. However, in the context of the Biblical narrative and culture, this is not the universal feeling of those who became slaves. They are rather content, even happy, with the arrangement and see Joseph as a hero. They are now part of Pharaoh's household. They work to support his household and are given sustenance through him. In this context, slavery is a means to earn a living.

nations have willingly made themselves servants of Joseph's master. The nation of Egypt sees that life is gained through Joseph and so they give themselves over to his master, to serve his purposes and to be supplied by his riches.

Table 17

Correspondences to Israel's exodus from famine

	Sarai in Egypt	Israel to Egypt	Exodus
(1) Famine	Gen 12:10	Gen 41:54	Gen 45:4–13
(7) Blessing: fruitful, multiply		Gen 46:3–4	Lev 26:3–10; Deut 11:7–16
Pursuit and overtaking		Gen 44:4	Ex 14:5–9
(4) Come out with mixed multitude and possessions	Gen 12:16; 13:1–2	Gen 46:5–6	Ex 12:35–36, 38
Prepared speech to secure well-being	Gen 12:11–13	Gen 46:33–34	Gen 46:31–34
(6) Rested at Yahweh's garden/ dwelling	Gen 13:3, 18	Gen 47:5–6	Ex 15:17; Lev 26:11–12, Deut 11:8–12; Josh 21:44
(7) Act as Priests		Gen 47:7	Ex 19:5–6

Jacob Out of Egypt

INTERMINGLED WITH THE JOSEPH narrative is another exodus of Jacob. As previously mentioned, despite the fact that Israel's migration to Egypt was a means of deliverance from the current famine, when Joseph brought his family to Egypt, he brought them into a place of exile from which a later generation would need deliverance. With their movement to Egypt comes the expectation of their exodus back into Canaan, as Yahweh had promised (Gen 15:13–16). As Jacob leaves Canaan to meet Joseph in Egypt, he is met by Yahweh (Gen 46:2). Yahweh promises Jacob that this place of exile will be a place of multiplication and that he will bring Jacob back to Canaan, to Yahweh's land, after he dies in peace with Joseph. This promise to bring Jacob back from a land of exile should bring the reader back to Gen 28:15, where Jacob is promised that he will be brought back to Canaan from Paddan-Aram. This link within the text creates the expectation that another exodus cycle has begun for Jacob. Jacob comes down to Egypt, meets his long-lost son, and, as his fathers before him, allots blessings to his sons before his death.

JACOB'S BLESSINGS

Though the blessings of Jacob are not directly related to Jacob's exodus out of Egypt, they are worth discussion as they relay the final developments of the story of the elect one in Genesis. As Jacob gives his blessing during his stay in Egypt, just before his death, this seems to be a fitting place for their inclusion.

In Gen 48, Jacob begins by adopting Joseph's sons alongside Reuben and Simeon, in order to increase the children of Rachel (Gen 48:5–7). In this, Jacob compares Joseph's sons with his chronologically first-born sons. Jacob proceeds to bless his newly adopted sons, putting the younger, Ephraim, over the older, Manasseh, as firstborn (Gen 48:14, 20). Jacob gives the blessing that his name be carried on in them, which is the name of Abraham and Isaac. Jacob gives to Ephraim the name which is to be made great by Yahweh through one of Abraham's descendants (Gen 12:2; 48:16). He also pronounces that Joseph's sons (though more so Ephraim) will be the most blessed of Israel. Jacob concludes his blessing on Ephraim and Manasseh by giving them an allotment of land in Canaan rather than giving any land to the other brothers. It seems that Jacob has made Ephraim the firstborn of Israel and given him the Abrahamic promise of being a blessing to the nations.

This notion seems to continue as Jacob blesses Joseph (Gen 49:22–26). Joseph's blessing contains "bless" or "blessings" six times, whereas the lemma does not occur in the blessings of the other brothers. Jacob blesses Joseph with the blessings beyond the blessings of himself and his parents. Jacob puts these blessings on the one who was "set apart (נְזִיר, nzyr)" from his brothers. As was done when Joseph shaved his head to meet Pharaoh, Joseph is associated with a Nazir, one who is separated and dedicated to Yahweh (Num 6). In this blessing, Jacob again seems to intend that Joseph, and therefore Ephraim, obtains the blessing of Abraham and the promise to be a blessing to the nations. This blessing, however, seems to create tension with the blessing of Judah.

The blessings of the other brothers largely discuss the fate of the tribes as they enter the land and live out their time as a nation[1], creating expectations for each tribe as the Biblical narrative progresses. Reuben, Simeon, and Levi, the oldest three of Jacob's sons, each are passed over for the right of firstborn due to their actions earlier in the book of Genesis. Judah, as next in birth order and as one that has been refined by the events of Gen 38, receives the firstborn blessing from Jacob. Per the blessing, Judah's brothers will bow down to him (Gen 49:8). Previously, Joseph had dreams which deemed him the firstborn and predicted that the sons of Israel would bow to him. Now the brothers will bow to Judah[2]. The tribe of Judah will produce a king that will rule nations (Gen 49:10). Through this blessing, the firstborn status seems to have moved from

---

1. See Hamilton, *Genesis Chapters 18–50*, notes on Genesis 49:1–33; Pulse, *Figuring Resurrection*, "Chapter 3," §Genesis 49 for analysis of the blessings and their potential fulfilments.

2. Emadi notes that, by describing the ruler that comes from Judah in similar terms as were previously applied to Joseph, Joseph becomes a "narrative prefiguration" of the Judahite king (Emadi, *From Prisoner*, 60–61).

Joseph to Judah. Joseph has lived out the life of the elect one to whom the brothers bow. As Judah now inherits that role, the reader may look to Joseph as an image of what the tribe of Judah will become.

Judah's king will also have his garment washed in wine and in "the blood of grapes" (Gen 49:10). This choice of words is significant given the events of the Joseph narrative. Though here, blood is used as a metaphor for wine, the washing of a garment in "the blood of grapes" recalls the dipping of Joseph's garment in the blood of the goat. It is possible that the author intends for Judah to not only take the role of firstborn but to also take the role of the Goat for Yahweh, slaughtered by and for the sake of his brothers, as symbolically happened to Joseph.

Through his blessings, Jacob has given both Joseph and Judah pre-eminence in Israel. In part, these blessings may have been the rationale behind the rivalry between Ephraim and Judah throughout the period of the split kingdom. However, Jacob has ultimately given his favorite son, Joseph, the firstborn status and given him blessing upon blessing (1 Chr 5:2). Concerning Judah's blessing, Jacob has also created an expectation that one will come from Judah who will rule all Israel and the birthright will be transferred to him by Yahweh's election (cf. Ps 78:67–68; Col 1:15). Joseph is made the firstborn in the current generation, but one day, Yahweh will choose one from Judah to rule Israel and the nations from Zion.

THE EXODUS MOTIF: JACOB OUT OF EGYPT

The scene of Jacob's blessings opened with Jacob nearing death (Gen 48:1). Now he has given his blessings, his final testament, and is ready to die. In hope of Yahweh's promises, Jacob commanded that he be buried in the family tomb in Canaan and is then "gathered to his people" (Gen 49:33). It is now left to Joseph to give his father exodus from Egypt back to Canaan. Joseph prepares Jacob's body with a forty-day embalming process (Gen 50:2). While the embalming process may have required forty days, it is significant that Jacob spent forty days undergoing post-mortem preparation in Egypt. (1) These forty days under Egyptian embalming should call the reader's mind to the 400 years that Israel would spend in Egypt as slaves (Gen 15:13). After this period of embalming, Joseph requests of Pharaoh that he be allowed to go bury his father and then he will return (Gen 50:5). Though Joseph does not use the word typically used to link to Moses' request (send, שלח, *šlḥ*), his request does echo Moses request to be sent out by Pharaoh (Ex 5:1, 3).

Both request are to be given leave by Pharaoh to leave Egypt, to go to Yahweh (or his land), and return (though the return is only implied by Moses). Upon Pharaoh's permission, they leave. (4) Joseph carries Jacob out of Egypt and into Canaan with a mixed multitude made up of Israel and high-ranking Egyptians (Gen 50:7–8). The author points out that, as Joseph and much of his family went to bury Jacob, they left their children and livestock in Egypt (Gen 50:8). This displays the impermanence of this exodus and their intent to return. Taking all the family and livestock was explicitly requested by Moses to Pharaoh (Ex 10:24–26) after Pharaoh requested that the livestock stay in order to ensure that Israel would return. Once the mixed multitude crosses the Jordan, the Egyptians mourn for seven days again (Gen 50:10), just as they had mourned for seventy days in Egypt. It is possible that the author intends these mourning events to mimic the future Passover event in Ex 12. The author explicitly says that the Egyptians mourned, and no mention is made of Israel's mourning alongside them. It would be more natural that all mourned in this situation, but if Passover is in view, the mourning of the Egyptians only would be significant.

Joseph successfully brought Jacob out of Egypt and to the land of Canaan. He buried his father in the tomb of Abraham as Jacob had requested (Gen 50:13). During the burial, the reader is reminded that this tomb is (6) "east of Mamre" and of the narrative of Abraham's acquisition of the tomb. These reminders recall the Edenic connotation of the tomb which it acquired throughout Abraham's story. Yahweh's promise to give Jacob exodus is complete (Gen 46:2) as he is laid to rest in an Eden-like place, in the dwelling of Yahweh.

Now that Jacob is dead, the brothers fear that Joseph will take vengeance on them for attempting to kill him and selling him. They continue to use deceit to obtain forgiveness, mistrusting Joseph's loyalty to them thus far. However, Joseph overlooks this deceit and maintains unity with his brothers. He assures them that Yahweh has indeed frustrated the plans of the wicked (Gen 50:20). Yahweh has taken that which is bad, that which is in ruin, that which is aligned with the waters, and made it into good. Yahweh has done what he continually does; coming to the darkness and chaos and forming them into good. In these words, Joseph partially fulfills the hopes of Lamech, comforting (נחם, *nḥm*) them (Gen 50:21). Lamech hoped that his chosen son would give rest (נחם, *nḥm*) to humanity (Gen 5:29) just as Yahweh had rested (נחם, *nḥm*) humanity in the Garden (Gen 2:15). Here these Edenic hopes find some fulfillment in Joseph as this elect one announces peace and loyalty to his deceptive and frightened brothers.

Joseph then continues to live to the ideal Egyptian age of 110, signifying fullness of life and righteousness[3]. Before Joseph's death, the author tells the reader of Joseph's deathbed reminder of the coming exodus from Egypt and of the oath that he made his family take that they would remember this hope and bring his bones to Canaan as he had done for Jacob. The book comes to a close with the tested, proved, and exalted elect one dying in a good old age and passing his hope of the coming exodus to the next generation.

Table 18

Correspondences to Jacob's exodus from Egypt

	Jacob in Paddan-Aram	Jacob out of Egypt	Exodus
Promised presence and return	Gen 28:13–15; 31:3	Gen 46:3–4	Gen 48:21; Ex 33:14
(1) Exile	Gen 29:1	Gen 46:6	Lev 26:14–27; Deut 28:15–68; 2 Kings 17:6–18; Micah 1
Request to be sent	Gen 30:25	Gen 50:5	Ex 5:1
Bride sent out	Gen 30:25; 31:42	Gen 50:6	Ex 5:1; 12:31–32
(4) Come out with mixed multitude and possessions	Gen 30:26; 31:16–18; 32:10	Gen 50:7–9	Ex 12:35–36, 38
(6) Rested at Yahweh's garden/ dwelling	Gen 32:1–2	Gen 50:13	Ex 15:17; Lev 26:11–12, Deut 11:8–12; Josh 21:44

3. Hamilton, *Genesis Chapters 18–50*, see comment on Gen 50:22

Moses

THE EXODUS MOTIF: MOSES THROUGH WATERS

WHILE THE LIFE OF Moses is clearly not within the book of Genesis, he does undergo the last exoduses before the exodus of Israel. Therefore, the exoduses of Moses may be worthy of discussion within this work. Moses, unlike other elect ones, very quickly, in narrative time, goes through two exodus events. The first happens within the first ten verses of Ex 2, allowing for little room to include the standard motif markers. Therefore, the author first unmistakably likens this small exodus event to that of Noah, then foreshadows Israel's exodus.

When Moses was born, the current Pharaoh had (1) issued a decree that all male babies were to be put to death. However, Moses' mother "saw that he was a fine child" (Ex 2:2). Literally she *saw* that he was "good (טוֹב, *twb*)." This echoes Eve's *seeing* that the fruit of the Tree of the Knowledge of Good and Evil was "desired" (lit. "good, טוֹב, *twb*") to make one wise. However, in this instance of seeing that something is good, Moses' mother acts in defiance of the oppressor and in loyalty to her son whom Yahweh has created as his image. In seeing that her son is "good," she has inverted the fall motif and has judged well. Following this inversion Pharaoh's daughter will be the one to "take" the boy as a form of rescue (Ex 2:5). Moses' mother placed her son in a "basket (תֵּבָה, *tbh*)," which is the same Hebrew word used to refer to Noah's ark. Furthering the connection with Noah's ark is the fact that, just as Noah's ark was "covered (כפר, *kpr*)" with "pitch (כפר, *kpr*)" (Gen 6:14), so Moses' ark is "daubed (חמר, *ḥmr*)" with "bitumen (חמר, *ḥmr*)." Both arks share a similar wordplay regarding the waterproofing of the vessel. Moses' mother places her son's ark in the water, among the reeds. By the reader's knowledge of the previous story of Noah, the author has created the expectation that Moses is going to be delivered through the waters as Noah was. Not only is Moses to be delivered through the waters in an ark, but through waters among the reeds, foreshadowing his later leading of Israel in their deliverance through the Sea of Reeds.

As Yahweh will send Moses, his servant (Ex 14:31; Num 12:7–8; Deut 34:5), to rescue Israel, the daughter of Pharaoh sees this child in the midst of the waters and sends her servant to bring him out (Ex 2:5). Pharaoh's daughter, through her servant, draws (משה, *mšh*) Moses (משה, *mšh*) out of the water and (5) names him (Ex 2:10), giving him a similar deliverance from Pharaoh as the children of Israel will soon experience. Later in Israel's history, David will look back on this event, loaded with the new creation and exodus imagery seen in Noah's flood, and describe his own exodus from his enemies as having been "dr[awn] (משה, *mšh*) out of many waters" (Ps 18:16).

By his deliverance through the waters and being given a name, with Pharaoh's daughter playing the role of Yahweh in this deliverance and naming, Moses is made a new creation. He has passed from the waters of death to new life. Through these events Moses has been marked as the latest elect one within Israel and he has been prepared beforehand by Yahweh for the task he will receive. This deliverance through the waters is also Moses' first of two exodus events.

Table 19

Correspondences to Moses' childhood exodus

	Flood	Moses' Birth	Exodus
(1) Oppressed		Ex 1:16, 22	Ex 1:8–14
Ark	Gen 6:14–19	Ex 2:3, 5	
Reeds		Ex 2:3, 5	Ex 13:18; 15:4
Servant Sent		Ex 2:5	Ex 14:31; Num 12:7, 8; Deut 34:5
(4) Delivered through waters	Gen 7–8	Ex 2:10	Ex 14
(5) New Humanity	~Gen 8:15–16	Ex 2:10	Ex 19:4–5; Isa 43:1

THE EXODUS MOTIF: MOSES THROUGH EXILE

Once Moses is grown, knowing that he is a Hebrew, goes out to see his people and discovers (1) an Egyptian beating a Hebrew. Moses (3) strikes down this Egyptian (Ex 2:11). While this event does bear similarities with Cain's striking of Abel, given that both are secret murders, Moses' striking down of the Egyptian is not to be seen in the same negative light. Cain murdered Abel out of jealousy, but Moses killed the Egyptian in defense of his brother. Moses has, though by his own schemes rather than by reliance on Yahweh, just displayed his loyalty to his people; to Yahweh's people. He has displayed his desire to deliver them from their slavery. However, as happens to each of the elect ones in Genesis, Moses is rejected by his brothers (Ex 2:14). Seeing that his killing of the Egyptian was known, Moses (1) flees from Pharaoh, just as Hagar fled from Sarai and Jacob from Esau. He comes to a well where another betrothal journey scene begins[1].

While sitting by a well in a foreign land, Moses once again shows his loyalty to the oppressed as he "saves (יָשַׁע, yš ʿ)" the daughters of the priest of Midian and allows them to water their flocks (Ex 2:17). Through the salvation he works for these women, he becomes accepted as family by the priest and one of his daughters becomes Moses' bride (Ex 2:21). With her, (7) he is fruitful and multiplies, having a son while in exile. Much of this narrative seems to loosely foreshadow the coming exodus of Israel. Moses is sent by Yahweh to save Israel, who will become, not Moses' bride, but Yahweh's. Moses also becomes a shepherd, following in the footsteps of his fathers, and it is during his time shepherding that he meets the Angel of Yahweh.

While in exile, Moses comes to an angel in a burning bush who says that he is "the God of [his] father" (Ex 3:6). This is the same Angel who met Hagar and Jacob in their exiles (Gen 16:7–13; 31:11–12), and is Yahweh himself. Just as with Jacob (Gen 28:13–15), the Angel of Yahweh promises to be with Moses (Ex 4:12, 15) as he comes out of exile and is sent to deliver Israel. Moses is not renamed within this scene nor have the new creation motif explicitly applied to him, but given the presence of the theme in other exodus cycles, it may be reasonable to here see Moses as becoming a new creation. Moses has been declared by Yahweh to be his instrument of deliverance for the people of Israel (Ex 3:10). He has been given a (5) new function by Yahweh and, ironically, it will be seen

---

1. Martin, "Betrothal Journey Narratives," 511–514

that Moses, he who has been drawn out of the waters, will be Yahweh's instrument to draw Israel out of the waters. If new creation is not the intent of the author in this section, Moses has at least already undergone new creation in his first exodus.

Having received his commission from Yahweh, Moses returns to the priest of Midian and requests permission to leave and return to his people, as he will soon request leave of Pharaoh for Israel. The priest of Midian allows Moses to leave and he sets out for Egypt. Moses came to Midian by himself and (4) now leaves as a sort of mixed multitude with his Midianite wife and son.

After Moses has begun his journey, Yahweh comes to Moses and tells him that if Pharaoh does not release Israel, his firstborn son, he will kill Pharaoh's firstborn son (Ex 4:22–23). Immediately after this Passover declaration, the author gives a very strange narrative involving the circumcision of Moses' firstborn, Gershom[2]. While Moses was on his way to Egypt, Yahweh sought to kill him (Ex 4:24), despite the fact that he just commissioned him to save Israel. Therefore, Moses' wife circumcised Gershom and touched the foreskin to Moses' "feet" (most likely a euphemism for "penis")[3] and this caused Yahweh to relent. The issue was that Moses had not yet given his own son the sign of the covenant of Abraham, and therefore had not identified Gershom (nor himself, possibly) with Yahweh's people. The Passover execution of the firstborn, which Yahweh had just detailed, is now going to be enacted on his chosen one who is going through his own exodus event. As the Israelites are about to leave the land, the Passover takes place and they are covered by Yahweh if they display the covenant sign of the lamb's blood on the doorpost. Meanwhile, those who do not identify themselves with Yahweh's people have their firstborn killed.

As Moses leaves the land, neither he nor his son have taken the mark which would identify them as Yahweh's people. Moses may be circumcised, and the text seems to imply so by not having him circumcised in this narrative, but this may be an Egyptian circumcision. Therefore, Yahweh is going to kill Moses, the elect firstborn. Zipporah remedies

---

2. I was introduced to the following interpretation of Ex 4:24–27 in Carmen Imes' Torah Tuesday videos inspired by her forthcoming commentary (Imes, "Torah Tuesday—Exodus 4:24"). A similar explanation of events can be found in Durham's work as well (Durham, *Exodus*, 56–59).

3. The term "feet (רֶגֶל, *rgl*)" is used often in the Hebrew Bible as a euphemism for genitalia (Warren-Rothlin, "Euphemisms and Bible Translation," 865–866). See also Durham, *Exodus*, 52–53, 56–59.

the situation, in the midst of Moses' Passover, by applying the covenant sign to Gershom and touching his circumcised foreskin to Moses' penis to apply the meaning of loyalty to the Abrahamic covenant to Moses' circumcision. She then states that Moses is a bridegroom of blood to her (Ex 4:25). By this statement, she is identifying as part of the covenant family. By her marriage to Moses, she has joined Yahweh's people and she states that she is loyal to Yahweh. Because of her actions, Yahweh let Moses alone. Through the encounter with Yahweh within this story, the author has established another significant correspondence between Moses' exodus and Israel's exodus. Both Moses and Israel go through respective passovers. Thanks to Zipporah, Moses's disloyalty has been dealt with through this confrontation. Yahweh then instructs Aaron to go meet Moses, supplying the assistance that was promised.

After coming through his exodus event, Moses, similar to Joseph, is reunited with his brothers and accepted (Ex 4:30–31). Also like Joseph, having been reunited with his family, Moses will lead Israel through their own exodus. The promise of deliverance that he brings incites worship to Yahweh. Moses then goes on to request leave of Pharaoh for the Israelites (Ex 5:1) and begin Israel's exodus narrative.

Table 20

Correspondences to Moses' exodus from Pharoah/exile

	Jacob in Paddan-Aram	Moses Flees	Exodus
(1) Oppressed	Gen 31:5–7, 14–16, 38–41	Ex 2:11, 15	Ex 1:8–14
(3) Enemies afflicted	Gen 31:9	E 2:12	Ex 7–12
Fled	Gen 27:43; 31:20–22	Ex 2:15	Ex 14:5
Spring/well	Gen 29:2, 10	Ex 2:15	Ex 15:25–27; 17:6
Exile	Gen 29:1	Ex 2:22	Lev 26:14–27; Deut 28:15–68; 2 Kings 17:6–18; Micah 1
Request to be sent	Gen 30:25	Ex 4:18	Ex 5:1
(4) Come out with mixed multitude and possessions	Gen 30:26; 31:16–18; 32:10	Ex 4:20	Ex 12:35–36, 38
(5) New creation		~Ex 3:10	Ex 19:4–5; Isa 43:1
Marriage/ covenant	Gen 29:23, 28	Ex 2:21	Ex 19:5–8; Jer 31:32; Ezek 16:8

Two Goats

THE TWO BIRDS

BEFORE MAKING SOME REFLECTIONS on the Two-Goats motif, it may be beneficial to explore another text that utilizes the motif shortly before Lev 16, perhaps to bring the motif to the mind of the reader before the all-important Day of Atonement. In Lev 14, instructions are given for the cleansing of a leper[1]. Once a priest has met the leper outside the camp to confirm that the leprosy has been healed, the former leper shall acquire two clean birds, cedarwood, scarlet yarn, and hyssop (Lev 14:4). One of the birds is to be slaughtered over a vessel of living water and its blood is to be drained into the water. The remaining bird is then to be taken, along with the cedarwood, scarlet yarn, and hyssop and be dipped in the blood-water mixture. The former leper is to be sprinkled seven times with the blood-water mixture and he shall be clean. Then the living bird shall be let go into the open field. Later in the same chapter, the same instructions are repeated for a house being cleansed of disease (Lev 14:48–53).

This ritual does not take place at the altar, but rather outside the camp or at the formerly infected house, so the slaughtered bird does not strictly conform to the instructions for the purification offering found in Lev 4. However, the two birds used in the cleansing of a leper or diseased house do bear similarities with the goats of the Day of Atonement. The slaughtered bird's blood, just as the blood of the goat for Yahweh and any other purification offering, is sprinkled on the thing needing to be cleansed[2]. The blood of a typical purification offering cleanses the

---

1. Parallels between the two birds of Lev 14 and the two goats of the Day of Atonement have also been noted by Mary Douglas (Douglas, *Jacob's Tears*, 52–54).

2. Compare Lev 4:6–7; 16:14 (Milgrom, *Leviticus 1–16*, 233–236, 1032)

sanctuary and altar (Lev 4:6–7 for example) and the blood of the goat which is a purification offering on the Day of Atonement is used to purify the Holy Place and the altar (Lev 16:15–16). Despite the added elements of water, red wood, yarn, and hyssop, the slaughtered bird's blood is similarly used to purify the leper or diseased house (Lev 14:7, 51).

After the blood purification is made for the diseased person or house, similar to the goat for Azazel which is sent into the wilderness, the second bird is sent out into the open field. Just as the goat for Azazel goes out from the community bearing the sins of the people (Lev 16:22), this bird is sent out bearing the impurity of the diseased person or house[3].

While space will not be devoted here to discussing the place of this ritual within the context of Leviticus and the rest of the Torah, it is interesting that the elements of the Two-Goat's motif appear again shortly before the Day of Atonement and in the context of cleansing. This appearance may be to bring the reader's mind to the motif before coming to the two goats of the Day of Atonement, preparing the reader to meditate on the similarities between the goats and the brothers of Genesis. The instructions for the cleansing of lepers and houses also reinforce the need for purification offerings and the carrying away of impurities for the purging of impurities and sin. This was seen within the motif in Genesis and culminated with both functions being performed by one character.

MEANING OF THE BROTHERS

As the Two-Goats motif appeared in the narrative, some comments were given as to the purpose of the motif. However, it would be beneficial to here summarize the uses of the motif and examine the differences and similarities of the uses throughout the narrative. As the motif becomes established within the text, the author changes aspects of the motif in order to teach the reader about its meaning and about the brothers.

The brother playing the role of the goat for Azazel has a fairly uniform pattern. (A) This brother, though typically older, is not chosen by Yahweh as the firstborn and carrier of the promise. Therefore, (B) this brother shows jealousy and acts against the elect brother. This brother begins to take the shape of the seed of the serpent who is at enmity with the seed of the woman. After their hostilities toward the elect, (C) they are given protection or a guarantee of safety by Yahweh and (D) exiled into

---

3. Milgrom, *Leviticus 1–16*, 840

the wilderness. In the wilderness (E) they are made fruitful and multiply until they become a people. (F) These peoples become nations which are hostile to Israel within the Biblical narrative.

With Cain, all of these elements are present. (A) Abel is chosen, (B) Cain murders Abel, (C) Cain is given a sign of protection, (D) he is exiled into the wilderness, where (E) he becomes a city that is (F) full of violence and is shown to be Yahweh's enemy via the flood narrative. Cain bears similarities with the goat for Azazel in that he bears his iniquities as the goat bears the sins of Israel.

With Ham, (A) Shem is chosen, (B) Ham attempts to usurp Shem by raping his mother, (E) he becomes many nations who are (F) major enemies of Israel throughout scripture. Though Shem is not linked to an offering, he does bear the burden, along with Japheth, of covering his father's failure. This mirrors Yahweh's covering of Adam and Eve's nakedness, which, among other things, signified Yahweh's desire to purify and forgive. Through this act of covering, Yahweh reinstated humanity as his royal representatives and Shem has carried out an act that mirrored Yahweh's.

With Lot, (A) Abraham is chosen, though Lot is not strictly Abraham's brother except in the Hebraic sense as part of his family. Due to this, jealousy of Abraham's position and promise is not part of Lot's narrative. Rather, what may fit into slot (B) is that he desires land that lies apart from Abraham's promised land, and is deceived like Eve, aligning himself with the seed of the serpent at that moment. This suggestion for slot (B) may be a stretch since Lot never shows hostility toward Abraham, making him the seed of the serpent, however, Lot's choosing of Sodom seems to be where we would expect slot (B) to be. Lot is then (C) protected as he is given exodus out of Sodom, (D) he dwells in a cave outside of the cities, (E) he becomes the father of Moab and Amon who (F) become enemies during Israel's wilderness wanderings (Deut 23:3–4).

With Ishmael, (A) Isaac is chosen, (B) Ishmael "laughs" at Isaac, (C) Hagar is promised that he will be blessed and become a nation, and he provides for them as well. (D) Ishmael is later exiled into the wilderness of Paran, (E) where he becomes the Ishmaelites who (F) sell Joseph and become Israel's enemies (Ps 83:5–6). As the goat for Azazel, Ishmael is explicitly exiled into the "wilderness."

With Esau, (A) Jacob is chosen, (B) Esau plans to kill Jacob, (D) Esau moves from Canaan to Seir and (E) becomes the nation of Edom who (F) attacks Israel (see Obadiah). Esau is further connected to the goat (שָׂעִיר, śꜥyr) for Azazel by his being hairy (שֵׂעָר, śꜥr) and moving to Seir (שֵׂעִיר, śꜥyr). As part of the reversals seen in the Jacob narrative, it can also be seen that some of the elements are applied to Jacob as well. (B) Jacob steals Esau's birthright and blessing, (C) is promised protection as he (D) goes through exile and (E) is made fruitful while in exile. Despite the fact that these elements are applied to Jacob, it does not seem that the author wishes us to see Jacob as the goat for Azazel, but rather to see how Yahweh works with this elect one who looks like a seed of the serpent in all except his ultimate hope in Yahweh.

Lastly, Joseph plays the role of both goats and reunites with his brothers rather than being permanently cast off from them. Therefore, element (B) includes wrongs by both parties and elements (E) and (F) are absent. (A) Joseph is chosen. Rather than there being one seed of the serpent who wrongs the seed of the woman in this narrative, (B) Joseph wrongs his brothers by flaunting his firstborn status and his brothers wrong him by attempting to kill and selling him. (C) The Lord is with Joseph, prospering him in his exile after (D) he is forcibly exiled into Egypt. As one of the patriarchs of Israel, Joseph does not multiply into his own nation who becomes an enemy of Israel. The fact that he does multiply into Ephraim who does become an enemy of Judah during the monarchical period (Isa 7:3–6) is not related to the motifs of Genesis under discussion.

As the Two-Goats motif is employed, it seems that the brother re-sembling the goat for Azazel becomes a standard character. There are differences between these specific goat-for-Azazel brothers, but they do not seem to be used for innovation within the story as their fates gener-ally remain the same. Each non-elect brother is exiled from their elect brother, from the promised land, whether by force or by choice, where they are made into a fruitful and hostile nation. The variances between each of these brothers and their circumstances are worthy of reflection, but it is significant that, given the pattern of hostility, Yahweh continues to bless and multiply these brothers. It would seem that Yahweh desires to bless his enemies in the hopes that the elect one would bring these now large families back to him (cf. Gen 12:2–3; Ex 19:5–6).

The markers for the brothers playing the role of the goat for Yahweh are more thematic than linguistic, and there are a select few who set the pattern that the rest fall into. The brothers playing the role of the goat for Yahweh are all chosen by Yahweh, as are the goats (Lev 16:8). Then these brothers, as part of their being chosen, are brought closer to Yahweh and his land by the end of their narrative. It can be argued that this part of the pattern does not apply to Joseph since he was not returned to Canaan until the Exodus of Israel, but within his narrative, he was brought to and exalted by Pharaoh, who played the role of Yahweh for Joseph. Within his narrative, Joseph becomes the climax and archetype of the goat-for-Yahweh brother in Genesis.

The most significant instances of the goat-for-Yahweh motif are those of Abel, Shem, Isaac, and Joseph; three of which are associated with an offering. Abel is associated with his purification offering via the metathesis between his name and the *fat* of his flocks which he chooses to slaughter. Some have also noted that Abel's blood being spilled is significant[4], given that the offering's blood is to be poured on the ground at the base of the altar. Additionally, the word "blood" is rare in Genesis and is also used to refer to the goat's blood in which Joseph's robe is dipped. These instances of blood are used to associate both Abel and Joseph with purification offerings. Shem is associated with a covering of sin similar to that which Yahweh performed for Adam and Eve, linking him, at least, with Yahweh's desire to purify and forgive humanity. Isaac was nearly sacrificed as a post-exodus burnt offering; as an offering of atonement and worship at the future site of Jerusalem. Lastly, Joseph is associated with an offering as his robe is dipped in goat blood in order to hide the sins of his brothers. Meanwhile, he was being carried into literary death.

Through the Two-Goats pattern it becomes clear that the elect one will be brought close to Yahweh and his dwelling, but the author suggests more through Abel, Shem, Isaac, and Joseph. After reading Abel's narrative, the reader has a category of an elect brother who is associated, at least linguistically linked, to a purification offering. Through Shem, the author suggests that the elect brother has the ability to bring about forgiveness and reinstatement of the fallen elect family. Since the next elect brother is not associated with a sacrifice or forgiveness, this may be forgotten as an oddity or simply a misinterpretation of the literary connections. However, this connection between election and atoning sacrifice is revived when the reader gets to Gen 22. Here there is not only an elect brother called by Yahweh to be a sacrifice for chosen Abraham, but this sacrifice takes place at the future site of the temple. Now the attentive reader is likely puzzled by these connections which have appeared only three times and in different ways but are nonetheless recurring.

4. Orlov, The Atoning Dyad, 12–13

When Joseph is associated with the blood of a slaughtered goat and sent through literary death, it would seem to suggest that the author is creating an expectation that the elect one will be associated with an atoning sacrifice. This is all the more significant since Joseph is the climactic elect one of the book of Genesis who passes through death to life, is exalted as king and priest, like his father Adam, and reunites the fractured chosen family. Not only this but he is also the greater exiled brother because he quite literally has the sins of his brothers put on him. He is not exiled due to his own sin or will but is sinned against and exiled. Ultimately, Yahweh turns these sins into good and Joseph forgives these sins that were committed against him.

As the reader continues through the Torah, perhaps this motif is recalled when reading Lev 14. Once again, one cleanses by its blood, and the other is exiled, bearing impurity. Then the reader reaches the Day of Atonement and reads of two chosen goats, one of which is exiled, bearing sins, and the other is offered as a purification offering that cleanses all Israel. The expectations and patterns created in Genesis are seen once again at the very climax of the Torah. Genesis has created the expectation that an elect one will pass from death to life through sacrifice in order to rescue Israel. By the end of the Torah, Israel is awaiting the elect brother, the prophet like Moses who will circumcise Israel's hearts and render the Day of Atonement unneeded. But until that elect one comes, the purification that the elect brother will bring is seen in and produced by the Day of Atonement goats.

Through these literary connections between the elect one and the two goats, the author of the Torah has created the expectation that an elect one will come who will be both the goat for Azazel and the goat for Yahweh. He will bear the sins of the people away from the camp and also have his blood shed as a purification offering for the people[5], perhaps even near Jerusalem. He will pass through death and come back to the land of the living where he will be exalted as king and priest. He will give life and blessing to the nations, and bring the brothers that act as the seed of the serpent back to him. This may be the pattern that is in the mind of

---

5. For example, Orlov discusses historical interpretations of Jesus as the goat for Yahweh in the Jesus and Barabbas scene while recognizing that Jesus plays the role of the goat for Azazel elsewhere in Matthew (Orlov, *The Atoning Dyad*, 58–64). Moscicke, while also recognizing that Jesus plays the role of the goat for Yahweh in Matthew, argues that Jesus is to be seen as the scapegoat as well. Moscicke, "Jesus, Barabbas, and the Crowd"; Moscicke, "Jesus as Scapegoat."

the author of Isaiah as he writes about the suffering servant who will be killed for the sin of the people yet will later live to see his offspring[6].

Before ending the discussion of the Two-Goats motif, a few words on this label are appropriate. It is clear that within scripture, this motif begins with the sets of brothers found throughout Genesis and is later found recapitulated in the goats of the Day of Atonement. It is also clear that the respective brothers have more similarities among themselves than they do with the goats. No non-elect brothers bear the sins of another to never return as does the goat for Azazel. The hope is always that the exiled brother would return to the elect family. Similarly, no elect brother actually affects blood purification from sin as the goat for Yahweh does. So perhaps to call this motif the *Two-Goats* motif is unfitting. However, this work has attempted to demonstrate that there is a pattern that is developed by these pairs of brothers, into which the goats fit at the climax of the Torah. While Joseph may be the greatest within this pattern in Genesis, the importance and purpose of the Day of Atonement makes that instance of the pattern significant. In order to maintain the connection between the goats of the all-important Day of Atonement and the brothers of Genesis, the label *Two-Goats* has been selected for this work.

6. Hamilton, *Typology*, 207–210; Hamilton argues that Isa 53–54 is recapitulating typological patterns from the binding of Isaac.

Reflections on the Exoduses in Genesis

THE BOOK OF GENESIS begins with Yahweh bringing humanity (and all creation) through the waters. He then brings Noah and his family out from a violent people and brings them through the waters; both of these looking forward to the culminating event of Yahweh making a new creation in Israel by bringing them out of an oppressive nation and through the waters. Yahweh continues through the book to rescue people out from under oppressors and violent people, who themselves are the ruinous waters through which Yahweh brings his people. He remains committed, through various circumstances, to give exodus to his elect and those associated with them.

Below is a concise list of the exoduses that have been seen before the exodus of Israel out of Egypt:

1. The exodus of creation
2. The exodus of Noah
3. The exodus of Abraham from Babylon
4. The exodus of Sarai from Egypt
5. The exodus of Lot from capture
6. The exodus of Hagar from the elect family
7. The exodus of Lot from Sodom
8. The exodus of Sarah from Abimelech
9. The exodus of Rebekah from the city of Nahor
10. The exodus of Rebekah from Abimelech
11. The exodus of Jacob from Paddan-Aram

12. The exodus elements applied to Leah and Rachel in the births of their children

13. The exodus of Jacob from Esau's army/the wrestler

14. The exodus of Dinah from Shechem

15. The exodus of Esau to Seir

16. The (potential) exodus of Tamar from Judah[1]

17. The exodus of Joseph from his brothers/slavery

18. The exodus of Israel from famine

19. The exodus of Jacob from Egypt

20. The exodus of Moses through waters

21. The exodus of Moses through exile

Not all of these exodus events are seen to be within the motif by their connection with other exoduses found in Genesis. Some of the exodus cycles in Genesis, such as the creation account and Lot's exodus out of Sodom, seem to have very little connecting them apart from a few conceptual connections. By themselves, these conceptual connections would be insubstantial. However, each of the exodus cycles examined share substantial linguistic and conceptual connections with Israel's exodus out of Egypt. Yahweh's deliverance of his people in their exodus out of Egypt becomes the culmination of all the previous exodus events, the lens through which previous exoduses are recognized as a unified motif, and the example of the full paradigm of the Exodus motif, encompassing all the exodus elements which had been utilized in previous narrative sections. The significance of the exodus of Israel surpassed all others, until that brought about by the Christ, and became the source from which the rest of the Hebrew Bible and New Testament drew as they pointed towards Yahweh's/Jesus' final deliverance of his people. For the purposes of this study, it is important to recognize the unifying and interpreting effect that Israel's exodus has on the Exodus motif within the book of Genesis.

1. This exodus may be implied since it is set in parallel with Joseph's exodus but the author has not made this point explicit by including clear Exodus motif markers in Gen 38.

NEW CREATION

Exodus and creation are generally thought of as two separate events, however, our study would suggest they cannot be disconnected. A majority of the exodus cycles discussed contain new creation elements; renaming, new purpose, beginning or promise of a new nation, or an actual (re)creation of the cosmos. The exoduses of Sarah, Rebekah, and Dinah from the houses of their captors do not contain these elements, nor does Jacob's post-mortem exodus from Egypt. However, each iteration of the motif need not contain all of the same elements. The Hebrew Bible often communicates meaning through the "manipulation of a fixed constellation of predetermined motifs"[2]. Even given the exclusion of the new creation element in the five exodus cycles mentioned above, new creation is seen to be part of the Exodus motif by its presence in the other fourteen exodus events. This point is strengthened by the fact that the new creation element was reasonably excluded from the exoduses of Sarah and Rebekah because their rescue was a necessity of their role in the act of new creation that Yahweh would work through them, i.e. birthing the nation of Israel. Sarah, additionally, has the new creation element applied to her through her naming elsewhere in her story. Likewise, Dinah did not need to become her own nation, but her exodus played a part in pushing her father to fulfill his vows to Yahweh in Bethel. Also, Jacob's exodus from Egypt was a brief foreshadowing of his children's future journey, and the new creation of a dead man would have been literarily unnecessary and perhaps counterproductive in light of him having already received a new name and purpose from Yahweh.

Through the reuse of the new creation element, and its inclusion in the paradigmatic exodus of Israel it can be seen that new creation is an integral part of an exodus event. The new creation itself needs to be qualified as well. Biblical creation is not about the creation of material out of nothing[3], but rather about the creation of nations through the separation of one family from their native people and designating them to be a new people. Creation is the act of pulling something out of the waters; taking someone from the violent nations, and decreeing for them and their seed a new destiny. It is the act of Yahweh taking people from a violent nation and starting his own kingdom with them.

---

2. Alter, *Narrative*, 60; see also Martin's exploration of variations on the betrothal journey type-scene. Martin, "Betrothal Journey Narratives"

3. Most notably, see Hubler, "Creatio ex Nihilo"

With that in mind, exodus and creation are not separate events. Rather, exodus is the means by which Yahweh saves and separates a people and creates them into something new. Likewise, new creation is a typical component and result of an exodus. As the motif of the exodus is studied throughout scripture, new creation should be looked for in the same context. It does not need to be in every recapitulation of the exodus, but the book of Genesis displays new creation as a common component of the exodus paradigm. New creation can, indeed, be found in the context of the Exodus motif in other places in scripture[4]. When a new creation is part of the Exodus motif in Genesis, it is most often in service of Yahweh's goal of forming a nation that would be a blessing to the nations and a kingdom of priests. New creation is intended, not just to make a new people, but to make a people who serve as Yahweh's royal representatives, spreading his rule and blessing to the nations. The new creation is intended to expand the boundaries of Yahweh's temple. As we look to our hope in Jesus, his defeat of the oppressive spiritual rulers of this age, his leading from death to life, and his forming of his people into a new creation, it would serve us well to remember that new creation is not the end. Rather, new creation is the beginning of a commission to continue bringing the nations into the mixed multitude which will follow Jesus to the city which he has prepared.

WATER AND SPIRIT

The story of the creation begins with water and Spirit, and from this beginning comes all creation and, most significantly, humanity. Noah also finds himself in the cosmic waters, which are restrained by wind (recall that this is the same Hebrew word as for spirit and breath), causing

---

4. For example: Isa 55 contains a new exodus and a new creation (Estelle, *Echoes of Exodus*, 179). 1 Pet 2:9–10, among key words and phrases which link back to the exodus, highlights that Jesus' people were "once not a people" but are now God's "holy nation" (Estelle, *Echoes of Exodus*, 294). Estelle also argues that new creation is the typological climax of the Exodus motif in Revelation (Estelle, *Echoes of Exodus*, 309–313). It is worth noting that, while further work is required to determine whether or not the Gospel according to John employs an Exodus motif at the death and resurrection, John does employ a new creation motif at the resurrection (Brown, "Creation's Renewal"), which is a key part of Jesus' deliverance throughout the New Testament.

This is by no means exhaustive but demonstrates that the new creation does appear in the context of the exodus later in scripture. More work will need to be done to examine its inclusion elsewhere and the various ways in which it is recalled in a given passage.

creation to reemerge and Noah to be delivered. Israel likewise is faced with waters which are parted by an east wind, enabling Israel to pass through the waters and be rescued. This pattern continues throughout scripture up to Jesus' baptism, in which he emerges from the Jordan (which has its own significance from Josh 3, which recalls the parting of the waters at Israel's exodus) and God's Spirit comes on him (Matt 3:16).

There is a pattern of God's people being delivered through waters by the work of the Spirit/Breath. Those who are loyal to Jesus, like previous iterations of the elect community, when they believe and receive God's Spirit, symbolically pass through the waters of death and emerge a new creation. They are baptized and join Jesus' new nation. Even Abraham, Jacob, and others are shown to have passed through the waters symbolically by their inclusion in the Exodus motif. They were given exodus from violent nations (compared with the waters elsewhere in scripture as discussed) and brought out as a new creation. While there is more to baptism than this pattern, the readers are intended to think of baptism in light of this pattern. This is why Jesus tells Nicodemus that he must be born of water and spirit in order to become part of God's kingdom (John 3:5). We must pass from death to life in the deliverance of Jesus, by the work of the Spirit, to emerge as Jesus' kingdom of priests. We must trust in Jesus' message, forsake our former kingdoms and gods and obey Jesus' call to become part of his people.

Conclusion

THE BOOK OF GENESIS does indeed give a history of the Abrahamic family, but that is not all that it is. It comes in the form of a crafted narrative which intends to convey more than simply a series of events. The book of Genesis is a story which is continually developing the same handful of tensions and themes, all of which contribute to the overarching plot. The book introduces the readers to Yahweh, his plans, the humans he makes, the world they live in, and the reasons that things do not seem according to his plan today. The story quickly introduces Yahweh's intentions towards his fallen humans as well. He desires to redeem humanity through a human. The rest of the narrative follows this hope; it follows the family that this redeemer is to come from. However, this family history simply becomes the backdrop of the narrative rather than the point of the narrative itself. This family becomes the object of a series of building and changing motifs throughout the book that display the relationship between Yahweh and humanity within the biblical world. As the motifs change or build, Yahweh is seen as committed to redeeming humanity and using them in his original plan to expand his dwelling to all the land.

SUMMARY OF GENESIS ACCORDING TO EXODUS AND TWO-GOATS MOTIFS

The book begins with the Exodus motif, which Yahweh consistently uses to deliver. In the beginning, the pre-creation state and Yahweh's actions conform to the pattern of events found in the Exodus of Israel. There, the motif is used as a means for Yahweh to create a good and suitable dwelling for both himself and his royal representatives. From there, humanity was intended to expand the boundaries of Yahweh's dwelling until all that is in a state of ruin is turned to good and under their authority. With their disloyalty to Yahweh, the desire for humans to rule creation along-side him was put out of reach. Humanity has come under the ruin they were to subdue, and even have become sources of decreation and ruin themselves. However, Yahweh still intends to have his human family rul-ing alongside him and the exodus pattern becomes the means by which the situation will be rectified. The exodus becomes the means by which Yahweh will create the family he will use to redeem the rest.

Abel becomes chosen to carry forward the promise of the redeemer, is brought closer to Yahweh, and is subtly associated with a sin offering. Meanwhile, his brother is hostile to him and becomes a violent nation, leading to the violence which precedes the flood through which Noah's family is brought.

Noah's story is one of the destruction and re-creation of the land and all that is in it, portrayed as an exodus event. Through this event, Yahweh brings the world back to only one family on a garden-like mountain with the blessings given to the original humans. The project of creation has been restarted with a descendant of the original human family. While de-stroying all humans and restarting would be a legitimate option for Yah-weh, he has made a promise to redeem his original humans and desires to have them redeemed. So Noah was brought through the flood; through his own exodus for Yahweh's creation project to be restarted in him. However, Noah and his family fell as well. Shem is chosen to continue carrying the promise while hostile Ham becomes nations which progress to the Tower of Babylon. From this, the project was again restarted in Abraham, not through destruction but through a desire to redeem all the rebellious humans. Abraham is brought through his own exodus to ac-complish this; to make him into a new people who would bring all people back to Yahweh where they could live out the original Edenic plan.

However, Abraham has his own act of disloyalty in leaving the land given to him and going to Egypt, where an exodus was required in order to save Yahweh's chosen family and get them back on track for the plan. Next, a member of Abraham's household, his own nephew, Lot, is por-trayed as having a fall narrative. As a result, Lot is carried away by oppres-sive nations and Yahweh enables Abraham to enact an exodus for Lot. The oppressive nations are defeated for the sake of one who belongs to the elect household. Once again Abraham and Sarah act with disloyalty and become oppressors toward their Egyptian slave, Hagar. This causes Hagar to flee as the Israelites do in their exodus. She is told to return and is blessed by Yahweh; he is delivering her by sending her back to the elect family and delaying her full exodus for the time being.

Once again, Lot finds himself going through an exodus by the intercession of Abraham. The oppressive city of Sodom is destroyed, while Lot and his family are protected from the destruction. Though Lot maintained a good relationship with Abraham, his earlier choice to separate himself from the elect one causes his exodus to result in an exilic multiplication just as has happened to the other hostile brothers.

Following these events, Abraham once again sells his wife for his safety, requiring another rescue for her. Yahweh gives her exodus ensuring that his promise to Abraham is not thwarted either by Sarah's absence nor by Abimelech's sexual advances. This story also enables Abraham to begin making covenants with the nations, as they see that Yahweh is with him. Once the promised seed, Isaac, came through Sarah, hostilities quickly arose between Isaac and Ishmael, creating a need for Hagar, along with Ishmael, to complete her earlier exodus and receive the promises made to her. Hagar and Ishmael are sent out, and Ishmael receives the fate of the previous hostile brothers; he lives in exile and becomes a nation. Isaac goes on to nearly be a mountaintop sacrifice at the future site of Jerusalem. At this point, Abraham has been through an exodus and made into Yahweh's new family; he has been tested and proven loyal; he has made his post-exodus sacrifice, which was nearly his son, and stands in the place of Noah as a restart of creation, through which the rest of creation will be redeemed rather than destroyed.

As the plan continues to the next generation of Abraham's family, Rebekah is given exodus so that she may join the elect Isaac and carry the elect family forward. She bears Jacob and Esau who are quickly hostile to one another. In this inverted story, Jacob steals the promise which was already to be his before he could correctly receive it from Yahweh. This sets the stage for his exile and his need for an exodus. However, Rebekah is given exodus first as Isaac repeats the mistakes of his father and sells her out for his safety. Once again, Yahweh maintains faithfulness to the elect family, and covenants are made with the nations because of Yahweh's blessings.

Jacob continues into his exile where he is blessed and multiplied, then given exodus from Laban. On his way back to the land, Jacob is also given exodus from the hostilities promised by his brother many years prior. Through these events, Yahweh has created the next generation of the elect family and brought them securely into his land. However, Jacob does not lead his family to Bethel where he is to fulfill his vow, but he takes them to Shechem after he departs from Esau. Esau, though he has left on good terms, is still separated from his elect brother, and therefore leaves Yahweh's land and becomes another nation.

While in Shechem Jacob's daughter is taken and becomes in need of an exodus. This exodus comes even through Dinah's deceptive brothers and their slaughter of Shechem. Fractures within the family are shown, and Yahweh reminds Jacob of his vows, telling him to go to Bethel.

Jacob's son Joseph then encourages the hostilities of his brothers by his arrogance. They send him into exile where he receives an exodus from the pit to a place of power (much of which was foreshadowed and paralleled by Judah and Tamar previously). Yahweh brings him through an exodus for the deliverance of the world and the testing and reconciliation of his brothers. He is associated with the Goat for Yahweh and for Azazel. He refines, forgives, and rules his family in this position. At many points, Joseph is shown to be a new Adam. The author has designed the book such that, although the ultimate resolutions are not presented in Genesis, the end of the book maps onto the beginning and resolves its long-standing tensions.

Once Joseph has united the elect family and they have received appropriate blessings from Jacob in Egypt, Jacob goes through another exodus after his death, as a firstfruits and foreshadowing of Israel's nearing exodus out of Egypt as the book comes to a close.

Finally, the book of Exodus opens with a new chosen one. As those who came before him, he must go through an exodus and become the firstfruits of the new creation that Israel would become. Yahweh elects and delivers Moses to lead Israel in their exodus out of Egypt and to his land.

While the summary given is inadequate in many ways; though I have left out much and nuance is needed at each point, the aim of the summary is to give an overview of the narrative structure in regards to the use of the Exodus and Two-Goats motifs. Yahweh is seen to consistently use the exodus as the means to bring the world from a state of ruin to a state of good. This begins at creation and continues in the lives of his elect ones, through whom he means to redeem humanity. The exodus is Yahweh's means of keeping his promise of redemption; of bringing the elect out of ruin and blessing him so that all the families of the earth can be blessed through him. Yahweh remains committed to this mission even if this means correcting the mistakes of his elect and delivering disloyal servants.

The exodus also becomes a means of displaying his blessings to the nations and enticing them to make covenants with his elect. Through the exoduses of the elect, the nations see Yahweh's commitment to his people and his care for them. Yahweh's power to deliver and protect is clearly displayed. His ability to bless and make fruitful is also shown to the nations who observe the elect coming through an exodus. As the nations learn of Yahweh through these exoduses and see Yahweh's elect as the recipient of his benefits, they are often drawn to make covenants of peace and loyalty with the elect. Through the elect, the families of the earth are brought back to Yahweh.

There are also those who perhaps unexpectedly go through an exodus, such as Lot, Hagar, Esau, or Dinah. They are not the elect ones, but their association with the elect family puts them in the care of the elect one and, therefore, in the care of Yahweh. He extends his care and blessing to those who are tied to the elect, and even to those who have broken ties with the elect. Yahweh's desire is not just the redemption of one family, though redemption will come through one family, but the redemption of all the families of the earth. Yahweh still gives exodus to those outside the line of the seed of the woman. He shows mercy, love, and blessing to other members of the humanity that he wishes to bring back into his presence.

Though some other than the elect are included in the Exodus motif, exodus is still seen to primarily be a means to accomplish the Edenic plan in Genesis. Someone within the chosen family is called out, passes through an exodus, and comes out as Yahweh's new creation, ready to pass on his promises to the next generation until the seed of the woman comes. It is not enough to simply be born to the elect family, one must be born of water and spirit; they must pass through their own exodus. This elect one then becomes a representative to Yahweh for his family. He becomes a ruler, a purification offering, one who removes sin, a tester, a reconciler, and a deliverer. All who place themselves within his household and maintain loyalty to Yahweh and his elect, take part in the blessings of Yahweh. As the prophets saw these patterns of the Exodus motif and the Two-Goats motif, the book of Genesis shaped their hope in Yahweh's future deliverance.

It seemed that the expectations of a new exodus had come in Ezra and Nehemiah's day[1] but were not fulfilled until Jesus came to lead an

---

1. The return from exile and the construction of the temple are portrayed as a new exodus (Fox, *Reverberations*, 74–93)

exodus. Jesus first passed through the waters of the Jordan and was tested, preparing him to lead the exodus from death to life. He simultaneously bore the sins of the people, killing their sins in his death, was multiplied into a kingdom, and became a purification offering. Jesus was taken from the pit and ascended to rule and to deliver the world as our firstborn brother at the right hand of the Father. He defeated the gods of the world, brought humanity from their power, and enabled humanity to come into his household. He enacted the Day of Atonement cleansing that was needed and led (and still leads) any who would follow him from death to life. He makes his people into a new creation who, as the first humans, dwell with God (because of the Holy Spirit's indwelling), act as God's royal representatives, and are charged with expanding the boundaries of God's dwelling as they subdue the gods with the Gospel. This commission will continue until the final culmination of the exodus, when Jesus' people are brought out of the nations as a mixed multitude, with great possessions from the nations (Rev 21:24–26), and into the garden-made-city. Jesus will return again for a final deliverance in which the sea and darkness will vanish (Rev 21:1, 23), and need for another exodus will never exist.

GOING FORWARD

The motifs and narrative exploration presented within this book are far from the final word on the book of Genesis or the motifs within. Further study needs to be done on the presence of these motifs throughout the canon and their contribution to the literary strategy of the Biblical authors. It remains to be seen where and how these motifs, particularly the Two-Goats motif, are utilized and developed later in the Old Testament. However, my hope is that the exploration within this book will serve the reader with a more complete understanding of the book of Genesis and provide a foundation for devotional reflection as well as academic study.

These motifs play a large role within the structure of Genesis and are intended to shape the expectations of the reader. The book of Genesis is also the beginning of a long and unified narrative. It acquaints its reader with some of the narrative and literary strategies used by the Biblical authors and shapes the expectations of the reader accordingly. As we end Genesis and continue on in the Biblical text, we are looking for the elect redeemer who will pass through an exodus and be associated with the

Two-Goats motif. Genesis has created the expectation that the resolution to the problems it presents will come through these narrative and literary features. Therefore, we should continue reading looking for developments and resolutions of the tensions presented within these motifs. By the end of the book of Genesis, the Exodus and Two Goats motifs have not only been made an integral part of the book, but an integral part of the narrative expectations and eschatological hopes of the reader.

Appendix: "Desire" in Gen 3:16

As PART OF THE exploration of Gen 4 within this book, the meaning of תְּשׁוּקָה (tšwkh; translated as "desire" by the ESV) in Gen 4:7 was reexamined. However, the use of this word in Gen 3:16 was skipped over. Thanks to Macintosh's work[1] and given the significance of Gen 3:16, the use of תְּשׁוּקָה (tšwkh) in this verse deserves comment. Gen 3:16 reads:
To the woman he said,

> "I will surely multiply your pain in childbearing;
> in pain you shall bring forth children.
> Your desire (תְּשׁוּקָה, tšwkh) shall be contrary to your husband,
> but he shall rule over you."

It is worth noting that the word "contrary" is supplied by the ESV to help the reader interpret the passage. However, the Hebrew does not warrant its inclusion and, as we will see, it is an incorrect inference.

There are competing ideas regarding what sort of "desire" the woman will have for her husband. Often, Gen 3:16 is insightfully interpreted in parallel with Gen 4:7, since the words "desire" and "rule" are mentioned together there within a similar sentence structure[2]. This leads many to conclude that this passage means that the wife will wish to rule her husband but he will have mastery over her. (Bear in mind that this interpretation relies on the typical interpretation of "sin" being personified as a predator in Gen 4:7). Others take it to mean that she will have a sexual or reproductive desire for her husband, which will give him dominance

---

1. Macintosh, "The Meaning of Hebrew;" See prior discussion under heading "The Two-Goats Motif: Cain and Abel"

2. Hamilton, *Genesis Chapters 1–17*, comment on 3:16; Wenham, *Genesis 1–15*, Comment on 3:16.

over her[3] or will be part of her desiring of his leadership[4]. However, if the word translated as "desire" is reexamined, these interpretations are found to not suit the text. A better definition of הְקוּשְׁת (tšwkh) will allow for greater interpretive precision.

In the previous discussion of הְקוּשְׁת (tšwkh), it was noted that the word is a noun that refers to the giving over of one's self (i.e. one's "given-overness," submission, or devotion). Taking this into account, the second half of Gen 3:16 is more appropriately translated:

> And to your husband shall be your devotion (or submission) and he shall rule you. [AT]

In this translation, it is not declared that the wife will attempt to usurp her husband's authority, but rather it is declared that she will submit and he will rule. One of the effects of the fall for the woman is that the husband will rule his wife and she will, in most cases, lie down and take it.

Given that this verse is often used in the Complimentarian vs. Egalitarian debate, it is helpful to see what the verse does and does not say. My intent is not to advocate for a particular side of that debate here and now, nor give an exhaustive explanation of Gen 3:16, but simply to give clarity to a verse that has been often incorrectly interpreted and misused. This verse states that, because of the fall, the husband will rule his wife and she will give herself over to his rulership. The word translated "rule (משל, mšl)" can refer to both good and bad rulership (e.g. Gen 45:8; Judg 14:4) and, therefore, does not speak to the love or cruelty of the husband in his rule by virtue of the chosen vocabulary. It is announced to this woman that she will be in this relationship of submission/devotion regardless of the way her husband rules.

If this relationship of submission is announced as a result of the fall then the verse implies one of two things about the pre-fall relationship of the husband and wife. Before explaining these two pre-fall scenarios,

---

3. Wenham, *Genesis 1–15*, Comment on 3:16. Wenham also discusses the sexual interpretation but lands on the interpretation that the woman will seek to master the husband, taking the verse in parallel with the typical translation of Gen 4:7.

4. Davidson, *Flame of Yahweh*, 56–80; Davidson gives a treatment of Gen 3:16 in conversation with many Complimentarian and Egalitarian arguments. His own belief is that תְּשׁוּקָה (tšwkh) bears sexual connotations (because of its use in SoS 7:10) but the wife ultimately desires the protective rulership of the husband. He sees this verse as a blessing (Davidson, *Flame of Yahweh*, 73–76). The data from Macintosh's would suggest that *sexual* desire is not inherently part of the meaning of תְּשׁוּקָה (tšwkh). However, Davidson does end up being correct that the wife's willful submission is intended to be communicated in this passage.

it is worth pointing out that this pronouncement is given in the context of marriage and is not to be applied to men and women outside of this covenant relationship. One scenario is that before the fall, the husband possessed headship over the wife within the marriage. This hierarchy was the created ideal. Presumably, he ruled with fairness and care and the relationship was pleasant for both. However, due to the fall, that relationship has become warped. She will now be devoted to his wishes and will submit to them whether he is a fair or unfair ruler. Now that sin has entered the picture, the supportive structure of marriage has become a shackle for her.

Alternatively, it could be that the woman had full equality with her husband before the fall. This equality was the created ideal. Now that she has led her husband to eat the fruit; now that sin has entered the world, he will possess headship and she will submit. Gen 3:16 seems to introduce rulership and submission into the humans' relationship and does not seem to introduce an intensification of the husband-wife hierarchy. There is no clearly stated pronouncement of an increase or warpage of a previously existing rulership-submission relationship. Therefore, the second reading seems to be the most natural, but either scenario can be argued from other factors found within the verse's context.

The observations made do not settle the debates about the roles of men and women. The observations possibly only muddy the waters in regard to those debates. As said, my goal here is not to weigh in on either side nor to give a full commentary on this verse. The interpreter still must determine if Yahweh's pronouncement is predictive or prescriptive; universal or general; and where it lies on the literal-symbolic spectrum, among other things. My goal is simply to provide clarity to a commonly misunderstood element of this verse and allow for a higher degree of interpretive precision. As Gen 3:16 is better translated it will allow for better reflection on the verse, both in regard to the Complimentarian vs. Egalitarian debate and in regard to the various fields of Biblical studies more broadly.

Bibliography

Alter, Robert. *The Art of Biblical Narrative*. New York: Basic, 2011.

———. *The Hebrew Bible. A Translation with Commentary*. 1st ed. New York: W. W. Norton & Company, 2018.

Beale, G. K. *The Temple and the Church's Mission: A Biblical Theology of the Dwelling Place of God*. Edited by D. A. Carson: Downers Grove, IL: InterVarsity, 2004.

Brown, Jeannine K. "Creation's Renewal In the Gospel of John." *The Catholic Biblical Quarterly* 72, no. 2 (April): 275–290, 2010.

Chambers, Nathan. *Genesis 1 and Creation Ex Nihilo: A Reconsideration*, Durham Thesis, Durham University, Available at Durham E-Theses Online: http://etheses.dur.ac.uk/12443/, 2017.

Collins, C. J. *Reading Genesis Well: Navigating History, Poetry, Science, and Truth in Genesis 1–11*. Grand Rapids, MI: Zondervan, 2018.

Currid, John D. *Ancient Egypt and the Old Testament*. Grand Rapids, MI: Baker, 1997.

Davidson, Richard M. *Flame of Yahweh: Sexuality in the Old Testament*. Grand Rapids, MI: Baker, 2007.

Dorsey, David A. *The Literary Structure of the Old Testament: A Commentary on Genesis-Malachi*. Grand Rapids, MI: Baker, 2004.

Douglas, Mary. *Jacob's Tears: The Priestly Work of Reconciliation*. Oxford: Oxford University Press, 2004.

Durham, John I. *Exodus*. Edited by David A. Hubbard, Glenn W. Barker, John D. Watts, and Ralph P. Marlin: Waco, TX: Word, 1987.

Emadi, Samuel. *From Prisoner to Prince: The Joseph Story in Biblical Theology*. Edited by D. A. Carson: Downers Grove, IL: InterVarsity, 2022.

Estelle, Bryan D. 2018. *Echoes of Exodus: Tracing a Biblical Motif*.: InterVarsity, 2018.

Foreman, Matt, and Douglas Van Dorn. *The Angel of the LORD: A Biblical, Historical, and Theological Study*. Danoco, CO: Waters of Creation, 2020.

Foster, Benjamin R. *Before the Muses: An Anthology of Akkadian Literature*. University Park, PA: Pennsylvania State University Press, 2005.

Fox, Michael R., ed. *Reverberations of the Exodus in Scripture*. Eugene, OR: Pickwick, 2014.

Garsiel, Moshe. *Biblical Names: A Literary Study of Midrashic Derivations and Puns*. Ramat Gan: Bar-Ilan University Press, 1991.

Gladd, Benjamin L., and G. K. Beale. *Hidden But Now Revealed: A Biblical Theology of Mystery*. Downers Grove, IL: InterVarsity, 2014.

Goldingay, John. *Genesis*. Edited by Bill Arnold. Grand Rapids, MI: Baker, 2020.

Hamilton, James M. *Typology-Understanding the Bible's Promise-Shaped Patterns. How Old Testament Expectations Are Fulfilled in Christ*: Grand Rapids, MI: Zondervan, 2022.

Hamilton, Victor P. *The Book of Genesis, Chapters 1–17*. Grand Rapids, MI: Eerdmans, 1990.

———. *The book of Genesis, Chapters 18–50*. Grand Rapids, MI: Eerdmans, 1995.

Heiser, Michael S. *The Unseen Realm: Recovering the Supernatural Worldview of the Bible*. Bellingham, WA: Lexham, 2015.

Hubler, James Noel. *Creatio ex Nihilo: Matter, Creation, and the Body in Classical and Christian Philosophy Through Aquinas*. Dissertation, 1995.

Hyers, Conrad. *The Meaning of Creation: Genesis and Modern Science*. Atlanta, GA: John Knox, 1984.

Imes, Carmen J. "The Lost World of the Exodus: Functional Ontology and the Creation of a Nation." In *For Us, But Not to Us: Essays on Creation, Covenant, and Context in Honor of John H. Walton*, 126–141. Eugene, OR: Pickwick, 2020.

———. "Torah Tuesday—Exodus 4:24." Youtube. https://www.youtube.com/watch?v=5nQ4NRcXJ14, 2022.

Kalimi, Isaac. *Metathesis in the Hebrew Bible: Wordplay as a Literary and Exegetical Device*. Peabody, MA: Hendrickson, 2018.

Kline, Meredith G. "The Feast of Cover-Over." *Journal of the Evangelical Theological Society* 37, no. 4 (December): 497–510, 1994.

Köhler, Ludwig, Walter Baumgartner, and Johann J. Stamm. *The Hebrew and Aramaic Lexicon of the Old Testament*. Leiden: Brill, 2000.

LeFebvre, Michael. *The Liturgy of Creation: Understanding Calendars in Old Testament Context*. Downers Grove, IL: InterVarsity, 2019.

Leonard, Jeffery M. "Identifying Inner-Biblical Allusions: Psalm 78 as a Test Case." *Journal of Biblical Literature* 127, no. 2 (Summer): 241–265, 2008.

Longman III, Tremper, Stephen O. Moshier, and John H. Walton. *The Lost World of the Flood: Mythology, Theology, and the Deluge Debate*. Downers Grove, IL: InterVarsity, 2018.

Macintosh, A. A. "The Meaning of Hebrew." *Journal of Semitic Studies* 61 (2): 365–387, 2016.

Martin, Michael W. "Betrothal Journey Narratives." *The Catholic Biblical Quarterly* 10:505–523, 2008.

Mathias, Steffan. *Paternity, Progeny, and Perpetuation: Creating Lives After Death in the Hebrew Bible*. London: Bloomsbury Academic, 2021.

Meade, John D. "The Meaning of Circumcision in Israel: A Proposal for a Transfer of Rite from Egypt to Israel." *The Southern Baptist Journal of Theology* 20, no. 1 (Spring): 35–54, 2016.

Milgrom, Jacob. *Leviticus 1–16: A New Translation with Introduction and Commentary*. New York: Doubleday, 1991.

Mitchell, David. *Jesus: The Incarnation of the Word*. Independently Published, 2021.

Morales, L. M. "Crouching Demon, Hidden Lamb Resurrecting an Exegetical Fossil in Genesis 4.7." *The Bible Translator* 63, no. 4 (October): 185–191, 2012.

———. *Exodus Old and New: A Biblical Theology of Redemption*. Downers Grove, IL: InterVarsity, 2020.

———. *Who Shall Ascend the Mountain of the Lord? A Biblical Theology of the Book of Leviticus*. Carson: Downers Grove, IL: InterVarsity, 2015.

Morrison, Martha A. "The Jacob and Laban Narrative in Light of Near Eastern Sources." *The Biblical Archaeologist* 46 (3): 155–164, 1983.

Moscicke, Hans M. "Jesus as Scapegoat in Matthew's Roman-Abuse Scene (Matt 27:27–31)." *Novum Testamentum* 62: 229–256, 2020.

———. "Jesus, Barabbas, and the Crowd as Figures in Matthew's Day of Atonement Typology (Matthew 27:15–26)." *Journal of Biblical Literature* 139 (1): 125–153, 2020.

Niehaus, Jeffrey. "In the Wind of the Storm: Another Look at Genesis III 8." *Vetus Testamentum* 44, no. 2 (April): 263–267, 1994.

Orlov, Andrei A. *The Atoning Dyad: The Two Goats of Yom Kippur in the Apocalypse of Abraham*. Leiden: Brill, 2016.

Postell, Seth D. *Adam as Israel: Genesis 1–3 as the Introduction to the Torah and Tanakh*. Eugene, OR: Pickwick, 2011.

Pulse, Jeffrey. *Figuring Resurrection: Joseph as a Death & Resurrection Figure in the Old Testament & Second Temple Judaism*. Bellingham, WA: Lexham, 2021.

Sailhamer, John H. *The Pentateuch as Narrative: A Biblical-theological Commentary*. Grand Rapids, MI: Zondervan, 1995.

Schnittjer, Gary E. *Old Testament Use of Old Testament: A Book-by-book Guide*. Grand Rapids, MI: Zondervan Academic, 2021.

Schrock, David. *A Biblical-Theological Investigation Of Christ's Priesthood And Covenant Mediation With Respect To The Extent Of The Atonement*. Dissertation, 2013.

Smith, David I. "What Hope After Babel? Diversity and Community in Gen 11:1–9, Exod 1:1–14, Zeph 3:1–13 and Acts 2:1–13." *Horizons In Biblical Theology* 18 (2): 169–191, 1996.

Smith, Gregory S. *The Testing of God's Sons*. Nashville, TN: B&H, 2014.

Stanhope, Ben. *(Mis)interpreting Genesis: How the Creation Museum Misunderstands the Ancient Near Eastern Context of the Bible*. Louisville, KY: Scarab, 2020.

Sternberg, Meir. *The Poetics of Biblical Narrative: Ideological Literature and the Drama of Reading*. Bloomington, IN: Indiana University Press, 1987.

Verrett, Brian A. *The Serpent in Samuel: A Messianic Motif*. Eugene, OR: Resource, 2020.

Walters, Stanley D. "Wood, Sand and Stars : Structure and Theology in Gn 22:1–19." *Toronto Journal of Theology* 3 (2): 301–330, 1987.

Waltke, Bruce K., and Cathi J. Fredricks. *Genesis: A Commentary*. Grand Rapids, MI: Zondervan, 2001.

Walton, John H. *Ancient Near Eastern Thought and the Old Testament: Introducing the Conceptual World of the Hebrew Bible*. Grand Rapids, MI: Baker, 2018.

———. *Genesis 1 As Ancient Cosmology*. University Park, PA: Pennsylvania State University Press, 2011.

———. *The Lost World of the Israelite Conquest: Covenant, Retribution, and the Fate of the Canaanites*. Grand Rapids, MI: InterVarsity, 2017.

Warren-Rothlin, Andy. "Euphemisms in Bible Translations." In *Encyclopedia of Hebrew Language and Linguistics Vol. 1*. 865–869. Leiden: Brill, 2013.

Wenham, Gordon J. 2014. *Genesis 1–15, Volume 1*. Edited by David A. Hubbard, Ralph P. Martin, John D. W. Watts, and Glenn W. Barker: Grand Rapids, MI: Zondervan, 2014.

Wilhoit, James C., Leland Ryken, Colin Duriez, Tremper Longman III, Daniel G. Reid, Jim Wilhoit, and Douglas Penney, eds. *Dictionary of Biblical Imagery*. Grand Rapids, MI: InterVarsity, 1998.

Wyatt, Nick. *Religious texts from Ugarit*. New York: Sheffield Academic, 2002.

Scripture Index

Genesis (continued)

Genesis (continued)

Exodus (continued)

1:11–12	127
1:11	78
1:12	78
1:14	53, 124
1:16	123, 175
1:20	120
1:22	175
2	174
2:2	174
2:3	175
2:5	174, 175
2:10	175
2:11	176, 179
2:12	179
2:14	176
2:15	179
2:17	176
2:21	176, 179
2:22	179
2:23–24	43
2:23	90, 94, 125
2:24–25	90, 127
2:24	50, 61, 87, 129
2:25	79, 82, 84
3–4	109
3:2–4	133
3:2	101
3:6	176
3:7	78, 79, 82, 84, 90, 127
3:8	134, 139
3:9	84, 90
3:10	176, 179
3:16	101
3:17	78, 127
3:20	90, 139
4:1	101
4:5	101
4:12	176
4:15	176
4:18	179
4:20	115, 133, 179
4:21	78
4:22–23	177
4:24–27	177
4:24	177
4:25	178
4:30–31	178
4:31	127
5	53
5:1–2	115, 133
5:1	64, 69, 95, 115, 123, 133, 145, 172, 173, 178, 179
5:3	172
5:8	84
5:15	84
6:3	101
6:6	139
6:11	64
7–12	69, 76, 77, 95, 133, 145, 179
7:9–12	6
7:16	64
7:25	90, 139
8:1	64
8:8	115, 133
8:12	84
8:15	115, 133
8:24	85, 90
8:28–32	115, 133
9	87
9:15	90, 139
9:18	87, 90
9:23–24	90
9:23	87
9:25	87, 90, 139
9:27–28	115, 133
9:31	90, 139
9:33–34	90
9:33	87
9:34–35	115, 133
9:34	87
10:16–20	115, 133
10:21–28	2
10:24–26	172
11:1	64
11:16	84
12	85, 101, 172
12:8	85
12:12	90, 139
12:13	43, 50, 85, 90, 139
12:18	90
12:22–23	90
12:23	85, 90

Made in United States
North Haven, CT
08 July 2024

54529995R00135